THE PARTITIONS OF
MEMORY

for
KAUSHALYA AND BHAVANESH KAUL
and for
PRIMLA LOOMBA

The Partitions of Memory

THE AFTERLIFE OF THE DIVISION
OF INDIA

Edited by

SUVIR KAUL

INDIANA
University Press
Bloomington & Indianapolis

This book is a publication of

Indiana University Press
601 North Morton Street
Bloomington, Indiana 47404-3797 USA

http://iupress.indiana.edu

Telephone orders   800-842-6796
Fax orders   812-855-7931
Orders by e-mail   iuporder@indiana.edu

Paperback edition first published in North America in 2002
by Indiana University Press

First published by Permanent Black
D-28 Oxford Apts, 11 IP Extension, New Delhi 110092

This edition is for sale outside South Asia
by arrangement with Permanent Black

Library of Congress Cataloging-in-Publication Data

The partitions of memory: the afterlife of the division of
India/edited by Suvir Kaul.
        p. cm.
    Includes bibliographical references.
    ISBN 0-253-21566-8 (paper : alk. paper)
    1. India—History—Partition, 1947. 2. India—Politics and government—
20th century. 3. Dalits—India—Politics and government. I. Kaul, Suvir.

    DS480.842 .P384 2002
    954.04—dc21
                                                        2002023292

1 2 3 4 5 07 06 05 04 03 02

Contents

List of Abbreviations

NWFP	North West Frontier Province
AICC	All India Congress Committee
PPCC	Punjab Provincial Congress Committee
ANP	Awami National Party
NMML	Nehru Memorial Museum and Library
IOLR	India Office Library and Records
IESHR	*Indian Economic and Social History Review*
UP	United Provinces

Notes on Contributors

SUVIR KAUL

Suvir Kaul is Associate Professor of English at the University of Illinois at Urbana-Champaign. He is the author of *Thomas Gray and Literary Authority* (Delhi: Oxford University Press and Palo Alto: Stanford University Press, 1992) and of *Poems of Nation, Anthems of Empire: English Verse in the Long Eighteenth Century* (Charlottesville: University Press of Virginia and Delhi: Oxford University Press, 2000), and of essays on critical theory and contemporary Indian writing in English.

MUKULIKA BANERJEE

Mukulika Banerjee is Lecturer in Social Anthropology at University College London. She was trained at the Department of Sociology, Delhi School of Economics before doing her D. Phil. at Oxford where she held a Junior Research Fellowship at Wolfson College. She is one of very few Indian academics who have carried out extended fieldwork in Pakistan, and her monograph, *The Pathan Unarmed*, is forthcoming from James Curry Press. Her current project, based on field research in rural and urban West Bengal, is on popular understandings of democracy and the nature of political leadership in contemporary India.

JOYA CHATTERJI

Joya Chatterji, a sometime Fellow of Trinity College, Cambridge, is currently Lecturer in International History at the London School of Economics and Senior Research Fellow at Wolfson College, Cambridge. She is the author of *Bengal Divided: Hindu Communalism and Partition, 1932–1947* (Cambridge: Cambridge University Press, 1994) and is currently working on a second monograph on the implications of Partition for society and politics in Bengal since Independence. She is the recipient of a MacArthur Foundation Research and Writing Award in support of her work on the East Bengal refugees.

RAMNARAYAN S. RAWAT

Ramnarayan S. Rawat is a Doctoral candidate at the Department of History, University of Delhi and a Sephis fellow at the International Institute of Social History, Amsterdam. His Ph.D thesis is entitled 'Struggle for Identities: A Social History of the Chamars of Uttar Pradesh, 1881–1956.' His M. Phil. thesis (1996), which is the basis for the essay in this volume, was on the 'Making of Scheduled Caste Community: A Study of SCF and Dalit Politics in UP, 1946–48.'

SUNIL KUMAR

Sunil Kumar is Reader at the Department of History, University of Delhi. He has a Ph.D. (1992) from Duke University and his thesis 'The Emergence of the Delhi Sultanate (588–685/1192–1286)' is soon to be published as a book. He is the editor of a forthcoming volume on the fifteenth century regional Sultanates and is also completing a monograph called 'Sites of Power and Resistance: A Study of Delhi Sultanate Monuments.' He is Associate Editor of *The Indian Economic and Social History Review*.

RICHARD MURPHY

Richard Murphy is a journalist and social anthropologist who lives in New York City. He covered the Afghanistan conflict in the late 1980s; and his more recent journalism has appeared in the *New York Times Magazine, The Wall Street Journal, The New Republic*, and many other media. Murphy serves as editorial director of the Committee to Protect Journalists, a non-profit, New York-based organization that documents abuses of press freedom worldwide. He is currently directing and producing *Banned in Pakistan*, a documentary film about popular culture and politics in South Asia.

URVASHI BUTALIA

Urvashi Butalia is co-founder of Kali for Women, India's first feminist publishing house. She is active in the women's and civil liberties movements in India, and has written on issues of gender, fundamentalism, media, women's writing, censorship and the history of reading and writing. She also teaches a professional course in publishing at a University of Delhi college. She is the author of *The Other Side of Silence: Voices from the Partition of India* (Delhi: Viking Penguin, 1998).

PRIYAMVADA GOPAL

Priyamvada Gopal is Assistant Professor in English at Connecticut College; she will shortly take up an appointment at Cambridge University. She has a Ph.D (2000) from Cornell University, and is now revising her dissertation into a book, *Midnight's Labors: Gender, Nation and Narratives of Social Transformation in Transitional India, 1932–1954*. She has published an essay on the Bandit Queen controversy in 'Gender in the Making: Indian Contexts' (special issue of the journal *Thamyris*), as well as book and other reviews.

NITA KUMAR

Nita Kumar is a Fellow at the Centre for Studies in Social Sciences, Calcutta. A historian and anthropologist, she is the author of *The Artisans of Banaras* (Princeton: Princeton University Press, 1988), *Friends, Brothers and Informants* (Berkeley: University of California Press, 1992), *Lessons from Schools* (Delhi: Sage, 2000), and is editor of *Women as Subjects* (Calcutta: Stree, and Charlottesville: University Press of Virginia, 1994). She has recently translated and published *Mai (Mother): A Novel and an Introduction* (Delhi: Kali, 2000). Her recent work focuses on education and children.

Preface to the US Edition

As I write this Preface, Pakistan and India have been much in the news in the United States. This attention is the direct result of the terrorist attacks on US civilian and military targets on September 11, 2001, and of the US military response against the Taliban and their supporters in Afghanistan. In the days after September 11, the governments of both India and Pakistan, with alacrity in one case and with considerable misgivings in the other, opted to join the battle against 'global terrorism,' a target whose lack of precise definition allows nations with vastly different geo-political agendas to band together. In the last five months, Russia has seen in this anti-terrorist campaign a legitimation of its actions in Chechnya, Turkey has clamped down further on Kurds and members of Islamic fundamentalist groups, Singapore, the Philippines and Indonesia have moved against Islamic militants, Britain has tightened its laws against the incitement of religious hatred, and China has confirmed its actions against separatist groups operating in its western provinces. These are but a few instances in a long list of nations acting purportedly against global terrorism but more particularly in the service of their self-defined 'national' interests.

As can only be expected, India and Pakistan have both jockeyed for position in this high stakes race. Several of the *jihadi* groups originating in Pakistan who fought with the Taliban in Afghanistan regularly conduct operations against both state and civilian populations in the Indian section of Kashmir, and both the military dictatorship in Pakistan and the civilian government in India have moved to curb their power. However, they have done so opportunistically and for very different reasons—General Pervez Musharraf to consolidate his own and state power in Pakistan, power that has been diluted by the presence of very well armed religious and private militias, and the Indian government because President George Bush's repeated calls to act against the 'evil' of terrorism provide excellent justification for the recent history of state repression in Kashmir. And, in a vicious pattern that goes back to 1947, Pakistan and India still march in lock-step—at this moment, there are enormous troop mobilizations in effect on their shared border, border areas have been heavily mined, and other preparations for war are in place. Even if these activities are an exercise in brinkmanship, as are the missile tests conducted in the past week by India, the overwhelming impression is one of repetition: both the countries have been in this position several times before, have fought three wars (1965, 1971, 1999), have skirmished constantly (wasting tremendous national resources each time), and are still none the wiser about how to come to terms with past histories and to learn how to build a co-operative and peaceful future.

The devastating two-decades-long conflict in Afghanistan is a product of the Cold War rivalries of two western powers, the United States and the Soviet Union. The loose confederation of tribal and national authority that made up Afghanistan had survived the geopolitical ambitions of the British Empire in the area, but tribal and ethnic alliances fell apart under the pressure of the Soviet occupation and the determination of the US to convert Afghanistan into a Soviet 'Vietnam,' a battlefield where they would be bled to the point of no recovery. This is indeed what happened, but even as the Soviets withdrew, it became clear that the real casualties in this long-drawn-out war were the Afghans. This sorry history, compounded by the rise of the Taliban to power, and their offering a home to Osama bin Laden and others of his ilk, prepared the grounds for September 11 and the war after. I offer this summary, now well known to readers of this volume, to emphasize a simple, inescapable idea: a great many of the political and socio-economic difficulties that plague nations like Afghanistan, Pakistan or India were precipitated by British imperialism and confirmed by the geopolitical divides of the Cold War. To be sure, India and Pakistan were created not by the imperial cartographers who supervised the demise of the British Empire but by the nationalists who fought for independent states, yet a crucial reason for their present-day antagonism is Kashmir, an unresolved problem bequeathed by those map-makers who remade maps and communities with little regard for the people concerned. Today, Kashmir exists in two sections, one amalgamated into Pakistan and the other into India, and both nations lay claim to the whole.

The post-independence antagonisms of India and Pakistan are of course larger than the issue of Kashmir alone, and this volume addresses these larger oppositions and difficulties. Readers will, however, notice a curious detail: no matter how much the legacies of Partition in 1947 look like pointed disagreements across the Indo-Pakistan border, there is no disguising the fact that these are disagreements 'within' too; the afterlife of the division of India flickers in social, religious, communal-identitarian tensions that continue to play powerful roles internal to each country. Even as many Indians and Pakistanis routinely define themselves *vis-à-vis* one another, each state struggles with problems in internal self-definition: how does Pakistan, a nation born out of the conviction that the Muslims of British India needed not simply their own independent, but also Islamic, state, deal with its non-Muslim minorities, including the Ahmadiyyas? (Pakistan has, via parliamentary legislation, declared Ahmadiyyas 'non-Muslim' because of their conviction that the founder of their sect, Mirza Ghulam Ahmad of Qadian, is a prophet.) How does Pakistan deal with the reality that India has as many Muslim citizens as it does, and that India's continued functioning as a state acts as a rebuttal of the 'two nation theory,' which insisted that Hindus and Muslims could not live and work together? And how does India, a constitutionally secular state, find ways of making sure that its non-Hindu minority populations are allowed to live as equal citizens of the nation? Indeed, the problem in India is not only one of Hindu and non-Hindu citizens: today, the major challenge mounted against upper-caste Hindu domination is the political mobilization of those vast lower-caste populations historically oppressed by their upper-caste 'brethren.'

These internal fissures and historical divides within the nations of the subcontinent remind us that civil society is a fragile order always under pressure, that it is a compact constantly under renewal. This is a lesson that Pakistan and India (and Sri Lanka to the south, torn apart by decades of Sinhala-Tamil violence) have been forced to learn, but this is as well a problem now facing citizens in the United States. In the wake of September 11, Attorney General John Ashcroft and the Justice Department have launched a series of internal arrests—largely under immigration laws—where over a thousand men, almost all Arab and South Asian Muslims, have been incarcerated without benefit of counsel or the protection of the US Constitution and the Bill of Rights. The fear is of the enemy 'within,' the neighbor who is, to all intents and purposes, like many other such neighbors, indeed not unlike oneself, but who must now be the object of great suspicion. This is a paranoia that several of the essays in this volume touch or dwell upon—it underlies both generalized conditions of personal and collective suspicion, as it does public and state actions in 'defence' of the 'social order' (the 'way of life') or the nation. These essays address a variety of issues, to which my 'Introduction' serves as a guide, but if there is one collective concern they might hold out for the US reader who has a non-specialized interest in contemporary South Asia, it is the knowledge that political and cultural relations between states, and between subnational groupings, are changeable, and for that reason can be mobilized into confrontation and violence, in South Asia as in North America. Further, if there is one important lesson these essays reiterate, it is that the idea of the nation under threat is powerful and fungible, and most often invoked and manipulated—including by the state—to serve interests more local, and more sectarian, than claimed by the idea itself.

January–February 2002

Introduction

SUVIR KAUL

IN AN EXTRAORDINARY irony, on 11 May 1998, the Partition of the subcontinent was undone at Pokharan. The nuclear blasts that melted rocks beneath the earth's surface also in effect vaporized the carefully demarcated, barbed-wired, watch-towered 'lines on the ground' that is our shared national boundary. The systematic work of British colonial cartographers and administrators that led up to 14 and 15 August 1947, the protracted and embittered negotiations between 'Indian' and 'Pakistani' nationalists who belonged to the Congress or the Muslim League (or other pre-Independence political groupings), the 'choices' made by entire populations who moved voluntarily, or were forced to do so, all were reduced to naught by the power of mutually assured nuclear destruction. In fact, these borders, which have so often been confirmed by the spilling of blood—in riots and in pogroms, or in the unofficial and official wars waged by the states of India

I wish to thank Anita Roy for initiating this project, and Rukun Advani and Anuradha Roy for enabling its completion. I am grateful too to those contributors who turned in their articles and then waited remarkably patiently for news; yours were the acts of faith that made this volume possible. Neeladri Bhattacharya, Pradip Datta and Javed Malik offered advice (but no essays!), as did Ania Loomba—for that, and for other gestures of community, my gratitude.

and Pakistan—no longer stand for anything except the commonality of our fate. Arundhati Roy puts it trenchantly:

> Though we are separate countries, we share skies, we share winds, we share water. Where radioactive fallout will land on any given day depends on the direction of the wind and the rain. Lahore and Amritsar are thirty miles apart. If we bomb Lahore, Punjab will burn. If we bomb Karachi—then Gujarat and Rajasthan, perhaps even Bombay, will burn. Any nuclear war against Pakistan will be a war against ourselves.[1]

The nuclearization of India and Pakistan is thus an extraordinary moment in the narrative of Partition: both its telos, in that it confirms the national jingoism and the bloodthirsty hatreds that propelled the mass slayings and movements of populations in 1947 and after, and its inversion, in that it reminds us that our fates as nations have never been separate, that when we look across our borders we look into a mirror, that we are locked in an embrace so close that we must draw the same fetid breath. As the bombs exploded (it seems unnecessary, even gratuitous, to call them 'tests'), first 'ours' over two days, then 'theirs' over a few more, it seemed hard to avoid a feeling of *deja vu*: you kill one of ours, we'll kill two of yours, you explode five, we'll explode six. This is, after all, the comparative vocabulary of 1947. It led to apocalypse then (perhaps a million dead, ten million dislocated), and it continues to govern the vengeful discourse of border skirmishes and internecine conflicts now. An eye for an eye, a neighbourhood for a mohalla, a city for a city, and now, a population for a population. We seem to have learnt the wrong lessons from the horrors and the realpolitick of Partition, from the chauvinism that anticipated it, defined its contours, and offered post-facto justifications for it. The destructive legacies and nightmarish memories of Partition—its afterlife—still guide our public policy and inhibit our 'progress' from colonial state to post-colonial democracies. We have not forgotten, for we memorialize selectively, and thus produce the authorized histories of the time, histories that are sanctioned by the state and its institutions, or by smaller social collectivities. For the most part however (to use a psychoanalytic truism) we remember by refusing to remember. Is it any wonder then that the mushroom cloud that now blights our collective imaginations seems the apocalyptic return, a vicious bubbling to the surface, of the knowledge of the enormities of Partition so systematically repressed into our political unconscious?

Partition: Five Decades After

Three years ago we celebrated, with a mixed sense of pride and misgiving, fifty years of national Independence. We proclaimed once again, in a number of fora, the grand narratives of anti-colonial struggle and the coming of Independence, but we did not particularly engage with the political and social cataclysm that followed upon the creation of the nation-states of India and Pakistan. There is a simple and powerful reason for this: our memories of Partition are fragmented and painful. Yet Partition and its known and unknown legacies have played, and continue to play, important roles in the constitution of collective identity and thinking in India. In spite of the efforts of a number of writers and filmmakers and the work of some scholars and analysts, we remain, as a national culture, uncertain and anxious about the place of Partition in our recent history. In many ways, Partition remains the unspoken horror of our time.

But not quite unspoken, for each time Indians are killed in the name of religion, each time a pogrom is orchestrated in our cities, memories of Partition resurface. So many of the Sikhs interviewed by Urvashi Butalia in her *The Other Side of Silence* emphasized their despair that in 1984, in the wake of Indira Gandhi's assassination, they, who had borne the brunt of Partition violence and dislocation in North India, were returned to their original status as refugees in their own homeland. Butalia herself writes of the inescapable sense of repetition, post-1984, that dogged and sharpened her own efforts as a researcher on the human costs of Partition.[2] And we have the literary testimony of Ilyas Ahmad Gaddi's short story, 'A Land Without Sky', in which the tensions generated by the Sangh Parivar's Shilanyas ceremonies in 1991–92 cause two Muslim families who have lived for years in a predominantly Hindu neighbourhood to move to a Muslim area. 'An old bond's broken today,' says the protagonist, Kalim Bhai, compressing into that simple sentence, the narrator tells us, volumes of 'inconsolable pain'.[3] In contemporary India, the burden of Partition is known in its reiterations, in the continuing forced movement of families and local populations away from the neighbourhood, the city, the region that they know as home.

The enormous dislocations of that time have not resulted in a corresponding cultural and historical sense of important lessons to be learned. We have been better at accounting for the political and social events, and the official policies and procedures that precipitated Partition than we have been at examining the violence and displacement that constituted its human dimension. This of course is the common complaint voiced by almost all work on Partition produced in the last few years, and is the starting point for much recent writing, so much that flippant comments have been made about the making of a 'Partition industry'. Yet the facts suggest otherwise. The newspaper articles or essays in academic journals, and perhaps a dozen books, or indeed the two new feature films—Pankaj Butalia's *Karvan* and Deepa Mehta's *Earth*—produced in the last four years comprise at best a cottage industry, a scratching of the surface rather than the systematic exploration that this historic experience demands. This is so particularly as we continue to live in a polity that compulsively reenacts that original divide. Each time communal tensions vitiate our public sphere, or our Prime Minister takes to the ramparts of the Red Fort to speak of 'unfinished business' left over from 1947, or we play cricket against Pakistan, or we believe that our emasculated 'masculinity' has been restored by our possession of a new penile prosthesis—a nuclear weapon—we hear echoes of that earlier storm. Nor have we considered fully the social processes of healing and recovery, or of repression and forgetting. We still need therefore, in years to come, a systematic, multi-faceted exploration of what we might call 'Partition issues', for they define not only our past but, in crucial ways, our collective future.

There is much to be learnt about citizenship, political mobilization, and the practices of the state, in considering the local histories of events that led up to 1947 and characterized the years after. From the work

of historians and cultural analysts we have learnt of the culpability of
state authorities in hardening borderlines and boundaries that were
once flexible or porous. Various state agencies forced people to choose
between one nation and the other, or one religious identity and another, or, more often than not, made the choice for them.[4] Such instances of administrative fiat can be multiplied, but they are not told in
our 'official' accounts of Partition. On the other hand, there are stories
that have been told so often, including by historians, that they have
become the official memory of Partition itself. These stories produce
particular versions of Partition, and each presumes upon and furthers
ideas of collective subjectivity or religious identity. Each time we teach
the story of Partition in order to demonstrate Jinnah's guilt or the
culpability of the Muslim League, and ignore the role played by religious chauvinists within the Congress or other political and social
organizations, we tell a tale that deepens the divides signified by Partition.[5] Similarly, an uncritical humanism that concentrates only on the
pain and sorrow of the 'human condition' that resulted from Partition
will limit our understanding of the political and civic fault-lines revealed then, fault-lines of religion, gender, caste and class that still run
through our lives.

So much that happened during Partition needs to be catalogued.
Many members of the generation that lived through those times are
still alive, and they are an invaluable historical archive. Beginnings
have been made to collate their 'unofficial' accounts (oral histories and
testimonials) and thus to reconstruct events ranging from the micro-
level—the lives of individuals and families—to the mass movement of
populations. Work done already on such personal accounts of the
rampant abductions, killing, and looting during Partition has complicated all our definitions of the victims and the agents of violence.
When we hear of fathers slaying daughters in order to prevent them
from falling into the hands of the enemy, or we hear of women com-
mitting suicide to save community 'honour', or of abducted women
rejected by their relatives, or of others who 'chose' to remain with their
abductors (or their lovers), we recognize that the overlaps between
notions of family, community and nation are more coercive and

violent than our cultural and religious pieties would encourage us to believe.[6] Indeed these oral histories, particularly those of women, bring home to us not only the gender-biases of public policy then (and now), but the complicity of most official and nationalist historiography in perpetuating such bias.

From oral histories we learn also about the many and powerful reasons for people who suffered through Partition to repress the past. Researchers in the field have encountered a number of people resistant to sharing their memories, particularly since they have not spoken about these experiences even to younger people in their own families.[7] In a newspaper interview, one Rajendra Kaur, who was forced to move from Rawalpindi to Delhi, is quoted as saying:

> Why talk about evil days? In our religion, it is prohibited to talk about evil acts. . . . There's a saying that if you discuss ghosts and snakes, they visit you. This talk is about dead people: why invite their ghosts? . . .
>
> You have been repeatedly asking me why I do not want to speak about Partition. The reason is that the murderers were never caught. The people who killed and looted were strangers. Your world is very different from mine. When I was young I had never crossed the *dyodhi* (threshold) of my house barefaced and bareheaded. When the riots started, when the world was fleeing not just in trains but also on the top of train compartments, my husband's head was without a turban. I had no *chunni* to cover my head. Suddenly I was exposed to so many men's gaze. It was so frightening. Can you understand this?[8]

Rajendra Kaur's sense of violation is massive: neither the self nor the private or public sphere will ever be the same, especially since it is expressed so poignantly through her evocation of the everyday coordinates of domestic and public order (the lost turban, the missing *chunni*) scattered by the events of Partition. Partition *defamiliarized* the everyday; even if much in Delhi was the same as in Rawalpindi, what had changed utterly was the familiar relation between self and society.

If the pain of Partition is to be understood, as the often-used metaphor will have it, as the birthpangs of two new nations, then we have only begun to understand how the lives of the children of violence have been shaped by the circumstances of their birth. But there is another, more belligerent version of such a metaphorics of Partition, which is the claim that all nations are founded in blood and that porous boundaries are sealed only through violence; sacrificial blood-letting, that is, is necessary for the making of strong nation-states. The vocabulary of martyrdom (*shahidi*) is an important feature of such understanding, and for good reason: senseless deaths are recuperated, those who were killed, however randomly, are seen to have died for a cause, the guilt of those who survived (or who participated in violence) is assuaged. In this vision, the nation, or the *quam* (community) demands its *shaheeds*, and is strengthened by them. An articulate enunciation of such an understanding of the role of violence in the making of nations is available in Amitav Ghosh's novel of borders and partitions, *The Shadow Lines*, where Tha'mma, the narrator's nationalist grandmother, talks about the making of Britain:

> It took those people a long time to build that country; hundreds of years, years and years of war and blood-shed. . . . They know they're a nation because they've drawn their borders with blood. Hasn't Maya told you how regimental flags hang in all their cathedrals and how all their churches are lined with memorials to men who died in wars, all around the world? War is their religion. That's what it takes to make a country. Once that happens people forget they were born this or that, Muslim or Hindu, Bengali or Punjabi: they become a family born of the same pool of blood. That is what you have to achieve for India, don't you see?[9]

And yet what happens to such a 'making' of the nation when the war that is fought is irregular and internecine, not one that binds Hindu to Muslim or Bengali to Punjabi but one that separates Bengali from Bengali and Punjabi from Punjabi, polarizing them into Hindus and Muslims who must deny all other linguistic, cultural or socio-economic commonalties?

An enormous problem with such a polarized history is that the 'communities' which Partition forged—both religious and national—then shape not only the relations between but also within nations. In India the rhetoric of secularism has to constantly strain against the legacy of religious difference, a legacy sharpened to murderous point by

Partition, which insists on the violent separateness of 'Hindus' and 'Muslims'. Ironically, difference is reproduced and re-circulated even through the rhetoric of sameness: the very slogans of national unity (for instance 'Hindu, Muslim, Sikh, Isai/Sab hain milkar bhai-bhai') work by producing stereotypes of Muslims in fez caps or Christians with crosses hung around their necks. Further, any ultra-nationalist anti-Pakistan sloganeering in India necessarily taps into a tradition of anti-Muslim rhetoric, as anti-Indian propaganda in Pakistan is at once anti-Hindu. Once two nations have been founded on the idea of religious difference, then even the secular constitutional obligations of Indians, or the democratic aspirations of Pakistanis and Bangladeshis, are under pressure from the theocratic agendas of mullahs and pandits on both sides of the border. Fundamentalist groups derive political benefits from arguing that Hindus and Muslims—as indeed other religious denominations—are primarily products of pan-ethnic and pan-national religious identification. Thus, in the subcontinent, national identities are not affirmed by *erasing* pan-national affinities, but often by invoking them. The domestic politics that results allows less and less space for the articulation of minority voices or of divergent cultural and social practices: authoritarian and military priorities become acceptable political currency, in times of war and in times of peace.

Such developments have locked the states of India and Pakistan into an impossible sibling rivalry (it is hard to avoid metaphors of the family when writing about the birth and contemporary existence of the two countries). The hope is always that we will out-grow our rivalries, will learn to find rational ways to expand our mutual interests. But there is much that gets in the way: memories of dismemberment (here too there is repetition: British India into India and Pakistan; Pakistan into Pakistan and Bangladesh); the desire to be revenged (Kashmir being the most obvious symptom of this problem); the atavistic, destructive world-views of religious fundamentalisms that have become increasingly powerful in both countries in recent years. Our politicians and defence experts, at any rate, are locked into mirrored anxieties— each time they look across the border they see justifications for their continued hawkishness and belligerence. The psychological force of this rivalry has had great material impact, for state policy has been guided by fears legitimized by the processes of Partition. We thus need to ask not simply how Partition created the nation-states of the subcontinent, but also how these nations require Partition, or its more local reiterations, in order to justify state authority. It is clear, for instance, just how much the state needs the fear of Partition, and of future Partitions, to maintain its investment in externally and internally repressive agencies.

Insofar as Partition functions as a touchstone of our culture and polity, each time its stories are made and remade for us by different forms of documentary, fictional and even analytical representation, we learn about our changing social and political values.[10] But we are far from institutionalizing these lessons: there are very well known poems, novels, films and plays that feature issues and ideas connected with Partition, yet precious few of them are part of our official school and college syllabi. We are familiar with the furore over texts like *Tamas.* Surely that should convince us of the importance of teaching such novels and films in a way that will allow young people to understand both the passions generated by Partition narratives and the necessity of coming to terms with this passion. Even though a number of historians and political theorists have worked on Partition, it is, for the most part, glossed over as part of the regrettable history of the anti-colonial movement, and is not taught in the detail and density that its scale and historical importance might warrant. We thus teach our school-children a 'no-faults' nationalism that has extremely jingoistic roots. In this vision, the founding-fathers of our nation could do no wrong, just as the founding fathers of Pakistan, the 'anti-nation,' could do no right. This kind of uncritical and hollow patriotism, if it can be called that, is precisely what is interrogated by the events of Partition.

Though Partition had a very different impact on different parts of this country, with many regions not affected at all, its consequences have in fact defined our nation and our nationalism. Thus, it is important to develop critical and political vocabularies appropriate to the full exploration of the intellectual, human and material problems posed by Partition. Even today, over fifty years after Independence, we are not easily able to move from the certainties and fears of chauvinist and nationalist historiography (which are not, even for a moment, to be thought of as ethically or intellectually equivalent) far enough to write different accounts of Partition. Perhaps we need formal institutes and programs for the collection and study of Partition materials, and the equivalent of a Holocaust Memorial in which to house these scholars and archives. Or perhaps we need more local initiatives. In any case, we must know that Partition raised, in a spectacular and destructive form, many important questions about citizenship, national identity and the making of national and sub-national mentalities: it still demands from us a continuing search for answers.

Rethinking Partition Histories

It is a critical commonplace that the nature of the object or issue examined changes the nature of the observational and analytical method; indeed it makes feasible, and urgent, questions that the analyst may not be directed to in other instances. In this regard, one of the most important reasons to pay attention to Partition and its legacies is that they lead us to emphasize questions of sexuality and gender relations largely ignored by political or economic historians. Sexuality and gender have a *constitutive* centrality here—as critical axes, they provide an understanding that does not simply supplement more orthodox historiography but interrogates and rewrites its narratives. Two recent books on women in Partition make available this insight most convincingly: Urvashi Butalia's *The Other Side of Silence* and Ritu Menon and Kamla Bhasin's *Borders and Boundaries*. What emerges in these works is an object lesson in critical methods and in understanding the gendered dynamics of family spaces and memories amongst the people they speak to: Butalia writes that she had to circumvent the problem that women who tell tales of Partition are often corrected by, or give way to, the men of the family who listen to them speak. She also had to learn, as she puts its, to hear 'the hidden nuance, the half-said thing, the silences which are sometimes more eloquent than speech.' Butalia comes to believe in a 'gendered telling of Partition': 'From the women I learned of the minutiae of their lives, while for the most part men spoke of the relations between communities, the broad political realities' (p. 12).

But this division between personal details and 'broad political realities' is not the conventional and predictable divide between women and men, private and public, the domestic and the world outside, for it is women who became targets of a particular form of public violence, and whose dislocation and homelessness, rape and abduction is, in hindsight, at once the most visible, and the most repressed, index of the social, cultural and familial fragmentation that constituted Partition. In the same way, their recovery (a process which quite often involved coercion) and rehabilitation by agencies of India and Pakistan is an indicator of the methods employed by these new states to restore those 'benign' structures of patriarchal authority which had crumbled under the onslaught of mass male violence. Both *The Other Side of Silence* and *Borders and Boundaries* call attention to the fact that the abduction of women was understood as an attack on the 'honour of the nation, and of its men' (*The Other Side*, p. 143), and thus their recovery was crucial to the vindication of the emasculated nation. That some women wished to stay with the men who had married them was considered inconsequential. Muslim women were to be brought 'home' to Pakistan and Hindu and Sikh women to India; in each case their 'citizenship' was considered a simple function of their original religious identity.[11] Even more troubling were the choices forced upon women who were pregnant or had had children with their abductors or companions: in order to restore them to their families, and to an acceptable social 'purity', they were led to abortions or to giving up their children, either to the men who had fathered them (if they wished to retain them, that is) or to orphanages. Most often, those women who kept their children did not return to their families, and lived in ashram-style institutions as wards of the state.[12]

Since Butalia's book begins with the recognition that Partition was not a 'closed chapter of history—that its simple, brutal political geography infused and divided us still' (p. 5), her inquiries focus on 'ordinary people'—women, children, scheduled castes— particularly women, and she relies largely on interviews and oral narratives, and more occasionally on published autobiographies and first-hand accounts of the time. This is the method favoured by Menon and Bhasin too, with some surprising results. So many of those interviewed offer the same candid 'common-sense' explanation for the pathological violence unleashed by Partition—and I quote one instance from *Borders and Boundaries*:

> We treated them badly—practiced untouchability, considered them lowly. We wouldn't eat with them. . . . Everything was separate. . . . Untouchability was the main reason for Partition—the Muslims hated us for it. They were so frustrated and it was this frustration which took the form of massacres at Partition, of the ruthlessness with which they forced Hindus to eat beef . . . (pp. 246–7).

And this from a person who has immediately before this comment shown that she is cognizant of the class-divisions that had structured Hindu-Muslim relations: 'Muslims had their reasons for demanding Pakistan; they had been dominated by Sikhs and Hindus for a long time. They were the working class, we were the exploiters. Hindus and Sikhs were traders, shopkeepers . . . economic reasons were important' (p. 246). Haunting every story of family friendships between people of different religious persuasions, and every account of shared spaces and lives (and these stories are legion), is this perception that *untouchability* polarized and led to resentments so strong that they erupted into desperate, even inexplicable, violence.

Reading Partition Tales

I had earlier suggested that literary texts, cinema and the other creative arts bear witness to the entire 'business' of Partition, to the feelings of bewilderment, loss, and dislocation, to the horrific experiences to which entire communities were subject, to the cultural and economic insecurities and aspirations that motivated socio-political elites and subaltern groups in their search for new homelands. In fact, one of the spin-off benefits of the fiftieth anniversary celebrations of Independence has been the number of new anthologies of writing that respond to and memorialize Partition.[13] Such writing reminds us of the need for individuals to bear witness, to write descriptive, analytical and poetic accounts of a transformation so total that nothing seemed the same any more. But not simply to bear witness, for such writing is often angry and denunciatory—of common humanity, of the 'leaders', and of the gods that failed them. This is Faiz, for instance, on 'The Dawn of Freedom (August 1947)':

> Now listen to the terrible rampant lie:
> Light has forever been severed from the Dark;
> our feet, it is heard, are now one with their goal.
> See our leaders polish their manner clean of our suffering:
> Indeed, we must confess only to bliss;
> we must surrender any utterance for the Beloved—all
>   yearning is outlawed.[14]   (II.16–21)

And running through these anguished accounts is the often despairing desire to make *sense* of all that happened, and to articulate compensatory, supplementary, explanations that will make easier the psychic and material struggles of communities to come to terms with altered lives. Faiz again:

> Did the morning breeze ever come? Where has it gone?
> Night weighs us down, it still weighs us down.
> Friends, come away from this false light. Come we must
>   search for that promised Dawn.   (II.25–7)

Given the conflicted history of the subcontinent in the past half-century, such poems and stories speak with a continuing urgency and demand of us, fifty years later, a particular responsibility as readers: as Alok Bhalla puts it, 'How we, in turn, read these stories, based upon our own presuppositions, will determine the kind of politics we choose to practice in the future.'[15] We are still accountable to Partition and its attendant narratives; in the rest of this section I will suggest, via an analysis of one 'Partition' novel, one form such vigilant or *critical* reading might take.

Khushwant Singh's *Train to Pakistan* (1956) remains one of our most popular accounts of the impact of the political partition of the subcontinent on the small villages and communities of the Punjab. That a largely mediocre novel, thin in character and event, written in an idiom that must have seemed forced even in the 1950s (and which has certainly dated rapidly since), has achieved such prominence is surprising. This success is either a tribute to the novel's simplicity of conception and narrative, whose truisms and pieties provide a shielded, even comfortable, way for readers to think about the enormity and human horrors of the time, or, more likely, follows from the fact that there was so little else written in English about the Partition of 1947 that interested readers did not have much to choose from.[16] Novelistic achievement aside, however, *Train to Pakistan* still invites us to think seriously about the border communities ripped asunder by Partition, and about the cultural and social values that enabled mass violence.

The novel opens by describing a time when people's identities had been polarized into a simple, murderous, opposition: you were Hindu or you were Muslim, and you 'belonged' to India or to Pakistan. The forced migrations from one to the other resulted in a situation when 'all of northern India was in arms, in terror, or in hiding.'[17] All except for a few tiny villages like Mano Majra, where the Sikh peasant land-lords lived in amity with their Muslim tenant farmers. While Khushwant Singh does not provide a particularly thick description of the village community, his Mano Majra does include a community of sweepers, who are notionally Muslim but who sing Christian hymns (wearing sola topees!) with visiting American missionaries. And all of the villagers—Hindu (the village money-lender's family), Sikh, Muslim and pseudo-Christian—repair to worship 'a three-foot slab of sandstone that stands upright under a keekar tree beside the pond (p. 10).' I mention these details to suggest that the novel, even though it does not do very much with such observations (the village '*deo*' and the pseudo-Christians are never mentioned again), does provide a plausible sense of place and time.

Central to the life of Mano Majra are the trains, and this is as true of the many trains that do not stop at the small village station as it is of the few that do. The station is a small hub of commerce, but it is the extensive sidings, where goods trains linger, that lend a prominence to the railway in the life of Mano Majra:

> After dark, when the countryside is steeped in silence, the whistling and puffing of engines, the banging of buffers, and the clanking of iron couplings can be heard all through the night (p. 12).

These sounds, the scheduled regularity of the passing trains, the whistles that are blown as the trains cross the bridge over the Sutlej, all function in the novel as markers of modernity, their repetition a reminder that the looser diurnal rhythms of an agricultural people subsist alongside, and are occasionally regulated by, the 'clock-time' that regulates the larger world around them. In a long passage (pp. 12-13), Khushwant Singh describes these interpolated worlds, thus lending a metaphoric density to the title of the novel, and allowing the later disruption in train traffic and schedules to function as a sign of social chaos, of a world adrift from its normal moorings.

When the trains begin to run irregularly, Imam Baksh and Meet Singh are no longer certain when to start their prayers, people wake up late and retire early, children do not 'know when to be hungry,' and clamour 'for food all the time,' and there is no peace at night:

> Goods trains had stopped running altogether, so there was no lullaby to lull them to sleep. Instead, ghost trains went past at odd hours between midnight and dawn, disturbing the dreams of Mano Majra (pp. 92–3).

The breakdown of railway schedules is a vexing of reality into nightmare; when the first train full of dead bodies draws up at the station, hope flees the village. Thus, when Jugga cuts the rope designed to knock Muslims off the roof of the train to Pakistan, and foils the plans, he does so less as an act of individual heroism, and more as a despairing attempt to bring back order and humanity to a village swept away by the flood of fratricidal violence sweeping over the Punjab. If the train can be allowed to run as scheduled, much more than the lives of its passengers will have been saved.

The novel renders inescapable the role of violence, including sexual violence, in the lives of the villagers. Jugga and Nooran's affair, and their lovemaking, is far from mutual or playful—in the novel, Jugga almost rapes her:

> Juggut Singh shut her mouth with his. He bore upon her with his enormous weight. Before she could free her arms he ripped open the cord of her trousers once again . . . She could not struggle against Juggut Singh's brute force. She did not particularly want to. (pp. 23–4).

Notwithstanding the last sentence, which in the rhetorical manner popularized by Khushwant Singh's celebrated libido, suggests that a woman subjected to her paramour's sexual violence is in fact a willing victim, there is no gainsaying the gendered imbalance of power in this sequence. This model of sexual intercourse as an extension of male power also defines the trysts of the deputy commissioner Hukam Chand and the dancing girl Haseena. Hukam Chand may be conflicted in his desire for this child-like dancer (lachrymose thoughts of his own dead daughter interrupt his pleasure) but the novel makes clear that the entire business is sordid and tawdry: Hukam Chand forces the girl onto his lap, where she sits 'stiff and frigid'. However, the 'magistrate was not particularly concerned with her reactions, he had paid for all that.' Later, as he drags her onto a table, we are told that the 'girl suffered his pawing without a protest . . . She covered her face with the loose end of her sari and turned it sideways to avoid his breath' (pp. 42–3). Later in the novel, even after they have seen more of each other, there is little mutuality of response: 'He stroked her thighs and belly and played with her little unformed breasts. She sat impassive and rigid' (p. 107). Hukam Chand's feelings for Haseena do develop a greater complexity than that of customer and prostitute, but theirs is no love story to set against the violence done by men to women in the novel.

Most crucially, *Train to Pakistan* suggests the culpability of those who exercise state authority in perpetrating violence. Hukam Chand, who is the resident magistrate and chief civilian administrator, is not free at all from communal and anti-Muslim feelings. In an early conversation with the sub-inspector of police, he says:

We must maintain law and order. . . . If possible, get the Muslims to go out peacefully. Nobody really benefits from bloodshed. . . . No, Inspector Sahib, whatever our views—and God alone knows what I would have done to these Pakistanis if I were not a government servant—we must not let there be any killing or destruction of property (p. 32).

And when, towards the close of the novel, Hukam Chand recognizes the failure of his administration to protect its Muslim citizens, he rehearses, as if in justification, his memories of Hindu and Sikh friends, colleagues and acquaintances butchered or raped in Pakistan. He knows he has abdicated his duty, and can only cry and pray (pp. 201–4). The novel thus emphasizes the criminal complicity of administrative systems in making inevitable the movement of minority populations. This is true even of the Sikh army officer who arrives with his Pakistani counterpart to oversee the evacuation. He has no time for the fellow-feeling expressed by the Sikh villagers of Mano Majra for their Muslim brethren; indeed he rebukes them for their affection, and all but tells them that their duty is to revenge the killing of Sikhs in Pakistan (pp. 157–8). Similarly, when Malli and his gang are appointed the custodians of evacuee property by the army officer and promptly loot Muslim homes, the novel suggests the active participation of Sikh soldiers (p. 160).

In *Train to Pakistan*, close-quarters violence is endemic in the village even before the horrors unleashed by Partition: Malli and his gang beat and spear the money-lender Ram Lal to death, the police twist testicles and thrust red chillies up rectums in order to get information out of arrested men, Jugga grabs an opportunity to thrash Malli. The novel suggests, if only dimly, the continuity between such routine violence and that of mass murder; the same hot-headed village youth who offer to kill any outsider who disturbs the Mano Majra community rally around to attack the train carrying their Muslim friends to Pakistan. What all this means is that there is at least some attempt made in the novel to understand the social and religious roots of communal violence, to explore the connections between the daily life of the villagers of Mano Majra and the violence visited upon, and perpetrated by, them. To that extent the novel does not give in to the convenient temptation to blame some violent 'outsider' as the motivation behind all evil, which is of course the easy fiction, the scapegoat, that we offer for our own misdeeds.

The novel thus does not view the tragedies of history—the destruction of the community of Mano Majra—via a purely personal lens. Notwithstanding all its problems, the novel has found a large readership, which begs the question of what it is about the power of not very compelling writing (or indeed cinema) to keep us riveted, so long as the stories told are those of Partition? We hunger for these stories not simply because they address the religious and social divides of a time past but because they engage with painful contemporary realities; the effects of the partition of India and Pakistan malinger into today, and Mano Majras are still torn apart, literally and figuratively, as they were fifty years ago. We need these stories then to put to rest the ghost trains that wail in our sleep, but for that reason, we need creative and analytic production adequate to the burdens of our violence-haunted history. In 1956, *Train to Pakistan* tried to imagine (even as the novel featured acts of everyday violence and ended in despair) a near-utopian village community as a kind of retrospective solace for the violence of Partition. Four decades later, we might need such utopian longing even more, but not at the cost of fuller, more critically acute, accounts of the dismemberment of communities and places.

On This Volume

In the original 'Call for Papers' circulated for this volume, potential contributors were asked to address a variety of questions and themes.[18] They were asked, *inter alia*, to consider the ways in which the known and unknown legacies of Partition play important roles in the constitution of collective identity and thinking in India today. They were asked to examine how we remember Partition—if we remember that enormous trauma and dislocation at all—and how these memories effect our functioning and our institutions. The volume sought to encourage intellectual and cultural histories of the political and social events, official policies and procedures, violence and displacement that constitute Partition, but also of healing and recovery, repression and forgetting, or of re-enactment and reiterations of the original divide. Contributors were asked if they thought particular varieties of testimonial or evidence have been left out, or under-emphasized, in the histories of Partition thus far, and to think of lacunae in materials, and of the particular shape or nature of the many archives that have been studied by those would narrate and analyse Partition.

The overarching question was: What was happened since Partition that inescapably refers back to, or perhaps is shaped by, that event? How accurate is it to claim that constitutive elements of our post-Independence sense of the nation (of the national or collective self) originated in, or was confirmed by, Partition? Contributors were invited to think about the psychological dimensions of this question, but also about more material concerns: how has state policy been guided by fears legitimized by the processes of Partition? The 'Call for Papers' emphasised the need to study critically the forms and nature of intellectual and creative enquiry into Partition and its aftermath. Similar questions could be asked about the concerns and practices of certain academic disciplines. Of History, for instance: how might the dominant forms of nationalist historiography alter if the study of Partition provided crucial materials, paradigms and concepts? Further, if we recognize that Partition is made and remade for us by different forms of documentary, fictional and even analytical representation, what do we learn from our reading of particular instances of, or trends within, such representation?

I had also asked contributors to evaluate certain questions of method: what might be the critical or analytical vocabularies best suited to an exploration of what we might call 'Partition materials and issues.' Psychoanalysis might provide ready paradigms—trauma, repression (and the return of the repressed), mourning (and its incomplete variant, melancholia)—but how useful might it be to extend terms designed for the diagnosis of the individual psyche to collective identities and national narratives? Similarly, the notion of 'difference', so important to deconstruction and cultural studies, is one that seems to offer quick application to the self-other dialectic necessary to the constitution of national identity—or is this polarity too rigid and cumbersome to be of use in describing the play of multiple subject-positions in the subcontinent? Other academic disciplines have equivalent concepts central to their operations: are such concepts flexible and powerful enough to enable textured accounts of the human and material problems posed by Partition?

Those were some of the questions posed; readers of this volume, however, will find that they have not always been answered, nor even provide the parameters within which contributors have worked. This has not proved a problem; indeed, contributors have widened the scope of the volume by bringing to bear their own concerns, often in areas that were not indicated in the 'Call for Papers', but which are, in overt or less immediate ways, all connected with the study of Partition and of its presence in our lives. Their essays, which I will introduce in this section, show just how foundational the material and symbolic histories of Partition are to so much that has been happening in the subcontinent after 1947, and how those divisions, or notions of those divisions, structure our public, institutional, and even private lives. In each case contributors are concerned with the perceptions—religious, cultural, political—that fed into, and were intensified by, the events of Partition. They study the divisions and dislocations of that time not only because they are a mine of historical information, but because they hold the key to understanding certain kinds of political consciousness or cultural activity today.

In 'Partition and the North West Frontier', the first of the two essays dealing with culture and history in what is now a part of Pakistan, Mukulika Banerjee fuses anthropological fieldwork with a historian's awareness when she speaks to survivors of the Khudai Khidmatgars (the famous Pukhtun Red Shirts). They offer poignant testimony to the fact that an extraordinary political and ethical movement in the North Western Frontier Province was treated with great suspicion by the colonial authorities, as by the Muslim League and the Congress, with the result that much that they stood for was marginalized by narrow nationalistic politics in pre-Partition India and then proscribed by the government in independent Pakistan. What energized them was Khan Abdul Gaffar Khan's vision of a non-violent, cooperative, multi-communal anti-imperialism, a vision co-opted by the Congress but abandoned by them when it came to agreeing to Partition, and certainly a vision that found little place in Pakistan after Partition. As Banerjee discovers, it is the memories—however meandering or imperfect—of the rank and file members of the Khudai Khidmatgars which function as a now-corroded bulwark against the precise narratives of histories authorized by the state, narratives which would deny them a place within the received tradition of Pakistani political history.

Joya Chatterji's 'Right or Charity?' goes back to the discursive and ideological differences (and the commonalties) between the relief and rehabilitation measures offered by the central and state governments to Bengali refugees in the years after Partition and those demanded by the refugees themselves. What governments might have considered their charitable obligations, Bengali Hindu refugees claimed as their right, a right granted to them by their having sacrificed their interests in what became East Pakistan so that Calcutta and West Bengal could be designated part of India. Chatterji observes how the specialized claims of the refugees (as refugees) broadened into a series of demands made on the grounds of *citizen's* rights, thus contributing immeasurably to the growth of democratic—and Left—consciousness in Bengal. Her interest in this debate over rights thus expands into a recognition of the role marginal groups such as the refugees have played in creating alternative 'notions of legitimacy and citizenship in India' (p. 77). A history of displaced people, and a historian's enquiry into their lives, which begins with the upheavals of Partition ends in a story of changes in democratic consciousness that changed political and public life in Bengal (and by extension, left-wing politics in India as a whole).

Ramnarayan Rawat's 'Partition Politics and Achhut Identity' calls attention to a unique and formative phase in Dalit politics. He argues that discussions about the constitutional protection of minority rights sparked off by the prospect of Partition and Independence allowed Dalits to claim a political community and agenda that differentiated them, as a community, from caste-Hindus. Rather than choose between the two poles of identity—Hindu or Muslim—that the events of the time seemed to make inevitable, Rawat shows how a Dalit political organization like the Scheduled Castes Federation in UP worked to mobilize a separate Dalit identity, and saw in this mobilization the route to legislative and administrative power. He examines the SCF's anti-Congress politics (and its decision to ally itself, on occasion, with the Muslim League), and revisits Ambedkar's decision to join Nehru's cabinet as Law Minister in 1948 to suggest the nature of Ambedkar's pragmatism. He also describes the anti-*begari* agitation engaged in by Dalit rural labourers who refused to do 'customary' work without wages both for landlords and for arms of the state like the police, and sees in such agitation another source of the separate identity claimed by Dalit political activists. In general, Rawat's essay is a reminder that the politics of Partition need to be disaggregated more than they are in available historiography, which tends to see Dalit activism in the period as a negligible subset of 'nationalist' (that is, Congress) politics.

Sunil Kumar's essay, 'Qutb and Modern Memory,' is an investigation into the power of 'national' monuments to evoke—in symbolic shorthand—a historical past whose putative religio-cultural tensions continue to fuel communal divides in India. He seeks to understand 'the manner in which the Qutb complex is understood today,' (p. 141) an understanding that is produced by the visual impressions of visitors to the complex (who notice the 'redeployed temple spoils' used in its construction), the Archaeological Survey of India billboards describing the monument, but especially the historiographical practices that have authorized the conclusion that the mosque on the site is evidence of the monolithic and destructive power of 'Muslim rule' and 'Islamic piety' in medieval India. Sunil Kumar offers a methodologically complex argument which disaggregates 'Muslim rule' in that period into a series of competing states and local powers, and shows how forms of Islamic belief then (as now) contested each other's claims to purity or authenticity of religious practice. The long process by which different rulers (and their religious supporters) built, broke down, and re-built the Qutb complex shows just how historically inappropriate it is to think of a monolithic Islamic presence in medieval India (as it is to think of a single 'Hindu' religion or culture). He, in short, *historicizes* the construction and reconstruction of the Qutb complex to restore to us a history of the 'complex, fragmented political and religious world of India's Middle Ages, a time when there was considerable disunity and contestation within the groups defined as "Hindus" and "Muslims" ' (p. 175). Such a history, one which refuses the easy polarizations of an age-old 'Muslim' and 'Hindu' India in favour of an accurate reading of more local enmities and alliances between and within religious groupings, is of particular importance now, at a time when political ideologues travesty history in order to insist that 'wrongs inflicted in the past upon the Hindu community' need correction today.

In 'Performing Partition in Lahore,' Richard Murphy calls attention to the contradictions and ironies attendant on the choreographed, aggressive ceremonial exchanges that are a nightly feature of the flag-lowering ceremonies at the Wagah border crossing,[19]and in the comparatively recent phenomenon of Basant parties in Lahore. In the first case Murphy details the need to produce 'a pure theatre of difference' which will 'dramatize the political contention that India and Pakistan are two distinct and mutually antagonistic states.' (p. 185). In the second, he shows how the Basant celebrations are now explained by Lahoris in a way that suggests that this festival has no connection with similar earlier multi-community, particularly Hindu, celebrations in pre-Partition Lahore. In each case, what drives this play of similarity and enforced difference is, ultimately, the desire for a simplified nationalism in which 'the extreme cultural and religious pluralism of north India is flattened into a simple contrast between two distinct nations who, like the Pakistani and Indian troops at Wagah, constitute one another's negation' (p. 191). This is one of the two essays in this volume on the legacies of Partition in Pakistan today, and, as Murphy makes clear in sections of the essay, it is uncanny how religious nationalisms on each side of the border mirror each other's cultural and political paranoias.

Urvashi Butalia's 'An Archive with a Difference', takes her back to the kinds of non-conventional sources that she developed in her book, *The Other Side of Silence.* This time she does look at archived material—letters written by people directly affected by the miseries of Partition to those in civil and administrative authority, letters that ask for help, for succour and protection. These letters still read as the poignant appeals that they were meant to be, for they were written by ordinary people, displaced by events and decisions larger than themselves, looking to the new state and its representatives to redeem them from their difficulties, to give them a fresh start. Butalia reads from these letters accounts of the loss of community and the determined reestablishment of community; stories of families and individuals displaced as well as stories of their desire to create once again familiar activities, sources of livelihood, neighbourhoods. These letters convey an immediacy of concern that, Butalia points out, is lost in retrospective accounts of those traumatic times; here, people worry about the everyday details of life, details that are massaged over by the operations of memory many decades later. Fifty years down, no one expects from the state what these letter-writers—hopeful citizens of the new nation, for which they had sacrificed much—expected and demanded then. Theirs was the experience of many disappointments, not least of which was the recognition that the new nation and the state would not be able to solve all their problems, big and small.

Priyamvada Gopal's essay, 'Bodies Inflicting Pain', offers a compelling reminder that Manto's celebrated and vilified explorations of the traumas of Partition focused not only on the victimage of women but on crises of masculinity, especially as that masculinity was reconfigured in the theatre of sexualized mass violence. In her reading Manto's response to 'catastrophe and breakdown' was 'to grieve. At the same time, however, he found himself preoccupied with the question of reconstruction: could different ways of being and relating emerge out of the destruction and disorientation he saw around him?' (p. 245). Manto's stories, in this case 'Thanda Gosht', make clear that such psychic transformation 'would require not only the "emancipation" of female subjects but also the reconstitution of male subjects and psyches.' These stories thus make visible 'manliness and masculinity—terms that tend to be unmarked in progressive and, certainly, nationalist discourses of gender.' (p. 253) Manto understood the disturbing power of chaotic libidinal energies in the transformation of psychic and political life; Gopal argues that it is this insight, enacted in some of his stories, that caused the state and its magistrates to rule on their purported 'obscenity'.

Nita Kumar's essay, 'Children and the Partition,' uses an ethnographic method to meditate on the gap between the secular, modernizing, universalistic pedagogic agenda of the nation (as made available in 'mainstream' schools) and the more specific, limited and sectarian instruction provided, in one instance, by a Barelwi madrasa in Banaras. But her interest is not so much in school curriculi or teaching methods as in the play between the 'histories' that are taught in these different schools and the life-experiences of young students. The Ansari children who study in (and most often drop-out mid-way through) the madrasas may know little about the modern anti-colonial history of India, but they are encouraged to feel themselves part of a living local community whose history goes back to the coming of Islam to the region almost a thousand years ago. The children in the 'progressive' schools certainly know more about the history of the modern nation, but this does not mean that they feel personally implicated in its narratives, even when they are the children of refugees who came to Calcutta during Partition. There exists a distance between the prescriptions of nationalist history and their own understanding of their relation to the nation, and Nita Kumar ends with the hope that educators and historians will learn to teach in ways that respect 'alternative wills' to individual and community action even as we teach the awareness necessary to modern citizenship.

This is a variegated cluster of essays, one whose disparate though linked concerns suggests the many ways in which the tangled skein of Partition might be unravelled. We have long recognized and debated the historical and ideological complexity of the issues that led up to Partition; we now need perhaps to rethink 'Partition' itself. Such a rethinking is in fact forced upon us by the shift away from the 'high political' histories of Partition. Any accounting of the human experiences that defined Partition, and the cultural and political tensions confirmed or exacerbated by its turbulent processes, moves us away from authorised narratives of Partition as primarily the colonial process that produced two (then three) nations on the subcontinent. Just as the 'causes' of Partition were many, its effects are myriad and lingering; indeed they are constitutive (in acknowledged or in repressed ways) of family, community and public life on the subcontinent. If one powerful meaning of Partition is the cleavage of the subcontinent, another is represented by the desire, expressed in story, in poem and in conversation, to cleave to near-utopian memories of undivided mohallas, communities and indeed of the undivided subcontinent itself. It is another matter that what is seen as a terrible fall into division and loss by some is seen as the beginnings of national possibility by others, that the lost unities mourned by some are seen as romanticized nostalgia by those who would emphasise the separateness of nations and communities. Human practices are changeable, as is, for that reason, 'history'—this is why we need the kinds of enquiry into our recent past, and our present, that this volume represents.

NOTES AND REFERENCES

1. Arundhati Roy, 'The End of Imagination', *Frontline*, 15:16, 1–14 August 1998, p. 13.
2. 'It took 1984 to make me understand how ever-present Partition was in our lives too, to recognize that it could not be so easily put away inside the covers of history books.' Urvashi Butalia, *The Other Side of Silence: Voices from the Partition of India*, New Delhi: Viking, 1998, p. 5. Ritu Menon and Kamla Bhasin open their book, *Borders and Boundaries: Women in India's Partition*, New Delhi: Kali for Women, 1998, by writing of the killing of Sikhs in North India in 1984: 'But here was Partition once more in our midst, terrifying for those who had passed through it in 1947. . . . Yet this was our own country, our own people, our own home-grown violence. Who could we blame now?', p. xi.
3. Ilyas Ahmad Gaddi, 'A Land Without Sky', in *An Epic Unwritten: The Penguin Book of Partition Stories from Urdu*, ed. and trans. Muhammad Umar Memon, New Delhi: Penguin, 1998, p. 347.
4. See, for instance, Shail Mayaram, 'Speech, Silence and the Making of Partition Violence in Mewat', *Subaltern Studies IX: Writings on South Asian History and Society*, eds, Shahid Amin and Dipesh Chakrabarty, New Delhi: Oxford University Press, 1996, pp. 126–63.

5. For an instance of the issues raised by, and the intellectual and political stakes involved in, contemporary discussions of Partition, see Ayesha Jalal, 'Secularists, Subalterns, and the Stigma of "Communalism": Partition Historiography Revisited', *IESHR*, 33:1, 1996, pp. 93–103.

6. See, for instance, Menon and Bhasin, *Borders and Boundaries*; Urvashi Butalia, 'Community State and Gender: Some Reflections on the Partition of India', *OLR* 16, 1994, pp. 31–67 and *The Other Side of Silence*.

7. See Ashis Nandy, 'Too Painful for Words?' *The Sunday Times of India Review*, 20 July 1997, pp. 1–3. Nandy claims that the silence about Partition violence was 'even more dismal in the case of Bengal. Though half the killings had taken place in that part of the world, the literary imagination there had obstinately refused to rise to the situation,' p. 1. For Nandy, Ritwik Ghatak's films contain a few passages which register such violence and terror.

8. 'The Long Silence', interview conducted by Meenakshi Verma, *The Sunday Times of India Review*, 20 July 1997, p. 1.

9. Amitav Ghosh, *The Shadow Lines*, New Delhi: Ravi Dayal Publisher, 1988, pp. 77–8.

10. The insistent need to link all discussions of Partition with the pressing socio-cultural and political issues of our day is played out—compellingly and usefully—in the essays collected in *Interventions*, 1:2, 1999, which features a 'Special Topic: The Partition of the Indian Sub-Continent', edited by Ritu Menon. Central to the conceptual method of many of these essays are metaphors of 'silence' that demand articulation, of a present 'haunted' by events and memories of the past, and of the 'traumatic' need to tell tales, to bear critical witness.

11. Jamila Hashmi's 'Banished', is written from the point of view of one woman who does not go 'home'. The story is a meditation on human dislocation and loss, but also on resignation, and to a lesser degree, reconciliation. In this story, as in so much of the literary corpus of Partition (as Manto's stories exemplify most powerfully), irony is a central trope—everyday reality is represented via its own inversion—as in this passage when the narrator explains why she must stay in the home of the man she is 'married' to:

> And besides, every girl must one day leave her parental home to join her in-laws. Well, maybe Bhai and Bhaiyya weren't present at my wedding—so what? Hadn't Gurpal [her abductor] rolled out a carpet of corpses for me? Painted the roads red with blood? Provided an illumination by burning down city after city? Didn't people celebrate my wedding as they stampeded, screaming and crying? It was a wedding, all right. Only the customs were new: celebration by fire, smoke and blood.
>
> (Memon, ed., *Epic Unwritten*, p. 102)

In debates on the recovery of women in the Indian Constituent Assembly, speakers often demanded that India go to war to recover its abducted women in the manner of Ram rescuing Sita from Ravan's court (see, for instance, Menon and Bhasin, *Borders and Boundaries*, p. 114). This mythic precedent shows up in Hashmi's story too, once again in a rhetorical reversal—this is the narrator explaining her decision to hide from government agents who came to recover women like her. 'Rather than embrace a second exile, Sitaji has accepted a life with Ravan', p. 104. Partition stories point out, like no other, the vulnerability of women in times of social turmoil.

12. This paragraph summarizes concerns and findings central to both the books mentioned here, which offer varied (and internally differentiated) examples along these lines.

13. See for instance (and I mention only anthologies of writing translated into English) Mushirul Hasan, ed., *India Partitioned: The Other Face of Freedom*, 2 vols, New Delhi: Roli Books, 1995: this is a collection of 'stories, poems, diaries, eye-witness accounts and excerpts from novels and autobiographies'; Saros Cowasjee and K.S. Duggal, eds, *Orphans of the Storm: Stories of the Partition of India*, New Delhi: UBS Publishers, 1995; Alok Bhalla, *Stories of the Partition of India*, 3 vols, New Delhi: Harper Collins, 1994.

14. Faiz Ahmed Faiz, 'The Dawn of Freedom, August 1947', trans. Agha Shahid Ali.

15. Bhalla, ed., *Stories of the Partition*, I: p. xxxiii.

16. All the problems of this novel are compounded in Pamela Rooks's 1997 film based on it, whose inane and weak screenplay makes the novel read like a mine of sociological, cultural and historical insight. The movie expends no energy at all in individuating or defining its locale, nor does it provide any sense of the role played by the railway in the collective consciousness of Mano Majra. The film is perhaps most thin in its understanding of the presence of violence, including sexual violence, in the lives of the villagers. Since it is committed to representing Jugga and Nooran's affair according to the romantic conventions of mainstream cinema, it prettifies their rendezvous in ways that the novel does not, and is oblivious to the forms of violence that are an unremarkable fact of life in the village.

17. Khushwant Singh, *Train to Pakistan*, New Delhi: Ravi Dayal Publisher, 1988, [1956], p. 10. All references are to this edition.

18. The 'Call for Papers' was sent out to a number of academics and writers in India, and to some in Pakistan and Bangladesh. As is usually the case, a number of promised contributions did not materialize; sadly, it proved impossible to elicit essays from Bangladeshi and Pakistani intellectuals.

19. In a recent documentary titled 'A Season Outside', Amar Kanwar (New Delhi/1997/Video/32 mins./The India's Quest Project) begins his exploration of the forms conflict takes in public and private life in India by focusing on the symbolic inter-national violence and threat enacted every evening at the Wagah border. The film is a meditation on the possibility of, and the importance of, non-violent activism in a public and private sphere saturated by everyday or more spectacular forms of violence.

Partition and the North West Frontier: Memories of Some Khudai Khidmatgars

MUKULIKA BANERJEE

T HE NORTH WEST Frontier may seem an unlikely site in which to explore the legacy of Partition. For a ninety-six per cent Muslim majority province[1] which became a part of Pakistan in August 1947, it seems a less problematic issue compared to other provinces where the proportion of Muslims and Hindus was not this straightforward. Nor was it like East Pakistan which the Muslim League bargained for and made part of Pakistan despite it being separated from its western half by the expanse of India. The Frontier on the other hand, was conveniently positioned, lying adjacent to the provinces of Sind, Balochistan and the Punjab, which formed West Pakistan.

On second thoughts however, there emerge several reasons for the need to explore the legacy of Partition in the Frontier. It was, for example, the only Muslim majority province to have three Congress ministries between the years 1930 and 1947 and was the site of one of the most remarkable historical instances of the practice of non-violence. The practitioners were the famous Pathan Red Shirts, the Khudai Khidmatgars, led by their charismatic leader Khan Abdul Gaffar Khan who is known to most in the Indian sub-continent as Badshah Khan or Frontier Gandhi. The Pathans had been allied to the Indian National Congress since 1930, were political and ideological opponents

of the All India Muslim League throughout and had an elected ministry in place at the time of the Third June Plan. Unlike other provinces
in British India, however, they were subjected to a referendum to decide whether they would join India or Pakistan.[2] Badshah Khan and
the Khudai Khidmatgars (hereafter KKs) found the referendum an
unfair imposition and boycotted it; the result of the referendum was
therefore unsurprisingly in favour of the NWFP joining Pakistan.[3]
Making nonsense of their geographical contiguity with Pakistan but
much of their ideological identification with the Congress, the KKs
often posed the rhetorical question in the 1990s that, 'If East and West
Pakistan could be separated by India, why could not we form West
India and be separated from the rest of India by Pakistan?' They repeated to me Badshah Khan's last words to the Congress, 'You have thrown
us to the wolves.'

A second reason for considering the legacy of the Partition in the
Frontier is to represent for the first time the point of view of the political actors in the Frontier which has been entirely ignored so far in the
historiography of the Independence movement. The KK movement
has been written about by a few scholars, but mostly from historical
records and literary sources and some interviews with political leaders
of the movement.[4] In my interviews with KKs in the early 1990s, I explored the praxis of the ideology of the movement and what the *bri-
colage* of Islam, Pukhtun custom and non-violence meant for ordinary
Pukhtuns. This was essential for an understanding of the KK movement
through which a sense of pan-Pukhtun identity was forged for the first
time.

Badshah Khan's appeals for non-violence were achieved through a
cessation of intra-Pukhtun feuding and the adoption of new forms of
loyalty and hierarchy that the structures of leadership and recruitment
in the movement brought about. These changes in Pukhtun society
were a revolution in themselves. What I hope to do in this article is to
use the testimonies of the KKs to focus particularly on their memories
of Partition and the independence they had fought so hard for.[5] Nearly
fifty years after the event, most of the KKs I spoke to shared memories
of betrayal, profound sadness, helplessness and bewilderment about

the way in which their struggle ended in 1947. Their betrayal was two-fold. They felt rejected by the Congress on the one hand for agreeing to the referendum on their behalf and by the Muslim League on the other, for they were never recognized as freedom-fighters in the new nation of Pakistan.

It is also interesting to explore whether the political machinations for negotiating the terms of Partition encoded assumptions and pre-conceptions about the Frontier on the part of all the major political players: the British, the Congress and the Muslim League. All the players had certain notions about the Frontier and its people and these were displayed in several statements they made about it. Fundamentally they, as most people in India today, worked with a stereotype of the Frontier which seems to be close to the image of the Pathan we get from reading stories such as Tagore's 'Kabuliwallah' or Kipling's *Kim*. This stereotype of the Pathan is of a hot-headed, fiercely loyal man with a fragile ego, prone to violent retaliation but also gentle, almost child-like, in his behaviour towards those he loves. C.F. Andrews described Badshah Khan thus: 'In the year 1936 I was privileged to spend many days at Mahatma Gandhi's village home in Central India, at a time when Khan Abdul Gaffar Khan was staying with him. He is one of the noblest Muslims I have ever met, as tender as a child and as brave as a lion.'[6] Nehru, in *Discovery of India*, observed, 'When it is remembered that a Pathan loves his gun more than his brother, is easily excited, and has long had a reputation for killing at the slightest provocation, this self-discipline [in the KKs] appears little short of miraculous.'[7] But he goes on, 'Changes of religion made a difference, but could not change entirely the mental backgrounds which the people of those areas developed.'[8] During the run-up to Partition, Gandhi warned, 'Any fight among the Pathans themselves, who were a martial people, would be most regrettable and they were endeavouring to find means to avoid the referendum and its consequences.'[9]

This conception of the Pathan may have had an important role to play when it came to deciding whether to bargain for the Frontier to remain in India or to allow it go to Pakistan. In the final instance, the elected ministry led by Dr Khan Sahib in 1947 was not consulted when the decision to hold a referendum was taken and ratified by the AICC. It is worth speculating why this was allowed to happen.

'Frontier and Partition': this title, a pairing of contradictions, provides another entry point. Partition creates boundaries of the kind which exists today between India and Pakistan: a no-man's land flanked by barbed wires, severely protected, a hysterical political desire to keep two sides of the same community hermetically sealed off from each other.[10] A frontier on the other hand, is a region of exchange of cultures, goods, ideas and people. The North West Frontier of the Indian sub-continent has remained just such a place. Indeed, even today, the Durand Line demarcating Afghanistan from Pakistan, dividing the Pathans between two nation-states, is a porous zone through which refugees, trucks, drugs, guns and news of war flow easily. This has been the case always. As one of my informants from the Tribal Areas said, 'There used to be regular crossings across the Durand Line . . . British law was disregarded.' The Durand Line is thus the opposite of a boundary. This fact was beautifully demonstrated during the death and funeral of Badshah Khan in 1988, a recent memory for most of the sub-continent. The Frontier Gandhi died in Peshawar but was buried in Jalalabad, Afghanistan;[11] for his funeral a day's ceasefire was called in the Afghanistan war, thousands of his mourners from Pakistan were allowed to cross-over into Afghanistan without any formalities and political Premiers broke with protocol to attend. A frontier cannot be easily partitioned because its very nature as a region of exchange does not allow it.

Finally, I offer a personal example of what it is like for an ordinary Indian to live and work in Pakistan. I visited Pakistan over three trips between 1990 and 1993, staying for several months during the second. I lived in the house of Khan Abdul Wali Khan, the most politically active of Badshah Khan's sons, and a well-acknowledged friend of India.[12] I had gone to the Frontier with the express purpose of looking for surviving KKs in order to talk to them at some length about their perspective on non-violence, why they chose it, how difficult it was and so on. I was lucky enough to find seventy of them after much searching and their stories form an important component of my research data.[13] I will draw on these testimonies in this article and would like to emphasize that these stories and opinions were shared with me not merely because I was a curious researcher but also because I am Indian. To them, I came from the country they had fought for: this they told me repeatedly, so I would understand. Being young, Hindu, Bengali, and a woman, made my situation curious to the authorities but unambigous to my informants. This convinced them that I was there not with any political agenda or to search for my roots but because I really wanted to hear their stories. My Pathan and Pakistani colleagues and friends were suspicious of what these old men said to me, impatient at my interest in the opinions of a bunch of toothless, ordinary peasants ('they were just blind followers of Badshah Khan!'). Comparing notes with some of them who spoke to some of my informants as well, I found that the stories and opinions that I was privileged to hear were not repeated to them.[14] As an anthropologist and as an Indian I maintain that it is crucial to understand their point of view to accord them their place in history. The struggle of KKs, their membership of the Congress, and their eventual inclusion in Pakistan at Independence turned them into 'traitors' in their new country. The Frontier was not partitioned, it is true, but it did isolate some freedom fighters forever, in their own country. KKs and their leaders ironically spent more time in jail perhaps after Independence than before it. When I met these old men in the early 1990s, they were a marginalized and forgotten lot among their own people. Most of them were not alive to witness the jubilee celebrations of India and Pakistan and perhaps that is a good thing. For it would have resurrected for them, even more profoundly, the irony of their situation.

The Frontier and the Congress

The relationship between the Congress and the Frontier was always fraught with ambiguities and misunderstandings. The KK movement was the culmination of nearly two decades of Congress and other political activity in the North West Frontier. Initially the Congress in the

NWFP was affiliated to the Punjab Provincial Congress Committee and came under its jurisdiction. But in 1928, the Frontier Congress decided to establish itself as an independent Provincial Congress Committee. The general secretary of the Frontier Congress accordingly wrote to Nehru, then secretary of the AICC:

> I am directed to say that according to the original constitution of the Congress, the NWFP was separate from the Punjab. In 1923 at the Cocanada session of the Congress, it was however, at the insistence of the Frontier local workers, amalgamated with the Punjab. Since then, though it has been connected with the Punjab, the PPCC have not been able to devote any time or attention to our province with the result that there has been no Congress work here worth the name. Under the circumstances, the Frontier local workers had no option but to stand on their own legs and organize the work themselves . . . On the evening of the 17th Nov. after putting up a very successful demonstration of 'Black Flags' . . . Frontier Provincial workers met under the Presidentship of Mr Abdur Rahim Khan . . . and formed their own provisional PCC.[15]

This show of initiative on the part of the NWF Provincial Congress took the high command by surprise and Nehru was firm in his objection. He wrote back:

> I am little surprised to learn that a separate Provincial Congress Committee has been established in Peshawar. Separate PC can only be established by a decision of the Congress in its annual sessions. No other organization has authority to do so. I have no doubt that the Congress in Calcutta will agree to your proposal but so long as this formal sanction is not obtained we cannot treat your committee as a PCC . . . I would therefore request you to continue to function for the moment as part of the Punjab Provincial Congress Committee . . .[16]

This exchange of letters provides some idea of the nature of relations between the AICC and the North West Frontier at the outset. Until 1928, the Congress organization in the Frontier was weak and quite unremarkable, with almost no mass support; it was regarded by Congress national HQ with a degree of suspicion and patronizing tolerance as representing what was, to Delhi and Calcutta, a little understood and rather enigmatic part of British India. Things were to change rather dramatically with the events in Kissa Khani bazaar in April 1930, when the sacrifice and the courage of the Pukhtuns was lauded and recognized for the first time at an all-India level.

It is alleged that British troops fired at a crowd of unarmed demonstrators at Kissa Khani bazaar. The news of this incident took some time to filter out of the Frontier and when it did, the AICC immediately sent Sardar Patel to carry out an investigation.[17] It also said in its monthly report of April 1930:

> News of the Peshawar incidents was withheld by the Government and only garbled versions were given to the public. Part of the truth leaked out, however, which electrified the whole country. The courage, the patriotism, the non-violent spirit of the war-like Peshawaris[18] became famous and earned for the whole province a unique place in the history of the struggle. Peshawar day was celebrated all over the country to commemorate the heroic deeds of that city.

It was after this event that the emerging KK movement was faced with a ban. Only an affiliation with an established, respectable, national political party could ensure its survival and prevent its being labelled 'Bolshevik', implying a violent and subversive revolutionary faction: 'We could do this only by joining the Muslim League or the Congress' [Haji Sarfaraz Nazim].* Badshah Khan, despite his personal links with the Congress, felt that as Muslims, the KK ought naturally to affiliate with the Muslim League. Though in jail at the time, he allowed two KK leaders to approach the Muslim League about affiliation: their request was rebuffed. They then turned to the Congress, who made no effort to conceal their scepticism at the idea of a non-violent Pukhtun movement. Sarfaraz Nazim narrated to me the incident when Mian Jaffar Shah and Mian Akbar Khan approached the AICC for permission to affiliate:

> Tyabji, the Secretary of the Congress at the time, wondered how non-violence and the Frontier were ever going to be compatible. Our leaders then convinced him that NWFP had more non-violence than the rest of India. Fazle Rahim Saqi remembered Mahatma Gandhi asking the

*The names in square brackets at the end of quotes refer to the informant I am quoting.

Pathans 'What do you want and how?' (And Mahatma Gandhi sent Patel to the Frontier later to check out what we said). Our representative said that we wanted the British out of our country and with non-violence. Only then did Gandhi agree to the affiliation.

This was the first of many occasions on which the KKs had to prove their worth to the Congress, as being capable of 'civil' resistance, not merely of unruly fighting.[19]

In 1930 when Abdul Gaffar Khan was appointed by the AICC to coordinate the all India civil resistance programme in the NWFP, it was not without some apprehension:

> The local Khilafat Committee has received a letter from Nehru asking for their proposals for carrying out the programme of civil disobedience. The letter laid stress on the importance of observing non-violence *in view of the traditional reputation of the people of the Frontier for the opposite characteristic*. The local committee has referred to Abdul Gaffar Khan, who has been in consultation with the Congress and Khilafat Committee of Peshawar. The only concrete proposal so far has been picketing of liquor shops. . . .[20]

The Government probably expected unruly mobs and noisy demonstrations and this early encounter with civil disobedience (picketing) must have seemed an anti-climax.

While affiliation to the Congress provided much needed official credentials for the KKs at the time, it carried with it a tension that was to last through its entire existence. The source of the tension was twofold. First, the KK movement was primarily a movement of rural Pukhtuns, who were effectively cut off from the rest of the Indian subcontinent, where the Congress had its mass base. There was thus little interaction between the activists of the two sides. Also, the Frontier was (and continues to be) a subject of curiosity for Indians who lived beyond the Indus, an enigma with strange customs of blood-feuds and tribal loyalty, and their view of the 'violent Pathans' was every bit as stereotypical as that of the British. My informants recalled several of their visits to India which they remembered with affection. They also remember being taunted by other Muslims in India for not being 'real' Pathans who fought with arms; they bore these taunts with irritation but great wit. The KKs were aware that 'incidents of firing by the police and their atrocities occured with far more frequency and closer to each other in the Frontier than anywhere else in the Indian sub-continent.' For many reasons therefore, the KK movement always remained exclusively a Pukhtun movement.

Further, Badshah Khan himself desired that the KKs remain discrete from Congress organization in the Frontier. It was his novel ideology, combining aspects of Islam and non-violence while keeping in mind traditional Pukhtun codes of behaviour, which had attracted a large majority of believing Muslim Pukhtun peasants. The organization had its civil and military wings; the latter consisted of the mass rural base who wore red uniforms and had all the trappings of an army, save the arms. The 'civil' or *jirga* wing mostly had older and literate people in it. While Badshah Khan admitted to being Gandhi's disciple, he was well aware that popular response in the frontier was to *him* personally and to his own non-Hindu articulation of non-violence. He thus needed to maintain the clarity of his leadership, without confusing it with that of the Congress. As Mohammed Gul put it, 'Badshah Khan . . . was to the Frontier what Mahatma Gandhi was to the rest of India.'

This was one of the reasons behind having two separate wings in the KK movement. The military wing was more populist, explicitly Pukhtun, and largely autonomous. The civil *jirga* wing kept far closer coordinating ties with the Congress Committee. The Governor, George Cunningham, accurately reported Badshah Khan's policy.

Abdul Gaffar Khan insists on absolute independence for the Red Shirts, and maintains that any support or allegiance accorded to the Congress party by Red Shirts will be given under his orders and that the Red Shirts will take orders from nobody else. To ensure that this procedure is followed in practice he has appointed his nephew, Rab Nawaz, as commander-in-chief of the Red Shirts—thereby providing a further insulator against Congress interference. In this connection a general tendency in Ministerial circles is noticeable to avoid interference by the Congress Executive in Provincial administrative affairs . . . Abdul Gaffar Khan . . . has not attended recent AICC meetings, and has of late become more parochial in his activities. These . . . go to show that the Red Shirts are determined to maintain their own independence as an organization . . . A corollary to this view is that the Congress executive will go a long way to retain the allegiance of the Red Shirts and that Dr Khan Sahib will be given a long rein in implementing his policy.[21]

The last sentence indicates the leverage that the KKs (or the Red Shirts, as the British and Indians preferred to call them) had with the Congress. They provided the mass Pukhtun following from which the Congress ministries derived their legitimacy in NWFP. That the Congress was governing there was a vital vindication of its claim to represent both Muslim and Hindu populations throughout India. Several of my informants could vividly remember visits by Congress leaders to the Frontier Province. For instance, Gul Rahman, who used to be the General Secretary of Pdang, recalled that several Indian leaders were at the camps which used to be held at least once in three or four months. Likewise, Waris Khan remembered that Vijaylakshmi Pandit laid the foundation for the Khudai Khidmatgar Centre in Sardaryab and Gul Samand Khan remembered Devdas Gandhi's visit to the Frontier.[22] However, if the Congress gained kudos, the KK movement itself tended to suffer from the Congress ministries' weak performance in Provincial government. Its inability to deliver radical land reform tended to demoralize the peasantry and weaken KK activism.

The decision about keeping the two wings separate was Badshah Khan's idea, but there was always ambiguity surrounding this decision. He needed to keep the KKs away from the Congress to avoid the effect of *realpolitik* on party discipline but also the Congress away from the KKs because he was aware that the KKs' first allegiance was to him as a Pukhtun leader. Badshah Khan appears to have used the confusion with skill. He was rarely blamed in the several tensions and disagreements between the Congress and himself, and even when criticized, neither his credibility and following among the Pukhtuns nor his allegiance to the Congress and Gandhi were ever in serious doubt. If Badshah Khan had definite reasons for keeping the two organizations separate, he did not state them. The rumours and the uncertainty surrounding the autonomy of the KKs kept the speculations going and Badshah Khan did not need to commit himself by admitting that his loyalties were divided, if indeed they were. Both wings had their uses in the political life of the Frontier and he seemed to have worked out a division of labour both with his brother and within the organization to keep the Congress and the KK functioning independently and parallel to each other.

When Gandhi visited the Frontier it was reported thus:

> Mr Gandhi's visit . . . not a great success . . . his object in coming here not very clear . . . he no doubt, feels great anxiety regarding the relation between the Congress and the Red Shirt Party. Abdul Gaffar Khan's attitude towards Mr Gandhi is curious. He persists in refusing to allow the Red Shirts to become a part and parcel of the Congress, and shows no sign of changing his tactics in this respect, indeed by doing so he would surrender his independent position as a leader. At the same time he continues to sit at Mr Gandhi's feet as a veritable 'chela'.[23]

Clearly, the 'success', or lack of it, of Gandhi's visit was measured by the colonial government in terms of resolving the perceived tension between the KK organization and the PCC. The real object of his visit seems to have eluded British officials: it was to ascertain how well civil disobedience and non-violence were working in the Frontier. In this respect the trip was successful, inasmuch as Gandhi returned from it greatly reassured of the adherence of the Pukhtuns in the KK to non-violence. Fazle Rahim Saqi's memory of Gandhi's visit is invaluable to gain an insight into what the visit achieved:

> Gandhi was very close to Badshah Khan. He came to the Frontier to meet this army that Badshah Khan had. He said that he wanted to meet the Generals of this army. So the Generals were summoned and 12 of them were introduced to Gandhi in the Khudai Khidmatgar office. Gandhi asked them, 'Do you follow Badshah Khan as your leader? Do you obey him totally?' And they all said a prompt and vehement 'Yes!' Then Gandhi asked them, 'What will your reaction be if Badshah Khan one day decides to change and start to believe in violence?' The Generals tried to tell Gandhi that he was making a mistake and that there was no way in which

Badshah Khan would ever change his ideology. When Gandhi still insisted, a General called Anwar, my father's brother's son, replied, 'We can
leave Badshah Khan but we cannot leave non-violence.'

This is believed to have impressed Gandhi very much. The visit also
achieved some familiarization on the part of the KKs about leaders of
the Congress. Gurfaraz Khan said about this or other visits:

> Gandhi came, Nehru came . . . Gandhi was a Hindu, he was in charge of
> the movement in other parts of India . . . he was a frail man and had a goat
> with him. Badshah Khan and Dr Khan Sahib accompanied him every-
> where; I personally saw him in Peshawar Cantt . . . he had come here be-
> cause we had invited him . . . without an invitation nobody comes to visit
> us . . .

Also note here (and in Mohammed Gul's statement that follows at the
end of this paragraph) the candid ease with which people in the
Frontier spoke of Gandhi. Never was he referred to as 'Gandhiji', the
more honorific term of reference in India, neither as 'the Mahatma' or
'Bapu'. Here he was another Congress leader whom they had seen and
formed their own opinions about. 'Gandhi was an intelligent politician
because he managed to bring the whole of India together . . . that was
not an easy task to have accomplished.'

What the Governor did not realize was that his earlier remark about
Badshah Khan being a 'veritable chela of Gandhi' was indeed true.
Badshah Khan's first allegiance was to Gandhi personally and only
secondarily to the All India Congress Committee. Dr Waris told me
that 'Badshah Khan used to say that he was Gandhi's soldier . . . he
even refused the title of 'Frontier Gandhi' because he felt it created a
sense of competitiveness.' On several occasions, he took Gandhi's side
against other Congress leaders. The resignation of all Congress Provincial Ministries in 1939 was one such example, where he agreed with
Gandhi that resignation was an important act of non-cooperation,
even though many of their colleagues were keen on retaining power.
In many ways Badshah Khan's role in the Frontier was similar to that
of Gandhi's in the subcontinent. They were both ideologues with great

crowd appeal. They both shunned office and left such tasks to Nehru and Dr Khan Sahib respectively, men who were themselves in fact similar (and good friends) and suited to executive duties. This is perhaps the reason why Mohammed Gul said, 'Badshah Khan will never be born again. He was to the Frontier what Mahatma Gandhi was to India . . . There was Dr Khan Sahib and Badshah Khan in the Frontier and Jawaharlal Nehru and Mahatma Gandhi in India.' It is interesting to note that Maulana Hamdullah Jan clarified that Badshah Khan was more akin to Gandhi than other Muslim leaders in the Congress, for example, Maulana Azad. When I pressed him to clarify why, he explained, 'The difference between Maulana Azad and Badshah Khan was that the former did not lead a simple life. He wore Turkish clothes, travelled First Class and lived in the best hotels.' Sarfaraz Nazim may have echoed the opinion of his comrades when he said, 'Badshah Khan and Gandhi were reformers born to this world which needed them. They were men who were unshakeable in their beliefs. Mountains would move but their beliefs would not. The Congress Working Committee had some of the best minds. The British were continually creating problems and these leaders always showed the way out of them.' The feeling among all my informants was that Badshah Khan and Gandhi occupied a status which was very special compared to the other leaders around them. This is certainly the feeling today in India too. The Government of India made this clear when it offered a final resting place for Badshah Khan beside Gandhi in Raj Ghat, Delhi, when his death was imminent in 1988.

Most rank and file KKs were aware of the tensions between the Congress organization and their movement and the repercussions these had for the success of their movement. But there was also among the KKs a great sense of pride in the impact they made on outsiders, particularly the Congress. When Nehru arrived in the Province on 26 May 1940 for a short visit, he said nothing sinister but they thought it evident he wanted all the credit for their actions to go to the Congress.[24] Akram Khan remembered one visit by Nehru:

> Nehru came to the Frontier in 1938. He went to Hazara and then came to Swabi. We received him by lining the streets, waving flags . . . we were

wearing our uniforms. Nasveen Kaka and me were told to remove the seats in the bus that Nehru was travelling in and make up a bed for him for the night. We greeted him next morning along with Salar Munir Khan and others. Nehru crossed the river in a boat that was decorated in red with a band on board and lots of photographers . . . You see, Hindus also followed Badshah Khan. When Nehru made his speech, he said, 'Thank you for the warm reception, which was not for me but for the President of the Congress.'

Shah Jahan Khan and Gul Rahman told me:

> When Gandhi visited the Frontier KKs lined the streets from Utmanzai to Charsadda. At the meeting that was held, Gandhi said: 'I congratulate you that you have the privilege of being led by Badshah Khan. I have been to several public meetings all over the country but the level of organization in today's meeting surpasses all of them. There is so much discipline . . . everybody is so quiet that one can hear the birds!'

The KKs appeared to be well aware of the image that outsiders, not least the leaders of the Congress, had of them as supposedly unruly Pathans. They told me about Gandhi's statement as a way of reassuring me that all they had been telling me about the organization and the peaceful activities of the movement was really true: it had happened, and *even Gandhi had acknowledged it.* Muffariq Shah, a *khan* involved in the movement, reiterated this: 'Our organization consisted of hundreds and hundreds of workers, totally disciplined and ready to carry out any orders given to them by their leaders. Gandhi and Nehru used to be amazed and scared of this army!' This amazement is evident in the following passage from *Discovery of India*:

> Of all the remarkable happenings in India in recent times, nothing is more astonishing than the way in which Abdul Gaffar Khan made his turbulent and quarrelsome people accept peaceful methods of political action, involving enormous suffering. That suffering was indeed terrible and has left a trail of bitter memories; and yet their discipline and self-control were such that no act of violence was committed by the Pathans against the Government forces or others opposed to them [in the Frontier, during the 1942 agitations]. There was firing on the demonstrators and the usual methods of suppressing popular activities were adopted. Several thousands of

people were arrested, and even the great Pathan leader, Badshah Khan was seriously injured by police blows. *This was extreme provocation and yet, surprisingly enough, the excellent discipline, which Abdul Gaffar Khan has established among his people, held, and there were no violent disturbances there of the kind that occurred in many parts of the country.*[25]

The alliance with the Congress was a process of reciprocity between the KK and the larger nationalist movement. As one of my informants, Haji Sarfaraz Nazim saw it, there was a clear symbiosis between the KK and the Congress. The Congress claimed to represent all communities and religions and the NWFP ministry made a crucial contribution to this claim as the province had a ninety-six per cent Muslim majority. In return, the KK was able to share in the Congress's respectability in British eyes and avoid the 'Bolshevik' label which had been used against it in the past. But as we have seen in this section, the alliance was not without ambiguities and as the principal leader commanding both the provincial Congress and the KK, Badshah Khan had continously to strike a balance between the approaches and claims of the two.

Memories of Allegations

One crucial theme in the narratives of the Khudai Khidmatgars was memories of the political opponents of the KKs who used the alliance with the Congress as an excuse to discredit the KKs as 'Hindus' thereby also implying their lack of martial valour or incapacity for 'taking an eye for an eye'. Non-violent civil disobedience was as new a method of protest to the Pukhtuns as to the rest of India and was clearly associated with Gandhi and the Congress. However, KKs in jail were repeatedly made to wear orange clothes to mark them as Hindu and worse still there were numerous mentions by my informants of their 'manhood being compromised in various ways for involvement with the movement.' Sarfaraz Nazim remembered a striking comment made by one of their opponents that 'Badshah Khan had turned Pukhtuns into eunuchs and lions into sheep.' The 'feminization' of politics and suffering through civil disobedience is a separate and well-known discussion; here it is important to note that this idea was repeatedly inscribed on the bodies of the men with some violence. Various organizations tried repeatedly to brand the KKs as *kafirs* for their so-called non-Islamic ways and Haji Sarfaraz Nazim Saheb remembered how during the '1946 elections . . . the British had a new plan for anti-propaganda. They created *Anjuman Asfiya* (consisting of religious elders) and declared Manki Sharif, a Muslim Leaguer, its head. A lot of elders of the sub-continent joined the organization. They held a conference in which they passed a resolution declaring that Badshah Khan and all Khudai Khidmatgaran were *kafirs.'*

Badshah Khan on that occasion called a KK meeting and clarified their position. 'He said that we were Khidmatgars of the people and not kafirs. As the elections were very close, Badshah Khan travelled through every zilla personally clarifying his position. But he never asked for votes.' Badshah Khan himself seems to have been the butt of accusation often. When he started a *gur mandi* to encourage enterprise, self-reliance and freedom from money-lenders, he was branded a Hindu by other khans, because thus far such trade had been the forte of Hindus. Badshah Khan had to come up with ingenious solutions to respond to these accusations peacefully. According to Haji Chairman Meherban Shah:

> There was a lot of propaganda against Badshah Khan saying that he was a Hindu. Badshah Khan had changed Pukhtun people you see. Earlier people used to stay and interact within the confines of their tribes. But Badshah Khan changed all that. The British and the mullahs opposed this and started a lot of propaganda against him. They used to say that he was a Hindu and that *halal* from his hands was not valid. He finally decided one day to take off his turban to prove that he was not a Sikh and never covered his head again.[26]

In another story, Jarnail Hazrat Gul recalled how:

> we were constantly told that we were Hindu supporters and therefore kafirs. Badshah Khan was constantly bothered with questions about his faith in Islam. He was once asked why he did not slaughter cows (because you know that Hindus don't) and he replied, 'I am not a butcher that's why.' However the man persisted in asking him the same question and after the

third time Badshah Khan said, 'Why don't you bring me one of the bulls from the pair that pull your plough and I will certainly slaughter him!'

Such repartee was not only the forte of Badshah Khan. When Jarnail Hazrat Gul was taunted by a bystander for being seen to be carrying a charkha, his quick retort was 'that it was not a charkha I was carrying but a cannon . . . I said it was a cannon that would exterminate London.' Interestingly, this was a metaphor used often by many of my informants. The metaphor encoded the militancy of civil disobedience and self-reliance that was vivid in the minds of their interlocutors. Despite all the allegations, the KKs remained defiant in their identification with the Congress. As Fazle Karim, who came from Pabbi, recalled with pride, because of its huge number of volunteers, 'Pabbi was nicknamed "Wardha" after Gandhiji's ashram.'

Thus we see that the KKs had to constantly prove to the rest of the Frontier that their political ideology was in fact wholly compatible with Islam. Their interrogators were not always fellow Muslims though. C.F. Andrews, a devout Christian, learnt in his discussions with Badshah Khan about

the higher bravery of suffering as an essential feature of Islam, because the Prophet in his days of rejection and persecution had placed his faith in God and God alone. All the saints and prophets, he [Badshah Khan] said to me, had been persecuted. It was the way in which God purified them in the fire of suffering until the dross was burnt away and they came out at last pure gold. 'Look at your Prophet', he said to me, 'how He was persecuted to the very end.'[27]

The alchemy of ideas that the KK produced made it a unique achievement of the nationalist movement in British India. When I asked Gul Samand Khan whether he still believed that non-violence was the best way despite all the stigma attached to it, he said rather simply, 'We *believed* in non-violence, we asked for our freedom with folded hands . . . with violence we could not have won.' When I asked him why, he surprised me by saying, 'Subhas Bose and Gandhi had disagreed on precisely this . . . we did not want violence because we were ready to die but we could not assume the responsibility of the sacrifice of the lives of others.' Thus the KKs were aware that Hindus too could be divided in their opinion about the efficacy of non-violence. Their belief was a self-conscious choice of a particular ideology which happened to be espoused by a Hindu, Gandhi.

A further reason why the KKs felt favourably disposed towards Hindus was because a number of Hindus were fellow revolutionaries. Gul Samand Khan who came from Bannu (which had a large population of Hindus) provided the following picture, 'The Hindus were also involved . . . they wore uniforms, went to jail . . . In jail when we prayed, they waved flies away and kept us cool with a hand-held fan and we did the same for them.' Fazle Rahim Saqi too remembered that, 'There were a lot of Hindus and Sikhs with us as well . . . we were all together in Haripur jail. I remember an old Hindu man in jail who hung a portrait of George VI upside down as an act of defiance. When we had been arrested he had started a "vow of silence" . . . he was released after six months but died at the door of the jail. . . .' It was touching that Colonel Mohammed Sayid remembered the names of dozens of his Hindu compatriots from among the hundred and seventy KKs who were with him in 1942 for two years. When I remarked that it was amazing he should still remember their names after all these years, he replied, 'They were my friends from our days in the jail! I cannot forget them!' The KKs seemed to convey this feeling of solidarity with Hindus and Sikhs in various ways. Ninety-year-old Haji Zamir Gul of Charsadda recounted how they were spared a punishing workload and poor diet in Haripur jail by the intervention of the Sikh jailer's wife. He said, 'The wife asked her husband to stop his boorish behaviour and give the inmates proper food and to buy a buffalo for them and so on. She was a Congressite, you see.' As one of the KKs put it, 'We used to go to jails illiterate but came out of them educated.'

The reason for this sense of solidarity was also strategic; Badshah Khan appears to have repeatedly emphasized to his followers the reasons why they should forge such alliances. Mukarram Khan said rather candidly:

The British said that on winning the war they would set our country free . . . in those days India was undivided and united . . . Badshah Khan used to explain by saying that after independence we will have to live with them [Hindus] and they are three times the population of Muslims so we should make friends with them.

Muffariq Shah remembered Badshah Khan explaining to them that 'in independent India there will be one army for the whole of the country. It will not be like it is now . . . the Muslim League beat the Hindus here and the Hindus beat the Muslims in India.' Colonel Mohammed Sayid recalled that Badshah Khan had told them that 'in an independent undivided India, in Hindu majority areas Hindu law would prevail and in Muslim-dominated areas Muslim law would be introduced.'[28]

The Partition then came as a betrayal of everything that they had been told and what they expected from the future. Nehru was always concerned about raids from the tribal areas on Hindus in the NWFP and so I asked several KKs about this. Could this have been a reason why the Hindus left? When I asked Mohammed Yakub Khan, a Waziri from the tribal areas[29] this, he said shortly, 'This is the one from 1938 I suppose . . . in your notes? There were large concentrations of Hindus and raids meant a means of making money. But in the raid of 1938, nobody was killed or robbed . . . definitely no looting . . . these raids were directed not at Hindus but at the homes of the British and the British loyalists.' This may or may not have been true of numerous other raids, but he wanted me to know that the Faqir of Ipi, the anti-colonial revolutionary leader of the Waziris 'told his people not to harm Hindus and that their battle was only against the British.' He insisted that British 'agents' in the tribal *lashkars* always spoiled things and gave the wrong impression. Nehru was right in stating that Muslims of the Frontier, unlike other Muslims who were in the minority in other provinces, were 'brave and self-reliant and have no fear complex . . . for they can stand on their own feet and have no reason to fear other groups.'[30] But Mohammed Yakub Khan, like so many of his comrades, seemed to convey a sense of embarrassment and regret that people in India or elsewhere should believe that the Pukhtuns had treated Hindus and Sikhs badly. In the end while they lost the right to be a part of the India they had fought so hard for, they felt vindicated that it was because of them that the Congress was not known to be an anti-Muslim group even if it was known as a 'Hindu Jumma'.

Memories of India

The KKs were very aware of the politics of the rest of India and had several stories about their visits outside the Frontier. They treasured memories of times spent there and had hung on to old photographs and letters of their political comrades in India. I felt that these were also produced for my benefit as if to welcome me from a place they, unlike younger Pakistanis, knew about. They had things to say about the Congress, political developments, and details of Congress intrigue. Several of them had visited India in the 1930s and '40s and were eager to tell me about these visits. Ghazi Khan from Pabbi recalled going to Lahore for picketing activities; Fazle Karim remembered a trip to Meerut where he met Charan Singh and was aware that Singh had later become Prime Minister of India; Sayyid Mohammed Fasi Badshah remembered meeting Devdas Gandhi in Multan Central Jail and even brought along a letter he had from him, to show me; Haji Saifur Khan had been to Meerut and had been sent to Ahmedabad by Badshah Khan with a message for Patel; Gul Samand Khan told me about his visit to India in great detail when I asked him if he was aware that their movement was part of a larger nationalist struggle. He told me how on one occasion:

> Badshah Khan took with him to Allahabad twenty men from every district. I went with one from Kakki. The meeting there had been called for two reasons:
>
> i. To decide who would form the Government once the British had gone.
> ii. To promise the public that the movement would end once the British left.
>
>   . . . The first day we ate at a *langar*. We managed to hoist our flag again in Meerut. Maulana Azad came to Badshah Khan and asked for some soldiers to guard the flag. But Badshah Khan said that he could not promise to 'give' anyone without consulting his Khudai Khidmatgaran. . . . Yes, we

knew that our movement was an all-India movement. We knew that everyone, Hindus, Sikhs and Muslims, were asking for independence. I know
that Tilak was Gandhi's uncle. The resolution for independence had been
passed in Deoband.

The above anecdote demonstrates a number of things. First, that KKs
were much sought after for their discipline to serve the purposes of
soldiers in civil actions. Hama Gul Pdang explained that their 'job was
to keep order at polling booths. The police used to try and stop us but
we would protest by throwing our canes away and surrendering ourselves for arrest. Our job was to collect the ballot papers from the
people and put them in the right boxes in an honest fashion. We were
asked to do this and people realized how Badshah Khan's army func-
tioned.' Wazir Mohammed remembered campaigning for Hafiz Ibrahim, who was against Jinnah.

Second, while Gul Samand may have got the relationship between
Gandhi and Tilak wrong, he was aware of them as political leaders, just
as he was also aware of major political events like the signing of the
Gandhi-Irwin Pact, and the rift between Gandhi and Bose; furthermore, most of the KKs felt that they had never had any trouble dealing with the people in India. In fact, Hama Gul remembered that,
'The people there were crying when we were to leave.' The instances
of hostility that my informants cared to mention to me were ones
which involved other Muslims and Pukhtuns in India:

> Some Pukhtun students came from Aligarh Muslim University to the
> camp and started to jeer at us saying that we were the 'non-violent types'.
> We got angry and said that 'We come from the Frontier and are always
> ready to fight.' We were asked how much we were paid to be with Badshah
> Khan. We were asked how many of us were in 'army'. We replied 'as many
> Muslims there are.'

Memories of Muslim League

Another important theme that emerges from the testimonies of the
KKs is their attitude to the formation of Pakistan and the Muslim
League. As I have mentioned before in this article, after Independence,

the new government penalized the KKs very heavily for their opposition to the Referendum. Eighty-year-old Mohammed Yakub Khan from Bannu was unequivocal in his opinion: 'No Badshah Khan supporters participated in the referendum for Pakistan, it was the Muslim League who did.' Raghibullah Khan stated clearly, they 'had believed in and fought for an undivided India'.

It is important to recognize that the reasons behind the KKs' boycott of the referendum lay in the history of their confrontation with the Muslim League over the past several years. Most KKs, like Dr Waris from Gallader, thought that 'The Muslim League, as far as we were concerned, were agents of the British. We had nicknamed the Muslim League, "Motor League" because of all the cars that they owned! We used to recite a *tappa* which said 'the stick that used to beat us now has a flag on it.' There were instances in the past when they had been let down by supporters of the League as is illustrated in an incident narrated by Gul Samand Khan:

One day the Assistant Commissioner came for an inquiry at one of our court meetings in the mosque. The ulema-in-charge was not present. There was only Hazrat Maulana Mir Sahib Shah present. The A.C. asked him on what basis was the law in our courts to be considered valid. Maulana Sahib said that it was based on the Koran and the A.C. looked shocked and said, 'But that is in Arabic!' Because of this incident the village of Kakki was surrounded by British troops and all the people of the village gathered together. One Khudai Khidmatgar stood on a string cot and asked the gathering, 'Who among the people present here wants independence?' Forty-eight people came forward. Nineteen maliks from our village went with the British. The British asked them if they thought that the British were likely to go away. They replied that they did not think that at all. The maliks added, 'We cannot do anything about them (pointing to us). Why don't you drown the lot of them in the river Sind?'

After this incident Special Courts were set up here and there was a new law by which any revolutionary was to be arrested and shot. Records were made and kept of these forty-eight people. This area was divided into six divisions and for each there was a malik and a British officer and a Dogra regiment assigned on duty.

The increased repression by the colonial regime here is directly linked to the attitude of the *maliks* (who were supporters of the League). They displayed a clear loyalty to the government rather than the KKs, as is expressed in their exasperated and cavalier comment about drowing the KKs in the Indus. These instances of betrayal and enmity formed vivid memories in the minds of the KKs even fifty or more years after the events.

In my long chat with Jarnail Hazrat Gul and Sadar Musa Khan someone mentioned an incident of poisoned tea at a KK camp. I was astonished that between them they reconstructed the entire sequence of events, the politicians involved and their future careers in Pakistan; they implicated people of no less stature than Sikander Khan, who they remembered was, 'the District Commissioner at the time and later went on to become the Governor General of Pakistan. Ibrahim Khan mixed poison in the tea that all the six hundred Khudai Khidmatgars drank. In return, we learnt, Sikander Khan managed to procure 4,000 *bighas* of land for Ibrahim Khan from the Sikhs.'

While Hazrat Gul was telling me this, Sadar Musa Khan intervened to add, 'Ibrahim Khan was in league with Dwarka Nath, a policeman. He had got Sarvar Khan, a Khudai Khidmatgar, arrested. There were several such incidents . . . therefore it was hard to tell whether Ibrahim Khan was a Khudai Khidmatgar or a stooge. When the poisoning incident took place naturally everybody suspected him.'

Hazrat Gul then continued, 'Sikander Mirza himself confessed that Ibrahim Khan was an informer for them. He said this to Ali Gul and to Yahya Jan.'

They may have misremembered some of the details but the memory of the betrayal was as fresh as events one week old. Like the incident in Aligarh recounted in the section above, KKs had constantly to distance themselves from co-religionists whose politics they did not share. Thus, Maulana Hamdullah Jan, a trained scholar, said to me with great pride, 'I am a political disciple of Maulana Azad and a disciple of Hazrat Maulana Syed Hussain Madani at Deoband. That is the radical school you know, involved in the Satsa agitation. This is not Aligarh which was full of British puppets. All of us used to spin the charkha.' He is thereby distancing himself from other non-Congress Muslim politics in the sub-continent. He obviously identified with Badshah Khan in this and quoted to me Badshah Khan's speech at the Congress centenary celebrations in 1985 when he had stated, 'My political life began here in Deoband.'

The KKs felt that they were different from other political supporters because they 'fully felt a part of the Congress', while the poorer supporters of the League were only part of it because 'the big khans forced their tenants to join the Muslim League.' However, the KKs also acknowledged the reasons why people succumbed to force. As Fazle Rahim Saqi said, 'The reason these people gave was that they had to tolerate a lot of beatings and torture from the British for being Khudai Khidmatgaran.' They also brought to life what happened when Congress supporters defected to the League. When their President in Bannu, Yakoub Khan, was convinced to join the Muslim League, 'his daughter and sister cried so much at this news that the whole village was at their door to find out the cause of the grief!' When such incidents took place, Fazle Rahim Saqi remembered trying 'to convince a lot of people not to join the Muslim League.' And when these prodigal revolutionaries changed their minds again, 'Badshah Khan had an amazing capacity of welcoming back defectors.'

From accounts such as these, we get a much better sense of the flux in the loyalty of Pukhtuns in the years of the struggle. People had various motivations for fighting for independence and tried to make the best choice of political party possible to them at any given time. This may explain to some extent why people did vote for Pakistan during the referendum in 1947 when rallies raised the slogan 'Islam in danger'.

When the details of the Third June Plan came to be known, Badshah Khan could only poignantly comment, 'The sacrifices the Pathans have made in the course of their struggle for liberty have borne fruit and we are on the threshold of freedom today. Now is the time to enjoy the blessings of freedom, but when I look at the prevailing conditions I fear that we may not probably be able to derive the full benefit from this golden opportunity.'[31] Despite their boycott, however:

During the polls for the Referendum in 1947 about the partitioning of the sub-continent, Khudai Khidmatgaran helped in maintaining discipline at polling booths in spite of the fact that they had agreed to boycott the Referendum. They did this to avoid bogus votes being cast; they did not want the foundations of the new country to be laid with cheating.

In this they seemed to have lived up to Gandhi's hope 'that the referendum in the Frontier was to be without violence. Khan Abdul Ghaffar Khan and Khudai Khidmatgars were pledged to non-violence. They were to show that they lived up to their beliefs.'[32]

The feelings of the KKs about Pakistan are therefore a result of both a sense of betrayal by the Congress for agreeing to a referendum in the Frontier as well as a deep sense of disappointment about the way their futures turned out after Independence. They repeatedly drew parallels between the colonial regime and the one after it. For instance, Gul Rahman, who is now confined to a wheelchair, said, 'We used to be amazed that the British did not in fact fire upon us when we stood up to them and were ready to face their bullets . . . that was certainly different from Abdul Qayyum's policy after 1947!' Haji Sarfaraz Nazim Sahib told me with regret that he could not show me the Khudai Khidmatgar Centre because, 'After 1947 the Chief Minister Abdul Qayyum auctioned off the building and it was later reduced to rubble by being blown up by dynamite.' Secretary Amir Nawaz Khan, whom I found after much searching, told me that as a 'secretary' in the movement his job was to keep minutes but I could not have them for my book because, 'All records of our movement have been destroyed . . . I have myself either buried or destroyed most of them.' Dr Khan Sahib's son by his first wife, Hidayatullah Khan, told me about the various publications of the movement, 'There used to be a magazine called *Abbasin*. And there was the *Chattan* in the 1930s. But I am afraid that you cannot read these magazines any more. They were searched out and destroyed after 1947 by the Pakistani police.' There are several other instances of peoples' land being confiscated, their being reduced to poverty, and their children denied an education for their fathers were in jail most of the time after Independence. Mohammed Gulab felt that 'it has only been a change of uniform after Pakistan was formed.'

When Wali Khan was put in jail by the PPP, a frustrated Hama Gul was moved to exclaim to Badshah Khan: 'I know it says in the Koran that if anyone wrongs you, forgive him, but is anyone going to forgive us or are we expected to do the forgiving all the time?' He says Badshah Khan's response was 'Violence will get us nowhere.' The greatest solace for the KKs therefore has been the knowledge that they fought a fair battle against the British and that they achieved Independence. Thus when I asked Mukarram Khan whether he thought that Badshah Khan managed to achieve his objective during his lifetime, he replied, 'Badshah Khan accomplished his mission . . . it was the liberation of his country.' Sarfaraz Nazim seemed to think though that the achievement was short-lived. He felt that, 'Badshah Khan wanted to humanize Pukhtuns. But later the influence of the Muslim League on the people ruined it all and ruined the values of the region. The Hindus were driven out.'

The formation of Pakistan therefore was a great disappointment for most KKs. The causes lay not only in their personal losses: they had believed that after the British, the law of *sharia'* would prevail, but it didn't happen; women stopped participating in politics—they could come out of purdah with the British but with the Muslim Government after 1947 it was not possible; Pakistan standardized dress so much that Yusufzais don't wear their traditional *khaliqs* any more; the name of the province was never changed from the British NWFP to one that reflected the people who lived in it; the Awami National Party led by Badshah Khan's son, Wali Khan, still has to demand the rights of Pukhtuns as the KKs did and finally, 'Partition itself is a lasting problem.'

To some extent we may be forgiven for thinking that their disgruntlement with the present is the same as that of eighty-year-olds in any society; things for them were always better in the past. But few remarks were made about rising prices, the morality of the new generations or the state of the country in general as elderly people everywhere tend to make. Their disappointment was always linked to the complete *volte face* that Independence brought. Their sentiments are beautifully captured in an anecdote that eighty-year-old Sher Khan recounted to me when I asked him whether looking back, he felt that they had achieved what they had been fighting for. He replied, 'There was an evening when I remember sitting with Badshah Khan by the Sindh river at dusk, talking . . . I remember telling him that I did not and could not accept Pakistan. I said that I wanted to kill off the "brown sahibs" . . . There was a man called Nawab who jumped into the Sindh saying, "O river! Carry me away to a place where they do not know the name of Pakistan." '

Memories and Narratives

In the testimonies as a whole we can see the influence both of older pre-KK narrative forms and of new post-Partition developments in a nascent KK oral tradition. Recall, for example, Rahim Saqi's story of the old Hindu man in jail who hung a portrait of George VI upside down as an act of defiance, and died at the threshold of the jail. Here we have a very vivid and amusing image of subversion, followed by a denouement of great pathos, whose combination of silence, martyrdom and thresholds again seems to resonate with older mythemes. As with this brief fragment, most of my interviews contained episodes varying in their content and mood and shedding light on each other. As Mills writes for the Afghans, it is 'part of the aesthetic of . . . traditional story telling . . . that stories of differing genres, scales of complexity and construction, as well as other kinds of discourse (proverbs, conversational remarks) are juxtaposed and caused to reflect on one another in a full-blown oral performance of varying verbal texture.'[33]

An obvious point noted by sceptics of oral material is that the greater the length of time between event and narrative, the more events and new people/generations will intervene to provoke alterations in peoples' perceptions and evaluations of the original event about which we want them to report. Analogous influences can be seen at work in my own fieldwork. We can point to two pivotal points in the pattern of memories of the KK. The first, a pivot explicitly identified by the KKs themselves, is their introduction to the work of Badshah Khan. Their testimonies repeatedly stress that before him the Pathans were unruly and divided, after him, disciplined and unified; before, they were ignorant and knew nothing; after, they knew more about the sins of the British and what is morally good behaviour.

The second pivot, more pertinent to the present argument, is Partition. The KKs as we have seen, had very strong links with the Indian National Congress. They were thus strong opponents of the Muslim League and of their programme for the creation of Pakistan; they opposed the partition of India. Thus, when the Pakistan movement was successful, the Pukhtuns and particularly KKs were regarded with a great deal of suspicion by the newly-formed Muslim government of Pakistan. The result was brutal repression of the Pukhtuns; KKs found their movement banned, their lands taken away, their leader Khan Abdul Gaffar Khan in jail, and they themselves placed under arrest on various contrived charges. The experience of Independence for KKs was thus far from their expectations as freedom-fighters. They experienced denunciation, suppression and imprisonment, and a far longer period of continued criticism and marginalization.

By the time of my visits, these intervening events seemed to have temporarily robbed the KK of their confidence in their actions and memories, after so many years of having been told they were mistaken and unpatriotic, of having been denied the support of memorials or memoirs or approbation. We may note here in passing the relevance and validity of the French sociologist Halbwachs's argument that individual recollections only survive by linking up with the memory of others: 'The individual's remembrance is the meeting point of a manifold network of solidarity of which he is part.'[34] My presence as an Oxford academic, and perhaps particularly as an Indian, seemed to galvanize their memories and convictions, and several explicitly said that my interest had reawakened both their recollections and their faith in the rightness of their actions; in some cases the effect seemed actually to bring about a brief improvement in their physical health. One can also see however, how Partition influenced their testimonies. The KK always viewed their pre-Partition activities in the light of their post-Partition disappointments and sufferings; their heroic tales are frequently followed by the wistful comment, 'But that was another time.' Since that time was clearly good for them, this comment in itself constitutes a veiled expression of their disappointments and critical attitude toward the post-Partition state. By their positive evaluation of 'before', the KKs reveal their distaste for the post-Partition chain of events, lamenting, if not actually re-inventing it. The KKs obtain a great part of their dignity and sense of self-respect from how they shape memories of their earlier political exploits. If they had said that the KK's aim had been an unpartitioned India or an independent pan-Pukhtun state they would have been conceding their ultimate failure. Accordingly, their aims and estimations of their achievements are framed predominantly in terms of the more narrow 'getting rid of the British', while most also stress their moral education under Badshah Khan, their cultivation of an ethic of non-violence, humility and service, as a great achievement in its own right. Thus there is a strong consensus among the old men about their aims and achievements: the removal of the British and the achievement of a non-violent ethic. To some extent therefore, some of the original means have been slightly re-emphasized, the original ends somewhat de-emphasized.

In the examples cited in this paper, we again see that processes of self-justification and self-presentation are not antithetical to the historical 'reality' but an intimate part of it, and we see how large scale political events influence more individual and personal memories, and how such events can act as defining points or pivots in the map of peoples' memories.

But if the passing years bring new events for comparison, each encouraging reconstrual and revaluation of older events, it should be remembered that the intervening years also bring age, and new domestic experiences and responsibilities, such that in a very real sense, the person recalling distant events is rather different from the person who participated in them. It seems reasonable to suggest that the stress upon the moral improvement and spiritual development which the KKs achieved under Badshah Khan is not simply a reaction to political disappointment. By the time of my interviews, these men had moved through fatherhood, grand-fatherhood and great-grand-fatherhood.

They had seen a half century of life, with all its pettiness, problems and little conflicts, and had had much opportunity for reflection upon it. Thoughts of specific political issues and enemies must have quickly faded in the grind of making a living. And now they were drawing ever closer to the brink of eternity, which must put politics in a certain perspective. It is not so surprising therefore that they should choose to emphasize the moral guidance which they had received from Badshah Khan, a guidance which seems to have influenced their approach to everyday life long after the British left, and the significance of which outlived the nationalist question. I felt also that they were clearly addressing themselves to contemporary life, what was surrounding them, many elements of which they find disturbing. An old man's impassioned defence of non-violence becomes highly resonant and understandable when one leaves his hut and encounters his grandchildren casually playing with Kalashnikovs, the availability of which has intensified feuding. Similarly, their emphasis on the KK's frugality seems to be directed both at venal and corrupt politicians and at a younger generation apparently seduced by foreign goods and a nascent consumerism. Recollections of the past are influenced by the changing responses of an individual over time. That is one reason why the elicitation of life histories can be so illuminating and intriguing.

As a general conclusion therefore, we can say that one of the reasons why the interpretation of oral sources about events gets more difficult over time is that there is more scope for other and disruptive events to intrude upon the memories, events which can range in scale from a civil war to the birth of one's child. However, the way in which recollections are influenced by these events is clearly itself of great potential value in shedding light on the social and political relations which have surrounded and are surrounding one's informants.

John Davis utilizes the Marxian phraseology of the social relations of production to signal his claim that historical statements are a type of commodity, a commodity moreover, that some people, due to their wealth or power, are far more able to produce and distribute than others. Accordingly, as with money and commodities, the pattern of distribution of particular historical assertions, including memories, will be greatly influenced by the structure and inequalities of the society in which they are produced. Davis argues through his discussion of Libyan history that, 'history is a social and cultural product, consisting of events plus the structure of relations among those who construe events.'[35] In particular, he contrasts the tribal history of the Zuwaya, which assimilates new events to a genealogy-based account of age-old triumph and glory, with a generational history which arose in post-Civil War Spain; one generation, raised in the war, turned their back on their parents' highly politicized view of events, only to see their own children reject the peaceful apolitical environment which they had tried to create after the war. Thus Davis contrasts 'the "never again" of Belmonte to the "always so" of the Zuwaya.'[36] The Libyan state, in contrast to the Zuwaya's small scale and lineage-oriented accounts, purveys a state-oriented nationalist account of the fighting against the Italians, stressing a trans-tribal unity of will and purpose, directed toward building a Libyan nation. In short, Davis's argument is that 'the social relations of the people who make history determine in some part the meanings that they attach to events: the typical products (texts) of villagers and tribesmen are different in specifiable ways, and these produce different actions (events).'[37] More particularly, control over access to historical sources and resources and the distribution of specific statements about the past are typically used to reinforce the authority of elders or the primacy of the state.

These phenomena are clearly present in the NWFP and its relationships with the Pakistan state. Initially, given the segmentary social structure of the area, one might expect something of a lineage-based set of memories of the KK and its activities. There is indeed something of this. The old men themselves often frame their recollections in terms of their uncles and cousins and their own feud-resolutions, celebrating particularly the defiant non-violent feats of other members of their clan, or suggesting that their clan or lineage had always been especially active and effective in struggling against oppressors. The young are more tolerant of their own KK relative than they are of his merely tiresome and senile comrades.

Nonetheless, in general, the pattern of recollections is more akin to a generational rather than a lineal one. The old men, describing what it was like to be swept up in the revolutionary and anti-British fervour, following an utterly charismatic leader, convey the exhilaration of self-sacrifice. But the children of the KKs, already themselves well into late middle age, were more eager to talk of the KK struggle which occupied their childhood in terms of hardship and deprivation, of absent fathers and uncles and the smell of prison visits. My informants seemed even more distant from their grandchildren and great grandchildren. They seem unable to communicate with the fast-changing younger generation who are swept up by the rhetoric of Islamic fundamentalism, entre-peneurship and 'foreign goods'. It is not easy to explain non-violence to youth surrounded by cheap weapons, and who witness nearby both ruthless military governments and heroic Afghan freedom fighters. Although most of the young have a vague respect for the old KKs as people who fought for the independence of the country, this respect is not a well-informed one—it is little more than a tacit and taken for granted social acceptance of their importance. Few under the age of thirty-five have any idea at all about the political life of the old men, about the exact role they played in the liberation struggle.

It is important to stress however that these differences are not the inevitable or 'natural' result of the age differences, of the fact that the KKs are now very old and speak slowly and quietly, their thoughts oc-casionally wandering. In fact there is a great and inherent respect for anybody of such advanced age. The problem rather is that the Pakis-tani state has systematically intervened, promoting its own vision of the nationalist struggle, a vision which criticizes and marginalizes the KK. The state's ability to do this has cut the younger generations adrift from their activist forbears. This is seen most clearly in the fact that the KK movement receives no mention in school history text books. There, the emphasis is very much upon Pakistan as a Muslim state, whose precursors run directly from Mohammed to Jinnah, a portrayal which leaves no place for the KK's sympathetic links to the mostly Hindu Congress or its opposition to Partition. Similarly, the emphasis on the unity both of the struggle for a free Pakistan (as led by the Mus-lim League) and of the contemporary nation, leaves no room for the

KK's opposition to the League and their calls for a free pan-Pukhtun homeland. Censorship has been very extensive. I was sternly questioned at Lahore customs about my illicitly acquired copy of Badshah Khan's autobiography, which had been published in Kabul (Afghanistan) and I had to feign indifference to it, saying it was a casual acquisition in a bazaar to help me learn Urdu.

After Partition, nearly all KK activists had their homes raided, and all personal papers were removed and burnt, including those of Badshah Khan. This was a clear attempt to destroy any source which might provide an alternative conception of events. Most other artifacts pertaining to the KK were also destroyed in this way; thus the Red Shirts and pictures of Badshah Khan which I occasionally encountered in peoples' homes had typically been preserved in great secrecy and at some peril, or been acquired very recently as posters of the ANP. The KK's central buildings were bombed in 1948, destroying the records there, along with the building and Badshah Khan's vegetable gardens. Speeches of Badshah Khan have been entirely memorized by some as I discovered in my meeting with Nabad Khan of Swabi. In India, though Gandhi remains pre-eminent, other nationalist leaders are also represented in the state history, especially where they had a regional following, such as Bose in Bengal. In Pakistan in contrast, all still remains focused on Jinnah, and in this minor cult of personality, his image continues to be omnipresent, and prefaces the nightly news programme. There have hitherto been no memorials to Badshah Khan, and no museums.[38]

In all these ways therefore, the State has denied younger generations access to the historical truth of the KK movement, and has presented a very critical and partial picture of it. In Davis's terms, we clearly see how state history has forcefully intervened in order to create a disjunction in the next generation's views of the past, in order to purvey a particular view of state and nation. It thereby prevents a lineal or tribal view of the nationalist struggle, which it fears would glorify KK ancestors and be too emotively connected to feelings of Pukhtun pride and autonomy.

However, the picture is not entirely gloomy. The course of events demonstrates the continued potency of historical images and their use in a counter-hegemonic vein. In recent years, the position of the long-dominant Muslim League ruling party had been weakened, firstly by the military rule of General Zia al-Haq, then by the rise of the Bhuttoist Pakistan People's Party (PPP). As part of this, the ANP, led by Badshah Khan's son Wali Khan, has significantly improved its political position both nationally and provincially, not least as third party power brokers. The first thing they did on assuming provincial office in NWFP was to begin changing the names of streets and buildings and to drastically increase the representation of Badshah Khan's image throughout the province with large and colourful posters and billboards. There are also plans afoot for a Badshah Khan memorial centre and archive. Much of the party's support stems from its claim to be the true heir of the KK movement, and the recent initiatives are clearly designed to re-emphasize and legitimate this claim. However, we should also note that the use of Badshah Khan's name is not monopolized by the ANP. Some of my informants invoked Badshah Khan and his moral standards specifically to draw a contrast with and make criticism of, the current generation of ANP politicians. As Mills remarks, 'didactic storytelling makes extensive use of oblique implications and implicit connections, especially from adult to adult, in communities where circumspection is a basic ingredient of polite conversation . . . Making points through narrative absolves the speaker of responsibility for direct confrontation. It is up to each listener to infer to what present persons or events the story might relate.'[39]

I have explored some ways in which social structure, high politics and struggles for power and authority intervene in the distribution of thoughts about the past. However, I want to re-emphasize the fact that such processes typically work through their penetration of even the most private and personal experiences and recollections, and this inevitably means that they also become connected to personal matters of prestige, personality, self-presentation and ageing.

It was very interesting to note that most of the seventy KKs whom I got to meet and talk with retained some symbol of their identities as Khudai Khidmatgars. For instance, several of them retained before their names the rank that they had in the movement. So I spoke to 'Secretary' Amir Nawaz, 'Jarnail' (General) Abdul Rahim, 'Lieutenant' Mohammed Wali, 'Sardar' (President) Musa Khan and so on. Further, several of them carried on their persons an article in the colour red—red painted walking sticks, a red turban, a red kerchief (not the usual accessories of Pukhtun men, I may add!)—to remind them of their identity as 'Red Shirts'. The lives of the KKs were an enduring legacy of the political activism of the colonial period. Several of them still kept up with international news through the BBC, they knew exactly how to handle my being followed by the Intelligence and their being interrogated; their children have names like 'Siyasat' (Politics). Their self-identity is clear as in the case of Haji Zamir Gul who specified at the beginning of our interview that he was a revolutionary first and a haji only later.

To evaluate the oral testimonies I gathered, I have had to consider them in the light of Pukhtun culture, imperial power, Islam, Afghan story-telling and rhetoric, the Pakistan state, five decades of post-Partition history, the nature of Pukhtun ethical and emotion terms, the life courses of old men, the experience of subsequent generations, the psychology of self-presentation etc. etc. This requires an imaginative restructuring of wide sociological significance and is a far richer approach than that of simply discarding or ignoring 'inaccuracies'. Anthropological history is (or should be) in the former position, and it is exciting precisely because it is not simply backward-looking but concerned to carve out a dialectical synthesis of past and present.

My Memories of the Frontier

As the principal players in the KK movement were British officials and Pukhtuns, I decided to consult any information that either side had produced. On the one hand, I consulted archival material in the India Office Library, London and the National Archives and AICC papers in the Nehru Memorial Library in New Delhi. The first two holdings are comprised mainly of fortnightly reports sent by colonial officials to the central government in New Delhi, the capital of British India, and to Whitehall. But report-writing and colonial administration have their own rules of facticity, not least the need to seem to have events under control, and as an anthropologist I was constantly aware of the dangers of taking the reports at face value. Ultimately, they provided not only a great deal of hard information, but also marginalia and parenthetical remarks that betrayed prejudice and occasional confusion, all of which helped in reconstructing the colonial government's perceptions of the civil disobedience movement and its methods of dealing with it.

Fieldwork in the NWFP on the other hand was a different experience. I talked to the old KKs usually in their own village, near the *hujra* (men's house). These conversations almost invariably attracted an audience of about twenty to fifty people. People came out of curiosity, to pass the time or to take a break between their tasks. Curiosity was sometimes shown in me—a young Hindu woman, an Indian travelling alone, who was interested in and wanted to write down their grandfathers' stories. At times I could sense the audience's incredulity or disbelief that I had gone through enormous logistical problems simply in order to have a chat with the oldest, most eccentric man in the village whom society took entirely for granted, or at best dimly respected for some now obscure sacrifice in the past. But interest in the content of the old mens' testimonies usually superceded their initial curiosity about the anthropologist. Some seemed to be hearing them for the first time, while many more seemed to be listening with new ears, as the stories transformed from old men's ramblings to revolutionary history, a transformation largely caused by my presence and interest and specifically, by my writing down the tales. Very often the interview became something of a performance as I had to live up to the image the local people had of me, a young woman, an Indian, a Hindu, an educated scholar, someone who knew life in the land of the English colonialists. My 'identity' was rarely that of an anthropologist.

The setting of the interview was always interesting because of the problem of where we could sit to conduct the interview. I usually arrived in a village with Habibullah, a Pukhtun, whose father was a respected KK, and who had generously agreed to help me locate my informants. Also present was the driver of my car, a young Pukhtun man. We could not sit in the hujra since respectable women were not allowed there. We could not sit in the jenana because men from outside the family were not allowed in. Most often therefore, a neutral space was found outdoors in the sun and a few string cots from the hujra were dragged out to serve as seating arrangements. I had to learn very quickly at which end of the cot I was expected to sit as the guest, because the less comfortable end would be occupied by the host. If I offered my seat to the old man as a mark of respect, I was blessed profusely but firmly overruled.

The difference in age between me and my informants was of course enormous. My knowledge of the KK movement was entirely secondhand and unlike older people in India I had not experienced undivided colonized India. I had not seen Badshah Khan except in pictures or in documentary films. Also because of the difference in our world views I could not immediately understand some of their ways of reckoning time. For instance, if I asked someone his age he might say, 'How old are you? . . . I had spun twenty set of clothes by the time you were born!' He expected me to know how long it takes to spin a set of clothes because I came from the land of Gandhi. In our conversations we had to zoom back over half a century, firstly, because that was the period I was trying to reconstruct, and secondly, because it was a genuine security risk to discuss the politics of post-Partition Pakistan, since I would probably face being deported for sedition. Of course, usually we had to go back much further than 1930, sometimes to the year when my informant was born, since most found it impossible to tell me about the KK movement and Badshah Khan without describing their own life histories along with it.

These conversations were in the nature of semi-structured interviews. I was looking for answers to some specific questions, but the chronology and format was guided entirely by the informant. Quite often, my informants did not even wait for me to ask them any questions; after the initial formalities, they started talking about the movement of their own accord, because by then word had spread about the reason I was there. The KKs usually drifted from one issue to another, guided by their memory and recall. I did interrupt occasionally for clarifications or to ask another question, but my general attitude was to be respectful and supportive. They did not always respond to my interventions and if they did, it was often indirectly. Thus their narratives largely took on their own structures, and their frequent use of emblematic episodes and tropes seem to be the beginning of a new 'traditional' corpus of stories about the freedom movement, a corpus created out of their disparate personal reminiscences.

Yet though I have spoken of narrative in this last section, it is important to emphasize that my interviews were often far from being smoothly produced narratives. As I have already said, the KK had been long-marginalized and there had been little occasion, opportunity or demand for them to tell their stories. Rather than pre-packaged reminiscences therefore, stories and facts often emerged gradually. Portelli makes the point that 'rank and file' histories are usually unlike the 'affirmative discourse' of official history, which is readymade, articulated and available. Instead, a vernacular version 'must piece itself together from scratch every time, and is burdened by the fear of disapproval and isolation . . . it is distorted, buried, deviated, and allowed to emerge only in between the lines, as dream, metaphor, lapses, digression, error, denigration.'[40]

One method which I hit upon of helping such things to emerge was provoking accounts through anger. Most of my archival research in the India Office Library was completed before I visited the Frontier to look for any surviving KKs. I thus had a fair idea of the British perspective on the KK before I spoke to the Pukhtuns themselves. Often, I would tell my informants of certain British statements or views. These were sometimes so divergent from the views of the KKs themselves that they found it difficult to believe the truth of my attributions and in defence I had to produce my file of notes, read out the relevant passages and translate them, in order to convince. This in itself was an interesting exercise and I began to do it regularly, for in responding to the 'allegations' of the British, their manner of discussion often became different from that of their earlier answers to my questions. 'False' claims made about their organization still angered them and

provoked them to state their points of view, clarify incidents or concede lapses with the clarity resulting from anger and pride. I had therefore quite inadvertently set up a sort of dialogue between the colonial
officials and the revolutionaries. This in retrospect has proved to be a
useful methodological tool in writing colonial history.

KK narrations of their past were helped by other stimuli as well. For
instance, when I posed my first question to Noor Akbar, instead of an
answer, he gave me orders to wait till he returned as he had just thought
of something. My two-hour wait was rewarded when he appeared
again dragging a slightly battered black trunk. I watched with growing
excitement as he slowly extracted his old uniform, his Sam Brown belt,
an old poster of Badshah Khan and other items of memorabilia. I
recognized what some of them were and my initial questions were
linked to them. As the discussion slowly moved to more general issues,
he repeatedly went back to the other obscure items whose significance
resided in his mind. He did not always explain to me what they were
and I did not always ask. They seemed to serve as mnemonic devices
and helped him recall information; that was enough to satisfy me.
While this was the most dramatic uncovering of the past, on other
occasions too, old uniforms were produced from well-hidden crannies,
and on one occasion I was even offered a uniform as a gift. When I was
talking to Sarfaraz Khan about their civil disobedience activities he
said: 'In 1942 we picketed the law courts. Thirty of us were arrested.'
He then produced an old notebook in which he had made a note of
the twelve 'generals' who were arrested along with him and imprisoned
for a period of three years in Dera Ismail Khan jail, and read out the
names to me. What till then had been a general and abstract conversation
about civil disobedience was at once grounded in his experience. The
writing in the notebook was his own and probably reminded him of
the time he had written it down, soon after the event or more likely
several years later when he felt that unless he wrote the names down he
would one day forget. The names in his book not only yielded hard information, they also triggered his thoughts about other associates and
other forgotten incidents.

On another occasion, I went to meet Gurfaraz Khan just outside

Peshawar city during the run-up to the general elections in Pakistan in 1993. On seeing my unfamiliar face, he assumed that I had come to solicit votes and began by apologizing for not helping with the elections. This was despite the fact that he was so ill that we had to conduct the entire conversation with him lying down. My informants often also felt the need to enact their activities as KKs, sweeping, spinning and marching while they described them to me. Their evocative gestures were the reenactment of previous revolutionary activities, making the contrast between their present setting and their past ideals starker. Also, they felt that I ought to visualize them as young, enthusiastic workers rather than the bent and toothless men they now were. In this desire they were indeed transformed as they enthusiastically supplemented the ever-increasing amount of information with their miming, striving to make the picture clearer to me. Their charades were the embodied memory of past actions.[41]

The search for the KKs was not an easy one either. There too I was repeatedly (and often pointedly) told that they were all dead. I nearly gave up on the project. No official lists of members of the nationalist movement exist and save for one district (Bannu) none of the local MPs seem to have any idea of the location of their 'political fathers'— further evidence of the KKs' marginalization since 1947. It required persistent searching and a little luck to find a Khudai Khidmatgar. But when I did find one, it was not only a richly informative session but a profoundly moving experience. Secretary Amir Nawaz had been bed-ridden for six months when I went to see him. By the end of our long chat he was sitting up and even saw me to the door. He insisted that he had suddenly found the will to live. At least someone was interested in his stories of the freedom struggle, he said ecstatically to his astounded sons, as he patted me on the head with tears in his eyes.

I also encountered problems in the search for local archives. As already mentioned, most of the personal papers of Badshah Khan and his family have been destroyed over the years in various raids by the Pakistani police. I tried to enter the offices of the regional archives in Peshawar but I was consistently denied permission, principally because of my nationality: 'If only you weren't Indian' was the oft-repeated apology. But I did consult the holdings of the National Archives and the Nehru Memorial Museum and Library in India, where the AICC papers yielded valuable information about the relations between the provincial and national organs of the nationalist movement.

Lastly, though I had begun my fieldwork as the interviewer, I ended as the interviewee. In the final month of my fieldwork, Pakistan security police came to one village and interrogated me about my excessively free-ranging movement in the province, clearly viewing me as employed in espionage (partly due to recent press reports that the latest wave of Indian spies were young women). After several hours they eventually accepted my oft-repeated account of my purely academic interests and my vow of not discussing post-1947 events; they even good-naturedly recommended that I read Macaulay on the Frontier. Upon returning to Delhi, the relief of being home was quickly dispelled by an 'invit-ation' from the head of the Pakistan desk of the Indian Civil Service to come for a 'chat' about my experiences in the Frontier, an invitation which, fearing a likely de-briefing, I nervously avoided. Thus I had come myself to be treated as an oral source on either side of the border, my interest in the old united sub-continent now caught up in post-Partition games of division and suspicion.

NOTES AND REFERENCES

1. 1921 Census.
2. Mountbatten's Third June Plan was for a partitioned sub-continent. Nehru agreed to Mountbatten's suggestion that two provinces be singled out for a referendum on the single question of whether they should join India or Pakistan upon Independence. Sylhet (Bengal) was the only other province forced to hold a referendum.
3. Khan Abdul Gaffar Khan and other Frontier leaders were kept uninvolved in the decision to hold the referendum. As a consequence they argued for India, Pakistan, and an autonomous Pakhtunistan, which was rejected. Since the Frontier leaders were ignored by the AICC in this as well as in the initial decision-making and the acceptance of the plan for a referendum, the new demand for Pakhtunistan was easily discredited by Jinnah.
4. These include works by Amit Kumar Gupta, Eric Jansson, Steve Rittenberg and Waqar Ali Shah. The last is a young Pukhtun historian who has recently

submitted his thesis about the movement. Interestingly, he has much the same attitude to the Khudai Khidmatgar as did historians before him. In his work, as in that of the others, we get a rich and detailed account of the workings of *realpolitik* in the Frontier; what remains missing is any enquiry into the motivations and activities of the rank-and-file of this vast political movement.

5. See Banerjee, *The Pathan Unarmed: Opposition and Memory in the North West Frontier* (James Curry, 2000, forthcoming) in which I have written about the movement in some detail, with particular emphasis on explaining the transformation of a segmentary-feudal Pukhtun society which usually settled conflict through violence into one that practiced non-violent civil disobedience for seventeen years.

6. C.F. Andrews, *The True India: A Plea for Understanding*, London: George Allen & Unwin, 1938, p. 34.

7. J. Nehru, *Discovery of India*, p. 381.

8. Ibid., p. 61.

9. 19 June 1947, *Hindustan Times*, 'Conflict Among Pathans'.

10. See Richard Murphy's article in this volume about the everyday rituals at this border.

11. Badshah Khan had specifically asked to be buried in the garden of his home in Jalalabad, where he spent several years after 1947 in self-imposed exile. His supporters saw this as his final rejection of the partitioned sub-continent.

12. I first got to know Wali Khan when he was visiting India in November 1988. I had spoken to his cousin, Mohammed Yunus, about my interest in the Red Shirts and I met Wali Khan at Yunus's house in New Delhi. My fieldwork was entirely possible because of Wali Khan's generous invitation to live in his house in Charsadda, for which I am grateful. It would have been impossible for me to have lived in the Frontier for as long as I did without the hospitality of his family and his constant and sometimes fierce protection! This paper is as much a tribute to his continued friendship with India as it is to the memories of the Khudai Khidmatgars.

13. I must add that there exist no records at all of erstwhile members of the nationalist movement. Unlike in India, 'freedom fighters' are not recognized or given a pension and thus locating them was not an easy task. See section below in this paper for a more detailed account of my searches.

14. For instance, their repeated references to the 'prophet-like' stature of Badshah Khan were never to be repeated to a young Pukhtun man, who would certainly see this as heresy from a Sunni Muslim.

15. 18 November 1928, AICC Papers, NMML.

16. 24 November 1928, AICC Papers, NMML.

17. Patel's team was however not allowed entry into the Frontier by the government, and he had to base himself in Rawalpindi (in Punjab) to carry out his investigation. The report was proscribed by the government.

18. Note Congress stereotype here.

19. One should note here that my informants clearly collapsed their later years of non-violence with the mood in 1930. Non-violence was a new idea for them in 1930, by their own admission, and I discuss elsewhere the long process of the adoption of non-violence. However, what is important in the statements quoted here is that they do remember Congress scepticism and their own initial guarantees being vindicated in the years to follow.

20. Chief Secretary's Report, 1930, IOLR, L/P&J/12/9, emphasis added.

21. Governor's Report, June 1938, IOLR, L/P&J/5/214.

22. In fact his exact words were, 'Devdas Gandhi came here . . . he was very young . . . I taught him many things' [Gul Samand Khan].

23. Governor's Report, July 1939, IOLR, L/P&J/5/214.

24. Chief Secretary's Report, June 1940, IOLR, L/P&J/5/216.

25. Nehru, *Discovery*, p. 486.

26. This is a telling example of Badshah Khan's early association with Akali leaders in the 1920s. I have argued elsewhere that the KK and Akali movement are not instances of the practice of non-violence by so-called 'martial' races but that there was an extensive cross-fertilization of ideas between leaders of the two movements. It is my contention that many of the lessons learnt during the Akali struggle were used during the KK one.

27. C.F. Andrews, *The True India*, p. 24.

28. Unfortunately we don't know much more about Badshah Khan's blueprint for a free undivided India and he may have kept his ideas deliberately vague to allow for the new idea of India to develop after Independence.

29. My meeting with him was an unexpected treat as he came specially to visit me in Bannu because I did not have permission to enter the tribal areas where he lived.

30. Nehru, *Discovery*, p. 530.

31. *Hindustan Times*, 9 June 1947.

32. *Hindustan Times*, 7 July 1947.

33. Margaret Mills, *Rhetorics and Politics in Afghan Traditional Storytelling*, Philadelphia: University of Pennsylvania Press, 1991, p. 21.

34. Quoted in Paul Thompson, *The Voice of the Past*, Oxford: Clarendon Press, 1988, p. 214.

35. John Davis 'The Social Relations of the Production of History', in Tonkin *et al.* (eds), 1989 ASA 27. *History and Ethnicity*, London: Routledge, p. 116.

36. Ibid., p. 113.

37. Ibid., p. 104.

38. This began to change in 1991 when the ANP formed a part of the Government at the Centre for the first time sharing power with PML (N).

39. Mills, *Rhetorics and Politics*, p. 121.

40. Alessandro Portelli, 'Uchronic Dreams: Working-class Memory and Possible Worlds', in R. Samuel and P. Thomspon (eds), *The Myths We Live By*, London: Routledge, p. 155.

41. See Paul Connerton, *How Societies Remember*, Cambridge: Cambridge University Press, 1989.

Right or Charity?
The Debate over Relief and Rehabilitation in West Bengal, 1947–50

JOYA CHATTERJI

I N THE HALF century since India was partitioned, more than twenty-five million refugees have crossed the new frontier mapped out by Radcliffe between East Pakistan and the state of West Bengal in India. The migration out of East Bengal was very different from the rush of refugees into India from West Pakistan, which was immediate and immense, as was the way the dispossessed were received by the country to which they fled. Unlike those from the west, the refugees from the east did not flood into India in one huge wave; they came sometimes in surges but often in barely perceptible trickles over five decades of Independence.[1]

The elemental violence of Partition in the Punjab explains why millions crossed its plains in 1947. By contrast, the causes of the much larger migration out of East Bengal over a much longer time span are more complex. That migration was caused by many different factors: minorities found their fortunes rapidly declining as avenues of advancement and livelihood were foreclosed; they also experienced

The author wishes to thank the John D. and Catherine T. MacArthur Foundation for its generous support of her research on the Bengal refugees, upon which this article is based.

social harassment, whether open and fierce or covert and subtle, usually set against a backcloth of communal hostility which, in Hindu perception at least, was sometimes banked but always burning. Another critical factor was the ups and downs in India's relationship with Pakistan which powerfully influenced why and when the refugees fled to West Bengal.[2]

Given this context, the strikingly different way in which the Government of India viewed the refugee problem in the east and in the west is not altogether surprising, although the refugees from the east paid dearly for it. The crisis in Punjab, government decided, was a national emergency, to be tackled on virtually a war footing. In September 1947, government set up the Military Evacuation Organisation to get Hindus and Sikhs out of Pakistan in a swift and orderly fashion. By 15 November, within just two months, the Government of India had escorted 1.7 million Punjab evacuees into its refugee camps.[3] From the start, government accepted that a transfer of population across the western border with Pakistan was a fact of Partition, inevitable and irreversible. So it readily committed itself to the view that refugees from the west would have to be fully and permanently rehabilitated. It also quickly decided that property abandoned by Muslims who had fled to Pakistan would be given to the refugees as the cornerstone of its programmes of relocating and rehabilitating them.[4]

The influx of refugees into Bengal, on the other hand, was seen in an altogether different light. In Nehru's view, and this was typical of the Congress High Command, conditions in East Bengal did not constitute a grave and permanent danger to its Hindu minorities. It was convenient for Delhi to regard their flight westwards as the product of fears, mainly imaginary, and of baseless rumours, rather than the consequence of palpable threats to life, limb and property. Well after it had begun, Nehru continued to believe that the exodus could be halted, even reversed, provided government in Dacca could be persuaded to deploy 'psychological measures' to restore confidence among the Hindu minorities.[5] The Inter-dominion agreement of April 1948 was designed, Canute-like, to prevent the tide coming in.[6] In the meantime, government saw the giving of relief to refugees from

East Bengal as a stop-gap measure since permanent rehabilitation was judged to be unnecessary; indeed it was something to be positively discouraged. So it set itself against the redistribution of the property of Muslim evacuees from Bengal to incoming Hindu refugees; the policy was to hold it in trust for the Muslims until they too came back home, *pace* NATO's latter-day plans for Kosovo. The official line was grounded in the belief that Bengali refugees crossing the border in either direction could, and indeed should, be persuaded to return home. Government clung to this view, in which optimism triumphed over experience, long after it had become patently obvious that the refugees in Bengal had come to stay and that their numbers would only increase. It was several months before the Government of West Bengal accepted that it had to do something for the refugees. When it belatedly set up a rehabilitation board, it was never given adequate resources to do the job. Even after the number of refugees in Bengal had outstripped those from Punjab, such relief and rehabilitation measures as government put into place still bore the mark of its stubborn unwillingness to accept that the problem would not simply go away on its own.[7]

This was what led the refugees to organize and demand that government give them what they regarded as their 'right'. Their movement of protest embroiled refugees and government in a bitter and long-drawn-out battle over what legitimately could be expected from the state. These increasingly entrenched positions were set out in official policy decisions and the campaigns against their implementation launched by refugee organizations. The nub of the matter, however, was quite simple: did the refugees have rights to relief and permanent rehabilitation, and did government have a responsibility to satisfy these rights? As both sides argued their corner, they were forced to spell out their own (often unexamined) assumptions on a range of critically important issues about the ethical prerogatives of citizenship and the imperatives of *realpolitik*.

This article looks at the main arguments that emerged from this confrontation and tries to tease out their inwardness. In examining what divided the government and the refugees, it will assess how far apart their positions were and how different the premises on which they were based. It will also locate what common ground, if any, they shared. In so doing, this enquiry may contribute to a better understanding of the ideological underpinnings of independent India and the role that marginal groups, notably the refugees, have played in creating notions of legitimacy and citizenship which came to challenge India's new orthodoxies.

Government Directives: The Construction of
Relief as 'Charity'

Campaigns by refugees against government *diktat* were a persistent and highly visible feature of political life in West Bengal well into the 1960s.[8] But their formative period coincided with the initial wave of migration between 1947 and 1950, which is the focus of this article. The issues began to crystallize after the Government of West Bengal decided, quite early on, to deny relief to 'able-bodied males' and to phase out relief camps. As soon as refugees demanded a say in their rehabilitation, the battle lines had been drawn.

Stopping free relief to able-bodied males was only the first of a series of measures to limit government's liability towards the refugees. The essence of the policy was to whittle down, by one device or another, the numbers eligible for help from the state. By November 1948, the surge in migration caused in large part by events in distant Hyderabad began to tail off.[9] As soon as the number of refugees entering West Bengal had slowed down government was quick to claim that the worst was over and some officials, adding their two-*anna* bit, even argued that the lure of handouts in the relief programmes was itself attracting migrants[10]—a convenient justification when government decided to stop providing the pitifully meagre relief it had reluctantly given.

In late 1948, government began to put a new and harsher policy into place. On 25 November 1948, Calcutta announced that only refugees, narrowly defined as persons ordinarily resident in East Bengal who had managed to get to West Bengal between the precise dates of 1 June 1947 and 25 June 1948, 'on account of civil disturbances or fear of such disturbances or the Partition of India . . .,' were to be entitled to relief and rehabilitation.[11] A second order published in December 1948 declared that refugees would not be registered after 15 January 1949, further cutting back the official definition of a 'refugee'.[12]

A month earlier, on 22 November 1948, the Government of West Bengal had decreed that:

> no able-bodied male immigrant . . . capable of earning his own living [would] be given gratuitous relief either in cash or in kind for himself as well as members of his family for more than a week from the date of their arrival at . . . camps.[13]

Relief with no questions asked would be given for just one week. After that, relief would be conditional 'only against works'—shades of the much-criticized famine relief policy of the British Raj; indeed Samuel Smiles could hardly have done better.

It was all very well for government to offer relief 'against works'. But there were no such 'works' to employ the able-bodied in need of relief, and government gave no assurance that it would create them. Instead, the official line was that the immigrant himself 'through his own effort [must] find work suitable to himself.'[14] Male refugees who were physically capable of working had, somehow or the other, instantly and miraculously to find themselves jobs, sufficiently remunerative to feed, clothe and house themselves and their dependent families, all within seven days of setting foot across the border. In this triumph of fantasy over fact, government outdid itself by urging refugees go anywhere in Bengal except to Calcutta and its suburbs, where casual employment was most easily to be found.

To begin with, government had allowed camp offices discretion to make exception in those cases where they felt that free relief (or 'doles', as they were called in terminology unattractively reminiscent of the Poor Law) was 'essential for preservation of life'. Put bluntly, government realized that it would not look good if people starved to death in its camps. Two months later, however, in the wake of refugee hunger strikes against its Gradgrind directives, it hardened its heart. On 15 February 1949, a government, brought to office by the sacrifices of generations of freedom-fighters, decreed that 'such able bodied immigrants as do not accept offers of employment or rehabilitation facilities without justification should be denied gratuitous relief *even if they may be found starving.*'[15] This breathtaking decision was blandly reiterated towards the end of March 1949. In a directive aimed at 'soft' camp superintendents suspected of being susceptible to pressures from refugees (or indeed to the imperatives of humanity), it laid down that free relief must not be given to anyone 'merely because he was found starving once, the underlying principle being that *an able bodied male must earn his own living, and should not be made to feel, under any circumstances, that he can at any time be a charge on the state.*'[16]

In July 1949, Calcutta announced that all relief camps in West Bengal must be closed down by 31 October 1949, just three months down.[17] A little later, the deadline was grudgingly extended by a further three months until 31 December 1949, 'with a clear direction that rehabilitation of the inmates of the camps be completed by that date and the camps be closed with effect from that date.' This time, the Government of West Bengal took pains to make it clear that while

there may be cases where refugees may show disinclination to move . . . [t]hat should not be any reason why the closing of camps . . . should be delayed. As soon as lands have been allotted and tents offered and railway warrants issued, refugees are expected to move to their new places of settlement. If they do not, they unnecessarily hold up rehabilitation. It should be made clear to them that by doing so they cannot continue the life of the camp which shall positively be closed.[18]

In one draconian step, Bengal's first national government spelled out its final solution. It asserted that it had fulfilled its responsibility to provide 'relief' to the refugees. From now on it would only 'rehabilitate' those few persons it chose to define as refugees. Refugees had to be made to understand that they should expect no further relief and that they would be entitled only to whatever crumbs by way of rehabilitation government decided to offer them. This was the first in a series of official announcements by which it was made unequivocally clear that refugees had no choice in the matter. They had to take what was offered or get nothing at all.

The thrust of what government set out to do, at least in the prospectus, was to encourage refugees to be self-employed. Categorized by their social background and training, refugees were to be offered soft loans of varying amounts to enable them to buy appropriate equipment, tools or supplies in order to set themselves up as entrepreneurs.[19] Those who felt they had neither the training nor the talent for entrepreneurship but wanted 'proper jobs' instead, those who preferred to stay on in camps and those who 'deserted' from the concentration camp-like conditions of 'rehabilitation colonies' were given no choice. They had to do as they were told or lose all claim to the meagre rehabilitation benefits on offer. Hardly surprisingly, this unattractive policy brought government into repeated conflict with the refugees.

These directives give an insight into the government's view of its responsibilities towards its refugee citizenry. The policy of the Centre and the state of West Bengal may have differed in emphasis, but more significant is the measure of consensus between them on this question. So the core assumptions that underpinned their common position need to be examined, as they have an importance that goes beyond the issue around which their thinking crystallized.[20]

By attempting repeatedly to restrict the definition of who could claim to be a 'refugee', government showed that it had to accept, however grudgingly, that it could not altogether avoid responsibility for those displaced by Partition and to acknowledge that it had some obligations towards the 'victims' of India's vivisection. The fine sentiment, frequently and platitudinously voiced in the documents of the Rehabilitation Department, was that 'to succour and rehabilitate the victims of communal passion is an obligation the country is solemnly pledged to honour.'[21]

In practice, however, government strove officiously to limit its liability and did so by cutting its definition of the term 'refugee' to the bone. A refugee, Calcutta declared, was a person who had migrated before the end of June 1948; to be classified as a refugee, he was also required to have registered himself as such before January 1949, and the small print further narrowed this straitened path for those who sought the status of refugee. In this enterprise, many were called but few chosen. A key device by which government was able to achieve its objective was by limiting its definition not only of refugees but also of 'Partition' itself, the *fons et origo* for such responsibility for refugees it felt it had to accept. By its own narrow edict, Partition was defined by official decree to be occurrences which began in June 1947 (or six months earlier in December 1946 if the refugee had happened to live in Noakhali or Tippera) and abruptly came to an end one year later in June 1948. That Partition was a process which began in 1947 but whose impact continued to unfold long after June 1948 was obvious to everyone outside the Writers' Building. But blinded by their own self-serving definitions, Bengal's new rulers were staggeringly myopic, and deprived themselves of the ability to anticipate and effectively to react to the ongoing problems caused by Partition and its aftermath. Not surprisingly, they were caught off guard by each new crisis.[22]

The stance taken by government also prevented it from seeing that the refugee problem was affected in vitally important ways by developments outside the two Bengals. Its choice of dates, by which only those who crossed the border before the end of June 1948 were recognized as refugees, was a deliberate act of policy, intended specifically to deny refugee status to the hundreds of thousands who had crossed over to India between July and October 1948 after the Hyderabad crisis. Government clearly planned to limit, in spatial terms, the scope of what it would accept as direct consequences of Partition. For officials in distant Delhi and those closer at hand in Calcutta, only events in East Bengal itself were to count as bona fide consequences of Partition for those who decided to flee that territory. But outside Lutyens' palaces and the rabbit warrens of the Writers' Building, refugees continued to be driven from their homes by happenings many hundreds of miles away, whether in India or in Pakistan, the consequences of faraway events which nonetheless had powerful reverberations upon communal relations in the towns and countryside of East Bengal.[23]

In a similar vein, the government decided to define in the strictest possible way what could be deemed to be the *effects* of Partition.

According to its taxonomy, 'civil disturbances' alone—that is communal violence or blatant discrimination against minorities—were accepted as genuine 'effects' of Partition. Only those who could prove that they had fled communal violence directed against themselves personally were regarded as 'genuine' victims of Partition and therefore as proper refugees entitled to protection (in however small measure) from the Indian state. But economic hardship in East Bengal, where famine stalked the land and where food cost much more than anywhere else in India,[24] was not accepted as a 'consequence' of Partition. It may have been obvious to others that Partition had directly and disastrously affected the livelihoods of millions of people, Hindus and Muslims, in both Bengals,[25] but migrants tossed across borders by the pitchfork of the Malthusian demon were not deemed by government to be 'genuine' victims of Partition or as 'true' refugees. So it followed that they were not in any sense the responsibility of the Indian state. This helps to explain why the Government of India treated the refugees from Punjab, where communal violence came close to being genocide, so differently from the refugees from East Bengal, where the violence was never remotely on that scale.[26] Such devices enabled the state to accept minimal responsibility, whether moral or practical, for the 'victim of Partition'.

But the official definition of the refugee as *victim* also deserves closer scrutiny, since this provides another key to assess the tenuous morality behind government's attitude towards the refugees. Only bona-fide 'victims' were entitled to relief and rehabilitation. To be eligible for relief, a refugee family had to register itself. This required giving 'detailed information', much of which was not readily at hand, to the registration officer. In December 1948, when government made public its decision to shut down registration offices by 15 January 1949, it justified the edict by arguing that refugees who were 'genuinely interested' had been given 'ample time' to register.[27] This introduced a new refinement to the horrors of Partition—what might be described as a 'desperation index' in the procedures by which a refugee was prevented from claiming the benefits of that status. If a refugee was truly desperate, so government argued, he would have found his way to a registration office by mid-January 1949. If he did not get to the office on time, that was proof positive that the person claiming refugee status could not have been sufficiently desperate (or destitute enough) to require relief. QED: such dilatory persons were not 'victim' enough to be classed as refugees. By laying down as the pre-condition for receiving state help that a person had first to be registered as a legitimate victim, government at a stroke cut down a huge problem to a size it felt it could handle. It mattered not a whit that in so doing it slammed the door in the face of so many refugees who had nowhere else to turn.

This had far-reaching implications for the way in which government responded to refugee demands once they came to be voiced in an organized way. By definition, since they are not the commanders of their own fate, victims are not agents. Rather they are the 'innocent', the passive: objects of persecution, casualties of fate. Significantly, the state's favourite euphemism for refugees was 'displaced persons', with connotations of innocent victims dislocated by events in whose shaping they had played no part. This helped government to justify treating the refugees from West Pakistan and East Bengal with such an uneven hand. Nehru's point was that the Punjabis had been 'driven out' from their homes. Bengalis, by contrast, by migrating in fits and starts, proved that they had the option of staying or of leaving. According to the official line, a true refugee or 'victim' had no choice and was not a free agent. He could therefore not be expected to exercise volition, or have any choice over where or how he was to live in the country in which he sought refuge. These were the only terms on which government was prepared to offer the refugees its helping hand.

By defining refugees in this way, government, without having to cross the road, could persuade itself that it had been a Good Samaritan. Furthermore, it could argue that it helped refugees not because of any binding obligation but voluntarily, out of the goodness of its heart. In this way it could claim the moral high ground while acting in ways that made a mockery of the ideals trumpeted in India's new charters and constitution. There is an unattractive undertone of self-congratulation in many of the official accounts of refugee rehabilitation programmes. Bhaskar Rao, himself a worker in this rather barren vineyard, thus describes the 'saga' of rehabilitation in smug hyperbole:

> the indefatigable effort to bring healing to these bruised masses of humanity, to wipe their tears, apply balm to their wounds, assuage their hunger and thirst, clothe their nakedness. And more, to set them on their feet and restore to them the dignity of man . . . What one needed here were virtues alien to bureaucratic routine—sympathy, understanding, great compassion, the urge to succour and sustain, attributes almost of divinity . . .[28]

Others may not have made such extravagant claims to godliness. But terms such as 'heroism' and 'courage' were frequently used by apologists to describe the efforts of rehabilitation officials who spent sleepless days in this endeavour, 'unflinching in the face of indomitable odds,' and other sanctimonious variations on the same theme.[29]

Stripped of its trappings, the message from on high was that the state had no obligation to give relief, but gave graciously at its pleasure. The refugee had no right to receive. Rather he had a duty to accept with humble gratitude whatever crumbs he was given. In effect, what the refugee received was charity. Since the recipient of charity has no right over how much or what he is given, so too the refugee had no moral right to relief, nor any say over what was doled out to him.

This construction of relief and rehabilitation as charity is seen most explicitly when government decided at a stroke to stop 'doles' for able-bodied males and to shut down its camps. In defence of the indefensible, government insisted that doles were simply a form of official charity. If able-bodied men accepted these handouts, this would erode their moral fibre and get them accustomed to a culture of dependency. 'Living on the permanent charity of doles' would, it was argued, make them 'sink into a state of hopeless demoralisation'. Camps, likewise, were seen as 'symbols of permanent dependence'.[30] At least to begin with, the Government of West Bengal had the candour to admit that it had other less high-falutin reasons for its stance, particularly hard calculations to do with money. It admitted that its 'financial resources would not permit a continued expenditure of Rs 24 lakhs a month on doles alone for an unlimited period.' But from the outset, government rather unconvincingly claimed that it was not a shortage of cash that determined its policy, but an overriding concern for the refugees' own good. In a press note worthy of an Orwellian state, Calcutta defended its order on the grounds that 'the Government of West Bengal feels further that grant of gratuitous relief for any length of time would be demoralising to the individual and would affect his self-respect.'[31] In time, official reconstruction of the government's rehabilitation efforts came to avoid any reference to the financial constraints which may have lain behind its decisions, and kept on the safe ground of high morality. So by 1956, it was commonplace for it confidently to be asserted in the publications of the Relief and Rehabilitation Department that it was 'in order to counteract the demoralising effect of prolonged stay in camps [that] Government introduced the scheme of keeping able-bodied men engaged in useful work. . . .'[32]

While the refugees starved, or at best survived on the barest rations, government was thus able to have its cake and eat it. It had, after all, a double-edged sword in its armoury. The state was able to represent its relief to the refugees as 'charity' (and to congratulate itself for being so charitable), and at the same time it was able to reprimand the refugees (or at least several large categories of them) for daring to *demand* 'charity'.

It might be tempting to see all of this as little more than a cynical tactic adopted by servants of the state to circumscribe, as far as possible, its responsibilities. But this would be to miss the point. The theme so dominates official thinking that it suggests it was the very touchstone of rehabilitation policy. In official pronouncements, the notion that charity breeds a demoralizing 'dependence' which is inconsistent with manly self-respect was seen as an obvious truth, and was elevated to the status of a self-evident, generally accepted and quotidian value in Indian culture.

But was this view of charity in fact a truism in a social milieu where *dana, dakshina* and *bhiksha* had long been carefully-regulated and vital elements of religious and social life,[33] and where the renouncer who lived on alms was customarily venerated at least as much as the house-holder?[34] It is by no means clear that it was.[35] By all accounts, these views were of recent origin, not hallowed by Indian tradition. Even in Europe, 'in the old days, the beggar who knocked at the rich man's door was regarded as a messenger from God, and might even be Christ in disguise.' According to Braudel, the origins of European attitudes which drove a distinction between the 'worthy poor, looking for work . . . whom one should succour' and the 'unworthy poor not seeking a living', the miscreants, vagrants and beggars who were 'idle, good-for-nothing, dangerous', deserving slavery and exile, are as recent as the seventeenth century.[36] By the late eighteenth century, accepting 'charity' had already begun to attract social odium; a century later, the wheel had come full circle and charity was seen as 'injuring' those it was intended to aid.[37]

Similarly in industrial Europe, 'dependency' came to denote a stigmatized condition, appropriate only for women, children and the infirm. When England put its New Poor Law onto the statute book in 1834, this attitude informed the amendment which aimed 'both to deter the poor from resorting to public assistance and to stigmatise those who did'.[38] By the early twentieth century, dependency had come to be taken as a mark of debility of character rather than a function of poverty.[39] So an able-bodied male who came to be dependent was seen as the epitome of the 'undeserving poor',[40] since it was not poverty, but a man's lack of self-respect, that caused his dependence. Dependence was thus a subjective condition. And because it was only acceptable for women and children to be dependent, an able-bodied dependent man was seen to have the perceived attributes of women and children: weakness, idleness, passivity and irresponsibility.

If these imported European attitudes towards charity and dependency were deployed with such great effect by the new India's policy-makers, it was because in their passage to Bengal, they assumed highly-charged local inflections and particular resonances of their own. In one of the deeper ironies of Bengal's modern history, this way of thinking happened to fit neatly with a pre-existing tradition among its colonial masters about the flawed character of the Bengali Hindu male, a hurtful caricature which now came to gain a new lease of life as the accredited political wisdom of the very people whom it had so cruelly mocked. In the nineteenth century, British officials had conventionally regarded physical weakness and lack of vigour, lethargy, effeminacy, and (not to put too fine a point on it) an absence of moral backbone as the very essence of the Bengali babu's being.[41] By the mid-twentieth century, even the babu's brave forays into terrorism, far from metamorphosizing him into an intrepid fighter, only underlined the weakness of his character in British eyes: the attributes of volatility, irresponsibility, immaturity and cowardice were simply added to the list of his irredeemable flaws. In gross stereotype, the Bengali Hindu male was thus seen by his imperial critic as a deplorable combination of the worst possible feminine and childish qualities.

Writing on rehabilitation by officers in Delhi and Calcutta unconsciously aped the prejudices of their erstwhile masters, thus bringing together two borrowed traditions—one from Europe and the other from colonial India's recent past—to produce a new and potent stereotype of the Bengali refugee. This characterization was drawn in counter-point to an equally hackneyed, but far more flattering, picture of the Punjabi refugee, whose 'toughness . . . sturdy sense of self-reliance . . . [and] pride' never let them 'submit to the indignity of living on doles and charity'. Even in his 'hour of supreme trial', the doughty Punjabi refugees

> . . . would not stoop to accept charity, never would their proud hands be stretched out to receive alms. No work, however seemingly low, would they despise . . . They represented the fine core of the Punjabi peasantry, to whom honest labour is the flower of human dignity. Rehabilitation, in their case, was easy, for they met the Government's efforts half-way. . . . They were of the breed of heroes, though their stories have not been told in epic and song . . .[42]

The Punjabi refugee, heir of the martial races who were the darlings of the post-Mutiny Raj, was thus held up by independent Indian officialdom as the model of the 'deserving poor'. The outrageousness of this statement—given that government allocated many thousand acres of land to the Punjabis, disbursed Rs 11 million among them for the purchase of livestock, and gave them a further Rs 44 million in grants, loans and advances—does not need to be underlined.[43]

The contrast drawn by the officials between the Punjabi and the Bengali refugee could hardly have been sharper. Blaming the 'character of the refugees themselves' for the failings of the rehabilitation effort in West Bengal, the same author who lavished praise on the Punjabis—admittedly no Bengali himself—condemned the Bengalis in prose reminiscent of the *Koi Hais* of Victorian India:

> . . . In the Western region they were tougher, more resilient of spirit and much more adaptable. . . . But the refugees in the East came from a different milieu; the influences that moulded their lives were different. East Bengal was a comparatively poor agricultural region, with an economy less diversified than West Punjab's. Also, what is more significant, the person displaced from East Pakistan had been exposed to devitalising, demoralising forces much longer than his western counterpart had been . . . he was completely shattered in body and spirit, all initiative, all capacity for self-adjustment drained out of him. . . .[44]

Describing the West Bengal Government's repeated but unsuccessful attempts to shut down the camps, Bhaskar Rao almost outdid Macaulay, in the fatuousness of his sentiments if not in the elegance of his prose, when writing:

> The more serious difficulty arose out of a certain psychological weakness or deficiency among a fairly large section of the camp population. Many showed a reluctance to forgo the advantage of gratuitous relief, a disinclination to embrace the rigorous discipline of independent existence. . . . Whether it was because the refugee sought sanctuary in India already broken in spirit as well as in body, or whether because long exposure to doles had demoralised him, here was a mood most frustrating to the rehabilitation effort. . . .[45]

The official view was that his very disposition rendered the Bengali male refugee prone to fall into a state of dependency and therefore incapable of breaking out of it. This, it was argued, made the task of government in West Bengal impossibly difficult and indeed justified policies that might, in other circumstances, be seen as ruthless or harsh. Whereas 'in the West, the refugee matched government efforts on his behalf with an overwhelming passion to be absorbed into the normal routine of living', in Bengal, 'the Government had to supply the initiative as well as the motive power. To overcome the apathy, even the sullenness, of the displaced person was itself no small task. It called for patience and tact, endless sympathy joined to occasional firmness. . . .'[46] In other words, India's new breed of Jacks in office, or self-appointed guardians, had no option but to be 'firm' in the male refugees' own 'best interests'.

Here, the thesis—if it deserves to be elevated to that status—brought together two different lines of argument. The first was that their qualities of character inculcated a psychological dependency amongst Bengali males. In turn, this rendered them incapable of making rational decisions for themselves.[47] Because they were dependent, any judgement of their own about themselves and their lives and times had no value: it was as feeble and untrustworthy as the judgement of women and children.

The second line of argument, again borrowed from the vocabulary of the Raj (albeit with unconscious plagiarism), was that the state's relation to this dross of humankind was that of surrogate *pater familias* or benevolent despot. Because the refugees had placed themselves in its care, government could decide—indeed it had a duty to decide—what was best for them. In this role, government assumed the moral authority to determine their fate; if need be by overruling the judgement of adult voting males about what they thought was best for themselves. In this same role, the state also accepted (albeit without much enthusiasm) responsibility for single 'unattached' women, the elderly, the infirm and their dependents. These categories of refugees were, it acknowledged, 'more or less a permanent burden on the government,' because they had no able-bodied male relative to support them.[48] In the case of the infirm, women and children, the state accepted 'permanent liability'. In other words, it saw itself as standing in for the male bread-winner in relation to these unfortunates and therefore entitled to assert all the moral authority over them that a male bread-winner enjoys over his dependants.

The official discourse moved easily between these two different positions. On the one hand it claimed that the state was the fountainhead of charity and on the other, it played the part of family patriarch, hardly missing a step as it straddled the divide between these very disparate positions. Indeed, often in the same paragraph, certainly within the text of a single directive, both arguments and models were deployed side by side. But of course, there are glaring contradictions between these two positions. The role of *pater familias* entails a far greater acknowledgement of responsibility and obligation (albeit of a patriarchal variety) than does the role of dispenser of charity. The material support extended to a dependent family member can in no circumstances be constructed as 'charity', which, by contrast, is purely voluntary. Unlike those at the receiving end of charity, dependent members of the family have socially sanctioned and legally enforceable rights to maintenance.

Yet the refugees never made an issue of these contradictions. One reason might be that from the point of view of a refugee, the impact of both constructions on their rights tended to be much the same in practice. If refugees were to be seen as dependent members of the national family, they could claim rights to maintenance only by virtue of their dependent status, and as dependents they were denied any other rights. If they were represented as recipients of voluntary charity, they had no claims whatever over the source of the charity. Indeed the very fact that they took charity showed them, in the official view, to be so 'psychologically dependent' that they were not fit to determine their own destinies. So the net effect of both positions—however mutually inconsistent—on refugees' rights, could be seen as not being significantly different.

But it is also possible that the refugees chose not to make much of this inconsistency because they saw opportunities in exploiting the grey areas in the official position to their advantage. If they had forced government to take a consistent line, that line—however government chose to define it—might have been so tightly drawn that the state could have disclaimed responsibility for refugees altogether. By leaving the ambiguity unchallenged, the refugee movement, whether by accident or by design, kept some room for manouevre in constructing its own definition of refugee claims as 'rights', and this eventually enabled it to wrest significant concessions from a reluctant government.

Refugee Claims: The Notion of 'Rights'

Perhaps because the first wave of East Bengal refugees were largely drawn from the bhadralok, with their lively traditions of political activism and organization, they were quick to organize themselves into pressure groups.[49] Middle-class refugees from the east who had neither homes nor jobs in Calcutta were particularly hard hit by Partition. In East Bengal they had been respectable people, with homes, lands, secure jobs and a distinctive way of life, even if its advantages were rapidly being eroded. Now as refugees, they often had no more than the clothes in which they stood. They were forced to jostle cheek by jowl with other destitutes of lesser status on the filthy platforms of Sealdah Station, where they waited to be transported to squalid, overcrowded camps. There, herded into barracks that robbed them of any semblance of privacy, they survived (for only as long as government permitted) on dry rations of stinking, inedible rice, or were left to die without dignity.[50] It is small wonder that they began so swiftly to organize themselves in protest against these appalling conditions.

To begin with, these organized groupings were a very mixed bag, heterogeneous in leadership and in political affiliation. Each camp or colony tended to set up its own Bastuhara Samiti (Refugee Committee) or Parishad (Council). By the middle of 1949, these numerous camp committees had begun to make the significant transition of forming themselves into larger umbrella organizations. Two such organizations, rivals to each other, were formed in 1950—the United Central Refugee Council (UCRC) and the Refugee Central Rehabilitation Council (RCRC). Although the Communist Party of India (CPI) and the Revolutionary Socialist Party (RSP) quickly began to try to establish their respective influence over these organizations, in 1950 they were still far from being party fronts.[51] In the period between 1947 and 1950 refugee organizations, as far as their political affiliations went, remained somewhat free-floating and disparate. Many had no allegiance even to the two umbrella organizations. Amongst those committees that did, a good number possessed no discernible party-political affiliation. Moreover, the parties which claimed support from the refugees were themselves ranged across the entire political and ideological spectrum, from the Hindu Mahasabha on the Right (which in these early days had a great deal of influence over several camp committees), to the Revolutionary Communist Party of India on the Left, which had as yet to capture a mass following among the refugees.

It would therefore be wrong to suggest that the refugees had a united and homogeneous programme, in ways analogous to government's policy and practice. Nevertheless, out of the somewhat amorphous refugee movement there came a distinguishable stance on the questions of relief and rehabilitation. Their position, which evolved during the course of many campaigns and was spelled out in endless slogans, pamphlets and demand-charters, was quite simple—as refugees they claimed a right to relief and full rehabilitation, as well as the right to decide what form of rehabilitation they preferred.

In the early days of the refugee movement, its claim to rights was usually defined and defended in a limited and rather sectional way. Their rights were seen as deriving from a specific if unwritten bargain made before Partition between the Hindu leaders of western Bengal and the Hindu minorities of eastern Bengal. The refugees argued that both the state government and the centre owed them a special debt, because the Hindu minorities of eastern Bengal had deliberately and unselfishly sacrificed their own well-being to help create a separate province of West Bengal from which their brethren in the Hindu-majority districts had mainly benefited.[52] As one pamphleteer it:

> The East Bengal Hindus have endured untold hardships in the cause of India's independence. When the freedom struggle had at last brought freedom within our grasp, then the scheming British imperialists together with the Muslim League put forward the Pakistan demand as an obstacle in the path of India's independence and worked to divide India. To foil their design, and to bring about India's freedom, the Hindus of East Bengal and

West Pakistan resolved to sacrifice everything—like Dadhichi, they worked against their own interests to enable India to become free. At that time, the leaders of the Congress, the Hindu Mahasabha, the Ramakrishna Mission, the Bharat Sevashram Sangha and many other organisations repeatedly promised to protect the life, dignity and property of East Bengal Hindus, and guaranteed them full citizenship rights (*nagarik adhikar*), birth rights (*janmagat adhikar*) and complete rehabilitation in India. Taking them at their word, we all threw our weight behind the campaign to divide Bengal, so as to prevent the whole of Bengal and the city of Calcutta ... from falling into the hands of the Muslim League and Pakistan. After the Partition of Bengal, we arrived in West Bengal, the independent homeland for whose creation we had sacrificed everything. For fourteen long months, we have waited in vain for that symbol of our hopes and aspiration, the 'Congress National Government' [to come to our aid]. ...[53]

Here, the claim to rehabilitation as a right was grounded in the notion of a pre-existing covenant between the Hindus of East Bengal and the political leadership of undivided Bengal, and by extension, underwritten by the Congress High Command. According to this 'pact', the Hindus of East Bengal had agreed to support the cause of a separate West Bengal province that was self-evidently antithetical to their own interests, and they had done so on the understanding that once Independence came, the state would compensate them for whatever losses they suffered as a result of being dispossessed in the east. In this construction, the Government of West Bengal owed the refugees relief and full rehabilitation as compensation or damages. But by failing to fulfil its side of the bargain, government had reneged on its pledge. This was breach of contract, no more and no less, even though the contract was unenforceable except in terms of a moral commitment.

This line, whatever its emotional appeal, was hardly a sufficient foundation upon which to base a secure claim to 'rights'. The argument was, first that the state owed refugees from East Bengal certain goods that it owed to no other class of its citizens. Secondly, it only owed them these goods because of a pre-existing contract. In other words, it could be seen as special pleading that gave the state scope to avoid accepting a *general* responsibility towards all refugees. In this sense, this was an even narrower definition of its liabilities than the government itself, however notionally or grudgingly, accepted.

This portrayal of refugee 'rights' as a special or sectional claim was never entirely abandoned by its protagonists. But as the movement gained momentum, it gradually came to be overlaid with other, more open-ended, meanings. The battle against the cut-back in the grants of doles to able-bodied male refugees provided a context in which refugee activists were forced to think afresh on the question of rights. In effect, the cut-back created two classes of camp refugees, those who were entitled to some benefits and those who were not. Those who resisted the government order insisted that dividing refugees into 'haves' and 'have-nots' was wrong, and they challenged it with a wave of hunger-strikes and *hartals* in camps all over West Bengal. But in the course of these struggles, they learnt how difficult it was to carry the 'haves' along with the 'have-nots' in a unified campaign. For example, at Chakdah camp in Nadia district, the two hundred families headed by able-bodied males who were affected by the order launched a *hartal*. But, as the officer on the spot reported, 'the attempts to dissuade persons from taking their legitimate doles by the refugees who are not eligible by the Government Order were made but without success.'[54] In effect, the refugee leaders found themselves waging war on two fronts, one against government for creating two classes of refugees—the dole receivers and the rest—and the other against those of their own dole-receiving brothers who took what they could and looked the other way.

The series of government orders which followed presented similar problems for refugee activists trying to bring about a measure of unity in their response. The thrust of the government's rehabilitation measures was to lump refugees into several different categories—able-bodied males, widows, the handicapped, government servants, medical practitioners, lawyers, etc.—and to offer each category a different rehabilitation package by way of help. Inevitably, some refugee families preferred to take whatever was on offer rather than to fight for more. For example, when refugees at Cossipore went on a fast-unto-death against the decision to shut down their camp, they had to contend with the difficulty that at least some refugee families in the camp were 'willing to leave the camp and go to their places of rehabilitation and to be settled on their land. . . .'[55] And again in Nadia, when 'the majority' of refugees at the Goushala and Chandmari camps refused to leave their camps for a rehabilitation site at Gayeshpur, they found that there were some refugees 'who [were] willing to accept the Government project. . . .'[56]

These circumstances forced refugee activists to begin to recognize the strategic necessity of arguing that the rights they claimed were held *equally* by *all* refugees. In this period, refugee organizations increasingly came to put forward the stronger line that the 'rights' of refugees were absolute and indivisible. The argument that these rights derived from a specific contract was gradually replaced by the claim that these were 'fundamental rights'. So, for example, at a meeting of 1500 refugees at Karbagan, organized under the aegis of the RCRC on 5 August 1950, 'the speakers criticised the Congress government for its utter failure to solve the *fundamental rights* of the refugees [*sic*]. . . .'[57] The following day, at a meeting organized at Hazra park by the Dakshin Kalikata Bastuhara Sangha, resolutions were passed making the usual demands—for free rations, free schooling and medicines and adequate sanitary arrangements in the colonies. Leaflets distributed at the meeting urged refugees 'not to make any compromise with the Government but to fight unto death for the vindication of their *rights*. . . .'[58] Inevitably, it became increasingly untenable for refugee organizations to insist that *only* refugees were entitled to these 'fundamental rights', and not every citizen.

In turn this raises the question, what specifically were these rights? Just as rights were asserted increasingly on the basis of an absolute and indivisible entitlement by all, so also there was a trend for the rights themselves to be interpreted more and more broadly. A perceptible shift can be seen, as time passed, from the assertion of specific, exclusive, and sectional, entitlements to more general, inclusive, rights. The list of demands put forward at various meetings and during successive campaigns have a familiar ring to them. Invariably they included both political and economic rights. Amongst the political rights claimed, two were common to every agitation by refugees. The first was their right to organize themselves politically. This was a response to the growing high-handedness of camp superintendents who picked on and punished those they saw as 'ring-leaders' of the agitations.[59] As the refugee movement became more and more closely associated with the Left-wing political opposition, this developed into a more general protest against the constraints on political freedom in independent West Bengal, particularly the Security Act and the Special Powers Act—which hurt all citizens, not refugees alone. So refugee pamphlets continued to make specific demands for the removal of a particular camp superintendent or the release of a particular refugee leader who had been detained, but increasingly these demands were linked with the broader campaign for the repeal of the so-called 'Black Acts'. Particularly after they fought pitched street battles with the police during Nehru's visit to Calcutta in January 1949, refugees formed increasingly visible and vocal contingents at protest marches in the city which denounced 'police *zulum*' and raised the slogan '*Yeh azadi jhootha hai*' ('this Independence is a sham').[60]

The second demand made by practically every refugee organization was the right to determine how, when and where they were to be rehabilitated. They demanded that families be given adequate notice before they were moved to rehabilitation colonies, and more importantly, that refugees should not be sent to 'rehabilitation sites' against their will. This eventually hardened into the demand that all refugees be rehabilitated within West Bengal. But here too, a trend towards expansion and inclusion can be detected in the way that the right came to be asserted. The refugee campaigns linked their demand that refugees be rehabilitated in West Bengal with a call for a state-driven programme to achieve economic reform and greater equality in West Bengal society as a whole.

The same trend towards greater inclusiveness can be seen in the demand for specifically *economic* rights. Every meeting reiterated the demand for certain basic economic rights: the provision of relief of *all* refugees, full rehabilitation, and entitlement to relief grants until full rehabilitation had been achieved. In elaborating these demands, the refugees showed that they defined both 'relief' and 'rehabilitation' in a broader way than government did. In their view, relief not only meant doles for all, but also free education for refugee children, free medical care and clothing, as well as clean and sanitary camps. Rehabilitation meant a brick-built 'pucca' house for each refugee household and regular, paid employment.[61] This particular demand went diametrically against the thrust of government policy on rehabilitation, since its central purpose was to encourage refugees to find self-employment, and not look to the *Sarkar* for jobs.

But here too, the trend in the refugee movement was to assert that these were not specifically refugee rights but the rights of *all* members of society. For instance, one pamphlet issued by the Nikhil Banga Bastuhara Karma Parishad appended the following 'long-term demands' (*deerghameyadi dabi*) to a list of demands specifically to do with refugees:

1. The zamindari system must be abolished without compensation, and the land must be distributed to the poor peasants, the landless and the poor refugees according to their needs.
2. . . . [illegible] arrangements must be made to ensure regular employment and livelihood for refugees and all other members of society (*ananya janata*) and to give their lives greater dignity (*jeebanmaan unneet korite hoibe*).
3. Free primary education must be provided and teachers must be paid a living wage. . . .[62]

In the same way, the demand for free rations for refugees was increasingly linked to a more general critique of the government's food policy and its failure to guarantee security of rations for the public at large.[63]

In these ways, the construct of rights which evolved out the successive refugee campaigns came to be part of an increasingly broad-based and inclusive political programme in a welfarist and even socialist mode, breaking with liberal and bourgeois traditions. This was partly a consequence of the fact that the refugee movement gradually but increasingly came under the influence of Left-wing political parties. But it is significant that this trend predates the 'capture' of the refugee movement by the Left, which (as Prafulla Chakrabarti has shown) only began in earnest after 1951 and was not achieved in full measure until 1959.[64] So the explanation has rather to be sought in the internal dynamics and logic of the refugee movement itself. To some extent, this logic was more semantic than substantial: in theory and in historical fact, the notion of 'rights' is based on the premise that all men are equal. So the rhetoric of 'rights' is a natural bedfellow of egalitarianism, since it is hard to sustain a claim to rights without claiming them *equally* for *all*.[65]

The refugee movement also soon realized that its own demands took it down the egalitarian path. Much of what the refugees claimed as of right was economic in nature: food, clothes, medicine, housing, education and jobs. It would have been difficult, if not impossible, to justify the argument that refugees had an entitlement to these economic 'rights' whereas other—and equally destitute—Indians, did not.

Practical considerations also encouraged the refugees to link their demands with a call for wider social change in an egalitarian direction. If they had insisted on fighting alone for their own particularist demands, they would have found themselves politically isolated and socially vulnerable. More to the point, a social and political transformation in Bengal was the necessary precondition for the realization of some of the refugees' most basic and unnegotiable demands. One example was their insistence that they be rehabilitated in West Bengal.[66] The government claimed that West Bengal was already too overcrowded to accommodate millions of refugees—that the state simply did not have enough uninhabited land to go around. If there was to be more land available for redistribution to the dispossessed, that could only come as the result of quite fundamental land reforms. So it is not surprising that refugees called for radical land reform, for the abolition of the zamindaris and for more equitable laws which imposed ceilings on the amount of urban land which the privileged could own.

In much the same way, the campaign against the eviction of refugee squatters brought the refugee movement into a head-on collision with entrenched rights to private property. From late September 1949, when government ordered camps to be shut down, groups of refugees began forcibly to occupy vacant plots and garden houses, chiefly in suburban Calcutta, in Dumdum, Naihati and Baranagar. They would stealthily enter these plots at night, and under cover of darkness rapidly put up makeshift shelters. They would then refuse to leave, while offering in many instances to pay a fair price for the land.[67] To evict them from these patently unused plots would have been particularly embarrassing for a government which had loudly proclaimed that there was no land available for redistribution. When it tried to evict the refugees, this inevitably led to ugly incidents. One incident which attracted wide publicity took place at Mahesh in Hooghly, where police were summoned to help a landlord repossess his vacant land which had been occupied by refugees. Characteristically, the police were brutal in enforcing the landlords's right of access but turned a blind eye when the landlord used thugs and bully-boys to oust the squatters.[68] The refugees could see only too clearly the galling contrast between the alacrity with which the state and its law-enforcement machinery responded to defend the rights of property-owners, and its vigorous denial that destitute refugees had any rights at all. Inevitably, refugees who had started out by acknowledging the right of the landlord to be paid for plots they had occupied ended up taking a more jaundiced view of the right to private property. Confrontations of this sort, which began with limited aims—often simply for a little space within the system in which individuals could survive—thus often rapidly developed into passionate indictments of the established order.[69]

The battle against eviction—which by implication was also a campaign against rights to private property—became fiercer after the public found out, through a leak in March 1951, about the secretly-drafted clauses of the Eviction Bill. The Bill, as the Chief Minister admitted at a Press Conference on 20 March, was essential if his government was to have the power to deal with squatter colonies which violated the right to private property enshrined in the Indian Constitution. But faced with a sustained campaign against the Eviction Bill and its no longer secret provisions, the Government of West Bengal was forced to retreat: the Bill was redrafted to include two significant new provisions. The first, Section 4, was reworded to include a pledge that a 'Displaced Person' in unauthorized occupation of land would not be disturbed 'until the Government provides for him other land or house . . . in an area which . . . enables the person to carry on such occupation as he may be engaged in for earning his livelihood at the time of the order.' The second was a new definition of the term 'bona fide refugee', which was broadened so as to include families who arrived in West Bengal before 31 December 1950.[70] This represented a major victory for the refugee movement, because it acknowledged that refugees had an absolute, inalienable, right to shelter, and that the government had a duty to provide it. It was also an admission that there were circumstances in which the right to private property could not be enforced.

It was also a great victory for West Bengal's Left-wing opposition. The communist parties (particularly the CPI) successfully refined the tactic of using refugee demands as the thin end of the wedge in their wider struggle. First they would press the case for the rights of refugees, whether to food, shelter or employment. And once the government (which acknowledged, however half-heartedly, that it had some special obligations towards refugees) had been forced to accept that the refugees did indeed have these rights, the Left-wing parties would demand the same rights for everybody. To change the metaphor, the Left used the refugees and their rights as a toe in the door that the government was trying to keep firmly shut.

This also explains why the sectional basis for the claim to refugee rights was never wholly given up. The very same pamphlet which demanded the abolition of the zamindari system began by asserting that 'before the Partition was brought about by the conspiracy of a pro-rich Congress, the leaders made pretty speeches promising that the refugees in West Bengal, in their capacity as free citizens would be able to live in comfort . . . it is clear that the Congress has completely betrayed this pledge. . . .'[71] In one and the same sentence, both the sectional and the general claim to rights is asserted. The Congress is alleged to have made a promise, and that was all and well, but it was '*in their capacity as free citizens*' that the refugees would live in comfort . . .' This could be interpreted either to mean that the refugees were rightfully demanding that the Congress fulfill its promises to them or to imply that all free citizens had the right to live in comfort. Here was the convenient ambiguity upon which the Left-wing leadership could, and did, capitalize, first asking for the fulfilment of the special obligation, and then quickly changing tack to demand the same treatment for all citizens. The refugee movement was thus the Trojan horse in the siege laid by the Left around the bastions of government in its battle to achieve a broader, more egalitarian, definition of citizenship.

Conclusion

In the chronicles of political science it is a commonplace that the refugees from East Bengal played a key role in the development of Leftwing politics in West Bengal. Yet the relationship between the refugees and the communist parties have usually been described in purely instrumentalist terms. The communists are accused of having used the refugees as mere cannon fodder in their campaigns. In his seminal study of the refugee movement in West Bengal, Prafulla Chakrabarti asserts that the communists used the refugees as 'plastic material' in their struggle for power, or as a mere 'footstool to mount the *gaddi*'.[72] This article has shown how misleading these analogies can be. In the volatile fifties, the refugees undoubtedly helped to advance a great many Left-wing campaigns in Bengal. Yet the crucial importance of their role was that they served as a test-case for the whole question of rights. It was precisely because government admitted, albeit in as narrow a way as possible, that it had some special obligations towards refugees, that the Left-wing opposition was able to push forward so many of their general claims for the citizens of India as a whole.

As this article has shown, there was *some* common ground between the government and the refugees: even if its extent was very limited. But this was the very ground on which the refugees stood when they successfully campaigned for their 'rights'. Once government had conceded the justice of some of their claims, the same claims were extended further and further by their Left-wing allies. In the process, more and more concessions were wrested from a reluctant government. And upon this ground, the communists and radicals would skilfully erect the claim that everybody had the same rights and entitlements.

It follows that the relationship between the refugee movements and the wider politics of the Left in West Bengal was more complex and symbiotic than the metaphors of cannon-fodder, plastic material or footstools would suggest. It will certainly not do to argue that the refugee movement was simply subsumed and exploited by the Left. The shift in their politics towards the Left was, to a substantial degree, a considered response by refugees to their distinctive experience as they organized their fight for survival. It was this experience—and not some unthinking adherence to a borrowed communist ideology—which persuaded them to articulate their demands in the particular ways that they did. In the final analysis, it was this experience, moreover—the public spectacle of their wretchedness and their incessant campaigns for rehabilitation and for a measure of human dignity—which created the moral and political climate in which so many aspects of communist ideology found a more general acceptance in West Bengal in the formative decades after Independence.

NOTES AND REFERENCES

1. The table below on refugees coming into West Bengal between 1946 and 1962, admittedly based upon official sources which always underestimated the numbers of refugees entering West Bengal, nevertheless gives an indication of the ebb and flow of the migration.

Migration of Refugees from East Pakistan to
West Bengal, 1946–62

1946	58,602
1947	4,63,474
1948	4,90,555
1949	3,26,211
1950	11,72,928

1951	47,437
1952	5,31,440
1953	76,123
1954	1,21,364
1955	2,40,424
1956	5,81,000
1957	6,000
1958	4,898
1959	6,348
1960	9,712
1961	10,847
1962	13,894
Total	42,61,257 (4.26 million)

Source: *Reports of the Committee of Review of Rehabilitation Work in West Bengal.*

2. The police action in Hyderabad in August 1948, the Bagerhat riots in East Bengal in 1950, the renewed agitation in Pakistan over the Kashmir issue in May 1951, and the introduction of a passport system between India and Pakistan in October 1952, each triggered off large-scale migration from East Pakistan into West Bengal. See *Report on how the millions who came from Eastern Pakistan live here. They live again.* Government of West Bengal, 1954, pp. 1–2. On the other hand, migration slowed down markedly after the signing in 1948 of the Inter-Dominion Agreement between Pakistan and India. It fell off again, after a sharp rise in February and March 1950 which coincided with the Bagerhat riots, once the Delhi Pact was signed in April of that year.

3. See U. Bhaskar Rao, *The Story of Rehabilitation;* issued on behalf of the Department of Rehabilitation, Ministry of Labour, Employment and Rehabilitation, Government of India, Faridabad, 1967, p. 15.

4. The official history of the relief and rehabilitation measures undertaken *vis-a-vis* the refugees from West Pakistan is set out in *After Partition* (Delhi: Publications Division, Ministry of Information and Broadcasting, Government of India, 1948); and Bhaskar Rao, *The Story of Rehabilitation.* A more scholarly assessment may be found in Gyanesh Kudaisya, 'The Demographic Upheaval of Partition: Refugees and Agricultural Resettlement in India, 1947–67', in *South Asia,* vol. XVIII, Special Issue, 1995, pp. 73–94.

5. Jawaharlal Nehru to Dr B.C. Roy, 2 December 1949, cited in Saroj Chakrabarty, *With Dr B.C. Roy and Other Chief Ministers: A Record Up to 1962,* Calcutta, 1947, p. 144.

6. The first Inter-Dominion Agreement was signed in April 1948 and provided for the setting up of Minorities Boards and Evacuee Property Management Boards composed of members of the minority communities in East and West Bengal. Proceedings of the Inter-Dominion Conference, Calcutta 15–18 April 1948. Government of West Bengal, Home (Political) Department Confidential File for the year 1948. (No file number). West Bengal State Archives.

7. By the end of 1951, the number of refugees in West Bengal was estimated to be 2.51 million, while those in Punjab only 2.4 million. By the beginning of 1956, the numbers in Bengal had grown to about 3.5 million. *Relief and Rehabilitation of Displaced Persons in West Bengal,* printed by the Home (Publicity) Department on behalf of the Refugee Relief and Rehabilitation Department, Government of West Bengal, 1956.

8. The last of the major refugee campaigns against government began in 1961, when the West Bengal Government ordered camp refugees to move to Dandakaranya in Madhya Pradesh. The order was vigorously resisted by 10,000 camp dwellers who simply refused to go.

9. The threat of conflict between India and Pakistan over the accession of Hyderabad had reverberations in East Bengal, where Hindus feared that in the event of war, they would face persecution. This fear prompted a sudden and sharp rise in the number of refugees fleeing East Bengal.

10. In 1947 and 1948, acute food-grain shortage and high prices were endemic in East Bengal and led to famine conditions in at least three districts: Barisal, Noakhali and Chittagong. See, for example, the reports in *The Statesman*, Calcutta, on 14 and 16 July 1947, and 9 August 1947.

11. An exception was made for refugees arriving from Noakhali and Tippera, for whom it was decreed that 'the time of leaving such residence shall run from the 1st day of December 1946' (i.e. when the communal rioting first began in these districts). Memo No. 5691 F.R./10M-87/48, from the Assistant Secretary, Relief and Rehabilitation Department, Government of West Bengal, to the Relief Commissioner, West Bengal, dated 25 November 1948. This and other government memoranda cited below have been culled from the voluminous *Weekly Reports on Relief and Rehabilitation of Displaced Persons from East Bengal,* contained in Government of Bengal, Intelligence Bureau (hereafter GB IB), File No. 1838/48.

12. Relief and Rehabilitation Department, Government of West Bengal, Memo dated 20 December 1948, in GB IB 1838/48.

13. Memo No. 5610 (13) F.R., from the Secretary, Relief and Rehabilitation Department, Government of West Bengal to all district officers, dated 22 November 1948, ibid.

14. Ibid.
15. Memo No. 800 (14) R.R., from the Secretary, Relief and Rehabilitation Department, Government of West Bengal, to all District Officers, dated 15 February 1949. Emphasis added.
16. Memo No. 1745 (10) R.R./18R-18/49, from the Secretary, Relief and Rehabilitation Department, Government of West Bengal, to all District Officers, dated 29 March 1949. Emphasis added.
17. Memo No. 4482 (13)-Misc./6B-3/49, from the Secretary, Relief and Rehabilitation Department, Government of West Bengal, to all Districts Officers, dated 11 July 1949.
18. Memo No. 8637 (13) Rehab., from J.K. Sanyal, Assistant Secretary to the Government of West Bengal to all District Officers, dated 9 December 1949.
19. 'Professional loans' of Rs 2600 and Rs 2100 were offered to doctors and lawyers respectively to set up practice; 'business loans' (of up to a maximum of Rs 100,000) to those who could persuade the authorities that they had the know-how and contacts required to set up industries; 'business or small-trades loans' and 'loans for artisans' of up to Rs 500 were offered to aspiring petty entrepreneurs in the rural areas. In addition, loans were on offer to weavers (Rs 600); there were also 'paddy-husking loans' of Rs 122 (intended especially for rural women) and 'horticultural loans' of Rs 630 and a bigha (a fraction of an acre) of land, which were designed 'especially for middle-class families' to live in reduced bhadralok circumstances, growing their own fruit and vegetables! *Report on how the millions who came from Eastern Pakistan live here. They live again*, pp. 29–30.
20. In the section that follows, unless otherwise specified, the term 'Government' is used to denote this common official position.
21. This quotation (from Bhaskar Rao, *The Story of Rehabilitation*, p. 229) is so typical an example of the dominant sentiment in the official record that it would be otiose to give detailed citations of other examples of this genre.
22. In practice, Government found it repeatedly had to extend the time limit as each new horde of refugees entered Bengal. Time and again, camps were closed down only to be reopened to take them in. But on each occasion, the same charade was played out of announcing cut-off dates, declaring camps closed once and for all, categorizing refugees according to those who arrived before (or after) certain dates, and all the other well-established devices. For details, see Prafulla Chakrabarti, *The Marginal Men, The Refugees and the Left Political Syndrome in West Bengal*, Calcutta, 1990; and Nilanjana Chatterjee, 'The East Bengal Refugees. A Lesson in Survival', in Sukanta Chaudhuri (ed.), *Calcutta: The Living City*, vol. II, Calcutta, 1990.
23. This is true even today: the demolition of the Babri mosque in Ayodhya

prompted a wave of refugees into India from Bangladesh. This is, of course, one of the central themes of Amitav Ghosh's novel, *The Shadow Lines*.

24. 'The Viceroy's Visit to Bengal: Note by the Viceroy', *Partition Proceedings*, Government of India Press, New Delhi, 1949, vol. I, p. 188 (C).

25. For a brief account of the havoc caused for the economic life of the border districts, see Joya Chatterji, 'The Fashioning of a Frontier: The Radcliffe Line and Bengal's Border Landscape, 1947–52', *Modern Asian Studies*, vol. 33, 1 (1999), pp. 185–242.

26. The Prime Minister justified to the Chief Minister of West Bengal the striking difference in expenditure per capita on refugees in the West and East by arguing that while 'there was something elemental' about the situation in West Pakistan, 'where practically all Hindus and Sikhs have been driven out', in the East it was more gradual, and many Hindus had been able to remain. Jawaharlal Nehru to Dr B.C. Roy, 2 December 1949, cited in Saroj Chakrabarti, *With Dr B.C. Roy*, p. 143.

27. Relief and Rehabilitation Department, Government of West Bengal, Memo dated 20 December 1948, in GB IB 1838/48.

28. Bhaskar Rao, *The Story of Rehabilitation*, pp. 2–3.

29. For instance, the (unnamed) author of *They live again* writes: 'Statistics cannot describe this story of misfortune, of mass human upheaval. It is too tragic for words. Nor can mere facts and figures relate the *magnificent* task of their rehabilitation. . . .' *Report on how the million who came from Eastern Pakistan live here*, p. 1.

30. Bhaskar Rao, *The Story of Rehabilitation*, p. 160.

31. Press Note dated 26 November 1948, GB IB 1838/48.

32. *Relief and Rehabilitation of Displaced Persons in West Bengal*, printed by the Home (Publicity) Department on behalf of the Refugee Relief and Rehabilitation Department, Government of West Bengal, 1956.

33. See for instance, Romila Thapar, '*Dana* and *Daksina* as Forms of Exchange', in *Ancient Indian Social History*, New Delhi, 1987 edn., pp. 105–21. Even if one accepts Raheja's arguments that a 'poison in the gift' tainted the (usually priestly) receiver in caste Hindu society, it does not follow that India had a tradition of contempt for those who received charity. See Gloria Goodwin Raheja, *The Poison in the Gift: Ritual, Prestation and the Dominant Caste in a North Indian Village*, Chicago, 1988.

34. On the distinctive role of the renouncer in Hindu society, see Louis Dumont, 'World Renunciation in Indian Religions', Appendix B, in Louis Dumont, *Homo Hierarchicus. The Caste System and its Implications*, trans. Mark Sainsbury, Louis Dumont and Basia Gulati, Chicago, 1980 edn., pp. 267–86. A critical reappraisal of Dumont's argument can be found in T.N. Madan, *Non-Renunciation: Themes and Interpretations of Hindu Culture*, Delhi,

1987. C.A. Bayly suggests that as late as 1880 religious mendicants of all sorts accounted for five people out of every hundred in northern India; in Banaras alone, the 40,000 or so Brahmins living on charity in 1810 accounted for almost one person in five of the city's population. In the last decade of the eighteenth century, Bayly surmises that there were as many as half a million Shaivite and Vaishnavite ascetics in North India, all living off alms. Nor were mendicant groups, such as the Gosains and Bairagis, in any sense marginal: indeed they played a critically important role in the economic life of the post-Mughal successor states, and were respected as much for their ritual status as for their commercial success. See *Rulers, Townsmen and Bazaars: North Indian Society in the Age of British Expansion, 1770–1870,* Cambridge, 1983, pp. 126, 183. Douglas Haynes, 'From Tribute to Philanthropy: The Politics of Gift Giving in a Western Indian City', *Journal of Asian Studies,* vol. 46, 1987; and Gregory C. Kozlowski, *Muslim Endowments and Society in British India,* Cambridge, 1985, show that traditional forms of charity and philanthropy persisted in the late colonial period.

35. The description of *dana* and *dakshina* in middle-period Bengal suggests that these practices were very much a part of the religious life of Bengal. See Ronald Inden, *Marriage and Rank in Bengali Culture: A History of Caste in Middle-Period Bengal,* Delhi, 1976, pp. 83–92. Tapan Raychaudhuri has shown that amongst Hindus of high status in early modern Bengal, the traditional norms of morality required them 'never to turn away a suitor for charity'. Tapan Raychaudhuri, 'Norms of Family Life and Personal Morality Among the Bengali Hindu Elite, 1600–1850', in Rachel Van M. Baumer (ed.), *Aspects of Bengali History and Society,* Hawaii, 1975, p. 21.

36. Fernand Braudel, *Civilisation and Capitalism, 15th–18th century,* vol. II. *The Wheels of Commerce,* London, 1985 edn., pp. 506–8. The literature on charity, philanthropy and welfare in early-modern and modern Europe is rich and voluminous; Hugh Cunningham and Joanna Innes (eds), *Charity, Philanthrophy and Reform from the 1690s to 1850,* London, 1998, provides a useful and comparative overview of the subject.

37. Raymond Williams, *Keywords: A Vocabulary of Culture and Society,* London, 1983 edn., pp. 54–5.

38. Albert O. Hirschman, *The Rhetoric of Reaction: Perversity, Futility, Jeopardy,* Cambridge, Massachusetts, 1991, p. 30, argues that the notion that well-intended welfare measures inevitably bring about results quite opposite from those intended, has been a central pillar of reactionary thought since Burke's reflections on the French revolution. The idea that welfare assistance, which is intended to alleviate poverty, actually creates the conditions which entrench poverty more deeply, belongs to this tradition, described by Hirschman as 'the perversity thesis', ibid., pp. 11–42.

39. See Nancy Fraser and Linda Gordon, 'A Genealogy of Dependency: Tracing a Keyword of the U.S. Welfare State', in *Signs: Journal of Women in Culture and Society*, vol. 19, no. 2, 1994, pp. 309–36.

40. Williams, *Keywords*, p. 55.

41. See John Rosselli, 'The Self-Image of Effeteness: Physical Education and Nationalism in Nineteenth-Century Bengal', *Past and Present*, vol. 86, February 1989; and Mrinalini Sinha, *Colonial Masculinity: The 'Manly Englishman' and the 'Effeminate Bengali' in the Late Nineteenth Century*, Manchester, 1995.

42. Bhaskar Rao, *The Story of Rehabilitation*, p. 38.

43. See Kudaisya, 'The Demographic Upheaval of Partition'.

44. Rao, *The Story of Rehabilitation*, p. 147.

45. Ibid., p. 155.

46. Ibid., p. 157.

47. This was reasoning similar to that which had informed the French Constitution of 1791, which excluded all categories of 'dependent' individuals (including wage workers) from the suffrage 'because poverty and dependency were thought to be obstacles to the possession of a reasonable will.' See Clause Offe and Ulrich K. Preuss, 'Democratic Institutions and Moral Resources', in David Held (ed.), *Political Theory Today*, Cambridge, 1991, p. 161.

48. Memo No. 8637 (13) Rehab., from J.K. Sanyal, Assistant Secretary to the Government of West Bengal to all District Officers, dated 9 December 1949.

49. Of the 1.1 million refugees who arrived in West Bengal before June 1948, it has been estimated, deploying the broadest of brushes, that 350,000 were members of the 'urban bhadralok', 550,000 of the 'rural bhadralok', 100,000 were 'peasants' and 100,000 were 'artisans'. Chakrabarti, *The Marginal Men*, p. 1.

50. Descriptions of the unspeakably degrading conditions in camps and colonies are commonplace in the newspapers and literary writings of this period. A brief and shocking account can be found in Chakrabarti, *The Marginal Men*, pp. 156–61.

51. The UCRC Central Council, formed in August 1950, included representatives from the CPI, the Forward Bloc, the Marxist Forward Bloc, the Socialist Unity Centre of India, the Revolutionary Communist Party of India (RCPI) (Pannalal Dasgupta's group), the Democratic Vanguard, the Bolshevik Party, the Socialist Republican party and the Hindu Mahasabha, ibid., p. 76. The RCRC was composed of representatives from the RSP, the RCPI (Saumyen Tagore's group), the Forward Bloc (Leela Roy's group), the Kisan Mazdoor Praja Party and the Socialist Party, ibid., p. 88.

52. For an account of the Hindu campaign for the Partition of Bengal in 1947,

see Joya Chatterji, *Bengal Divided: Hindu Communalism and Partition, 1932–1947*, Cambridge, 1994.

53. '*Amar Sankalp*' ('My resolve'), Nabadwip, 6 Agrahayan, 1355 B.S. This pamphlet was issued by Nagendranath Das of the Purbasthali Thana Bahirgat Punarbasati o Palli Unnayan Samiti ['The Purbasthali Thana Rehabilitation and Village Development Committee'] to announce his decision to fast unto death if government did not fulfil his demands.

54. Copy of a report dated 17 December 1948, by the Officer-in-charge, Chakdah Police Station, in GB IB File No. 1809–48 (Noida).

55. Report by P.K. Bhattacharjee dated 13 December 1949, GB IB 1809–48 M.F.

56. Report on the political activities of refugees and corruption in refugee camps for the week ending 4.12.1949, [hereafter RPAR W/E 4.12.1949, and so on], in GB IB 1809–48 (KW).

57. RPAR W/E 13.8.1950, in GB IB 1809–48 (KW).

58. Ibid.

59. The most spectacular incident occurred at Dhubulia camp in Nadia. In September 1950, after some 50 refugees of the camp set up a central committee, the infuriated camp superintendent dragged four of its leaders away from a meeting and held them captive in his office. In the resulting melee, several refugees were badly beaten and one, a young boy named Anakul Brahma, was shot dead by the police. The case gained wide publicity and became the focus of several refugee campaigns. 'Secret Report re: the incident at Dhubulia Camp on 19.9.1950', dated 25.9.1951, GB IB File No. 1809–48 (Nadia).

60. So on 15 August 1950, 'a procession of about 500 refugees from different refugee colonies such as Jadabpur, Tollygunj, Garia etc., . . . converged at Deshapriya Park where two meetings were held in succession under the auspices of the two factions of the Forward Bloc—Marxist and non-Marxist—to decry the Congress Government for the allegedly fake Independence achieved. . . .' On the same day, another refugee procession ended up at Hazra park to celebrate 'Anti-Independence Day'. RPAR W/E 20.8.1950, GB IB File No. 1838–48 (KW).

61. For example, a meeting of refugees in Srirampur at Purbasthali demanded that the government set up a mill at Nabadwip 'to enable the refugees to find employment'. RPAR W/E 10.9.1950, GB IB 1809–48 (KW). Similarly, at a meeting of refugees at Balurghat in August 1950, 'demands were made for employment of refugee youths', ibid.

62. *Desher janagana o bastubara bhaiboner prati Nikhil Banga Bastuhara Karma Parishader dak*, ['The Call of the All Bengal Refugee Council of Action to the People of the Country and to Refugee Brothers and Sisters'] (no date but

clearly published in or before July 1949, probably in Calcutta). GB IB File No. 1809–48 M.F.

63. The UCRC Working Committee organized meetings all over West Bengal on 3 September 1950, to discuss the 'food problem'. Similarly, at a meeting of refugees at Shraddhananda Park on 27 August 1950, 'speeches were delivered criticising the food and rehabilitation politics of the Government'. RPAR W/F. 27.8.1950, GB IB File No. 1838–48 (KW).

64. Chakrabarti, *The Marginal Men*, p. 407.

65. For a discussion of the history of the concept of rights and its historical and theoretical association with notions of equality, see Richard Dagger, 'Rights', in Terence Ball, James Farr and Russell Hanson (eds), *Political Innovation and Conceptual Change*, Cambridge, 1989, pp. 299–300.

66. This demand appears to have evolved spontaneously among the refugees, although it later came to win support from many political parties. For instance, a secret report on the objections of refugees in Nadia against leaving Bengal observed that 'this is purely their voluntary and sentimental objection. They say that they have been born in Bengal and will die in Bengal. There is no provocation or incitement from outside. Some of the refugees have even fled from the camp for fear of being transferred outside Bengal. . . .' 'Copy of a report of a District Investigating Officer of Nadia District', dated 23 April 1950. GB IB File No. 1808–48 (Nadia). After the summer of 1950, the refugees' worst fears were realized when those who had been sent to camps on Bihar and Orissa began to 'desert' in large numbers, bringing back horror stories of the conditions in the colonies from which they had fled. After this, the demand for 'rehabilitation in Bengal' became one of the central planks of the refugee movement's platform.

67. For example, the fifty refugees who occupied four bighas of private land at Jhil Road in Jadavpur 'were agreeable to pay a fair price for the lands occupied by them . . .'. RPAR W/E 8.1.1950, GB IB File No. 1838–48 (IV).

68. Chakrabarti, *The Marginal Men*, pp. 80–2.

69. Sunil Gangopadhyay develops this theme in his novel *Arjun*, which traces the radicalization and politicization of one refugee youth in the course of a property dispute between neighbouring landlords and the refugee squatters' colony.

70. *West Bengal Act XVI of 1951. The Rehabilitation of Displaced Persons and Eviction of Persons in Unauthorised Occupation of Land Act 1951.*

71. *Desher janagana o bastuhara bhaiboner prati Nikhil Banga Bastubara Karma Parishader dak.* ['The Call of the All Bengal Refugee Council of Action to the People of the Country and to Refugee Brothers and Sisters'].

72. Chakrabarti, *The Marginal Men*, pp. 426, 433.

Partition Politics and Achhut Identity: A Study of the Scheduled Castes Federation and Dalit Politics in UP, 1946–48

RAMNARAYAN S. RAWAT

'This is 1946, not 1932'[1]

THE YEAR 1946 was significant in the history of Dalit struggles, about which we still know very little. The Dalits had launched a popular movement against the Congress and the British government in different parts of Uttar Pradesh and outlined their agenda. Its importance was noted by a Dalit activist, Shankaranand Shastri. In November of the same year, he published *Poona-Pact or Gandhi*, which he claimed to be an authentic history of Dalit struggle from 1932 to 1946 (the second, revised edition of the book extended the narrative up to the events of 1965). Addressed primarily to Dalits, the book hoped to make them aware of the dubious and hawkish policies

I am grateful to Anil Sethi, Chanderbhan Prasad, Dipu Sharan, Dipankar Dass, Nilanjan Sarkar, Rohan D'Souza, Urvashi Butalia and Prof. Ravinder Kumar for their comments, suggestions, and support. I am very grateful to Suvir Kaul for his comments and generosity; to a very fine teacher Gyan Pandey for his support, tolerance and criticism, and to my Ph.D. supervisor Shahid Amin for his patience, comments and encouragement.

of the Congress. In an angry and combative tone, Shastri portrayed 'a scheming and corrupt Gandhi, Nehru, Malaviya and Company' and described the Congress as 'Brahmin-baniya Company'.[2] The timing of the book suggests Shastri's awareness of the crucial relationship between prevailing political equations and the fate of the Dalits in an independent India. As an activist's account of the Dalit struggle against Gandhi, caste-Hindus, and the Congress, the book offers a Dalit perspective on what we might describe as 'Partition politics', set in motion by the coming of Independence and the likelihood of Partition.

The Dalit agitation in United Provinces [UP], according to Shastri, was part of a wider agitation launched by the All-India Scheduled Caste Federation [SCF] between July and August 1946, that included the anti-*begari* movement in which rural labourers participated.[3] Shastri identifies two other 'satyagrahas' of the Dalit struggle: the Mahad Satyagraha of 1927 and the Nasik Satyagraha of 1930. He thus suggests a trilogy of Dalit struggles as a deliberate counterpoise to the trilogy of Congress struggles (1920–22; 1930–34; 1942) advertised by Congress spokespersons.[4] In all this, Shastri's work represents a Dalit reading of the recent historical past, an alternative to the Congress history of the 'freedom struggle'—it is a conscious effort to contest not only Congress politics, but also their 'politics of History'.

Shastri's central concern is to repeatedly assert a separate achhut identity and emphasize the leadership of Ambedkar.[5] Both were necessary, he urged, to protect the rights of achhuts. The book, in fact, seeks to document the 'betrayal' of the achhuts by 'Gandhi, Nehru, Malaviya and Company'. Shastri identifies the Poona Pact as the emblem of their betrayal.[6] He shows how the Pact ensures a continuation of Hindu domination over achhuts, obstructing any move towards the liberation of their community. He gives an account of the achhut struggle for rights, which caste-Hindus attempted to discredit by describing it as 'communal'. In the final section he discusses the contribution of Dr Ambedkar to political processes after Independence.

Is Shastri's book an aberration from the general mood of 'nationalist' unification that is supposed to have defined the times, or can it be considered one of the many subaltern initiatives which have been forgotten or are deliberately ignored by 'caste-Hindu' historiography? Existing writings on Partition and Independence seem to have no place for Shastri's text (or similar writing). Shastri's book, it seems to me, offers an alternative reading of the politics of the 1940s; one that takes seriously the attempt made by the UP Scheduled Caste Federation to formulate an achhut identity.

The prospect of Partition created a new and volatile situation, while constitutional discussions about Independence and the rights of minority communities in the new nation enabled, I will argue here, new forms of Dalit activism and struggle.

As a reminder of the issues at stake in such a discussion, we might turn to Urvashi Butalia's book, and in particular to the important question she poses: 'was there then a history of Harijans too at Partition?'[7] She provides the example of a woman from Punjab who was left unharmed by Muslim rioters once she disclosed her untouchable identity. In the context of the Partition riots in Punjab, Butalia suggests, the Dalits were in many ways 'invisible' or 'untouchable', and thus outside the polarized oppositions of Hindu and Muslim. I would suggest that we read this incident more specifically in the particular context of Dalit politics in the Partition years, and remind ourselves of their increasing assertion, at this time, of a separate identity. Indeed it is possible to speculate that the Dalit woman escaped because there was, for a while, a *formal* alliance between the Muslim League and the SCF in Bengal, UP and Punjab, and because of the support extended by the SCF to the demand for Pakistan. In Lahore, from early 1947, sections of Dalits had supported the League's movement, and demanded the resignation of the Premier of Punjab, Sikander Hyatt Khan, the restoration of civil rights and the establishment of Pakistan.[8] The Muslim League repeatedly vowed to protect the safety of the Dalits in Pakistan. In Punjab, many representations were sent by Dalits from various villages that they should form part of Pakistan.[9] These political developments may have shaped popular perceptions about the attitudes of Dalits towards the Muslim League and the Congress (perceptions which need to be addressed in discussions of Partition riots).

Sekhar Bandopadhyay has argued, however, that the Dalit electoral support to the Congress in 1946 and their role in anti-Muslim riots in Bengal suggests 'their merger with the Indian, predominantly Hindu nation.'[10] His study indicates that in response to the sharply polarized situation created by Partition politics, they opted for a Hindu identity. While the riots in Bengal perhaps provide compelling instances of such identification, his argument about national electoral support leaves too many questions unanswered. For instance, he fails to take into account the election to Primaries in which only the Dalits voted: in these elections, the SCF decisively demonstrated its popularity by winning most of the seats it contested in UP.[11] Other commentators too consider these years as insignificant to the history of Dalit politics. Mark Juergensmeyer's sympathetic account of the Ad-Dharmi's struggle is a case in point. He writes that 'during the final struggle for Independence and the trauma involved in the Partition of the Punjab, issues regarding the lower castes were all but forgotten in the chaos of migration and resettlement.'[12] Owen Lynch points to the initiative taken by the Jatavs in the 1940s to further 'direct political participation' by establishing the SCF, but discusses only the sociological aspect of the SCF; the political aspect of achuut identity as it was articulated in the new SCF agenda is not analysed.[13] In this respect, Juergensmeyer and Lynch share common ground with the historiography of Partition and Independence. Dalits figure in these histories solely as supporters of the Congress-led national movement. This has become received wisdom in Indian historiography.

I will point to the specificity of the Partition politics that enabled the Dalits in UP to raise the issue of their separate and communal identity; I take my cue from Shail Mayaram's suggestion that we 'look at how [the] identity politics of Partition' impinged on issues and politics which were not directly concerned with the demand for Partition.[14] Partition politics, we are told, fixed identities even for the marginal communities: the choice was between Hindu or Muslim. But this might be an inaccurate reading; I will argue that new opportunities for self-definition became available to marginal groups. The Dalits of UP, for instance, turned the new situation to their advantage. When necessary, they did not hesitate to establish an alliance with the

Muslim League to justify their demand for a separate identity. In doing so, they indicated the similarity of their politics with those of the League, and underlined the 'outcaste' status of their community. They further asserted their differences with the Congress in UP, especially in the urban areas, by voting for the SCF in the election to the Primaries in 1945. In contrast to existing historical accounts, I argue that in the context of UP, the SCF and the Dalits articulated a separate achhut identity forcefully enough to prevent it from submerging into Congress or national consensus, and one whose political concerns live with us still.

I

The SCF had expected constitutional safeguards from the Cabinet Mission. It hoped that the Mission would provide for the principle of separate representation for the Dalits by recognizing them as a separate community. This was the central demand that the SCF repeatedly raised in its resolutions after 1942.[15] The expectations of the SCF were not entirely unfounded; they were, in fact, based on commitments given by the Viceroys. In a letter to Gandhi, Wavell reaffirmed the British position, stating that they viewed the Scheduled Castes as a separate community whose consent was a necessary condition in the transfer of power. Earlier, Lord Linlithgow had made a similar statement about the Scheduled Castes in his speech on 10 August 1940 in Bombay.[16] According to Dr Ambedkar, the response of the Cabinet delegation to his proposals during their meeting on 15 April 1946 was positive.[17] The representatives of the Scheduled Castes, however, were not invited to the final discussions of the Cabinet Mission at Simla. The British, in the end, accepted the Congress proposition that the Scheduled Castes were part of the Hindu community. In line with this position, the Cabinet Mission Award of 16 May 1946 did not provide any specific safeguards for the Scheduled Castes.[18] The arrangement proposed by the Cabinet Mission for elections to the Constituent Assembly from the provincial assemblies recognized only three communities: a) General b) Muslims and c) Sikh; the SCF demand that the

Dalits be recognized as a separate community was not accepted. As a concession, the demands of the Scheduled Castes and other minorities were accommodated in the advisory committee to safeguard their interests in the proposed Constitution.

In his critique of the Cabinet Mission proposals Ambedkar protested that the 'Scheduled Castes were greatly surprised to find themselves lumped together with the Hindus.'[19] With the status and powers of the Advisory Committee undefined, he argued, the representatives of the Scheduled Castes in the Constituent Assembly represented the interests of the Congress and not those of the Scheduled Castes. He disagreed with the Cabinet Mission's defence that the Congress had won the Scheduled Castes' seats in the last election. Instead, he claimed, an examination of the elections to the Primaries in 1945 would show the limited extent to which the Congress represented the Scheduled Castes. In this phase of the elections the Scheduled Castes were provided with separate electorates, which was not the case in the general election. His analysis of the election results of the Primaries indicated that non-Congress Scheduled Castes secured 72 per cent of the vote compared with the 28 per cent for the Congress.

Jagjivan Ram, in his response to the Mission's Plan, asserted that the Ambedkarite politics of separate electorates had been rejected. Nevertheless he too articulated a position different from that of the Congress. He agreed that the Dalits had been treated unfairly by the Cabinet Mission, and reiterated the demand of the Depressed Classes League that 'the Scheduled Castes should be given representation in the Constituent Assembly and the Legislative Assembly in proportion to their population in a province.'[20] Ironically, this demand had first been raised by the SCF. Jagjivan Ram was aware of the similarities between his party's position and that of the SCF. The only difference between his party and the SCF, he said, was with regard to the position of the Dalits in relation to the Hindu community: he believed them to be a part of the Hindu community, while the SCF believed in Dalit separation from Hindu society.[21]

Jagjivan Ram had come to realize the importance of the changes in progress in the 1940s and therefore reassessed his position. The change in his attitude was also perhaps a comment on the Congress failure to deal adequately with the problems of Dalit society. It prompted him to agree with Wavell's characterization in 1944 of the Congress as a caste-Hindu party. When Gandhi protested against this description, Jagjivan Ram issued a public statement approving Wavell's position and describing Gandhi's statement as self-contradictory and surprising. He argued that the Poona Pact was a clear acknowledgement of two sections within the Hindus, the 'Harijan' and the 'non-Harijans and Hindus'.[22] This radicalism in a leading Congress Harijan leader underlines the changes taking place around this time in the character and temper of Dalit politics.

The inadequate representation of the Dalits in the Interim Ministry was portrayed as yet another instance of injustice towards them. In a statement, Ambedkar objected to the unfair and unjust composition of the Ministry. He protested that while the Dalits had demanded three seats, they had been allotted just one. Jagjivan Ram agreed, pointing to the iniquity of 60 million Dalit people, eligible for three seats, being palmed off with one. He complained that 'if three seats could be allotted to the Muslims, two seats to the Sikhs, then one seat for the Dalits is unfair and against the principles of the Cabinet Mission Plan.' Similar criticism was made by the UP Congress Dalit leaders Hari Prasad Tamta and Chaudhari Girdhari Lal.[23]

Criticism of the Cabinet Mission plan was not limited to the elite Dalit leadership. Even at the popular level there was a fairly widespread sense of betrayal by the Congress. The Dalits of western UP were among the first to register their protest against the award of the Cabinet Mission. In June 1946, the District Harijan Conference and the District Harijan Uddharsabha of Saharanpur passed identical resolutions.[24] They protested not only against the award of the Cabinet Mission *per se*, but also the acceptance of the award by the Congress. They accused the Congress of being unfair to the Dalit community. The resolutions were passed in response to a press statement by the President of the Congress, Maulana Azad, on 24 June 1946 in which he stated that the seats for the Dalits in the Constituent Assembly would be fixed in accordance with the proportion of their members in the Assembly of each province. Even the Congress Harijans (hereafter Harijans) of western UP disagreed with their Party's response to the Awards.

The two resolutions demanded that the Harijans be given 45 seats out of a total of 140 general seats in the UP Legislative Assembly. They had been allotted 20 seats in the Assembly, which they felt were inadequate in relation to the Scheduled Caste population in UP—11 million out of a total population of 55 million. The Harijans wanted the same rights in representation as had been provided to caste-Hindus, Sikhs and Muslims. The criterion enunciated by the Cabinet Mission for representation to the Constituent Assembly was one elected representative for every one million of the population. If this criterion could be applied to other communities, they argued, then why were the Harijans excluded?

What is significant for us is their articulation of Harijan differences with the Congress (and the implications of these differences for Dalit politics). They invoked the constitutional criteria by which the Congress accepted the rights of minorities, and thus, to reinforce their claim, compared themselves to other non-Hindu communities. While the Harijans were in fact careful to avoid any reference to their religious separateness from caste-Hindus, adopting a secular strategy to focus on a constitutional principle, they nevertheless underlined their separateness—as a *community*—from caste-Hindus. This sense of difference defined the notion of their own community and was enhanced by their invocation of, and comparison to, other communities. The positions articulated in the two resolutions were similar to the stand taken by the SCF.

The tension between the Harijans of Western UP and the Congress is a barometer of the changes in positions taken by Dalits in the 1940s. The two Harijan organizations were, however, equally keen to emphasize their preference for the Congress and not the Muslim League. To this end, they addressed the two resolutions, in order of preference, to the Congress leaders and the Viceroy. They chose to ignore Ambedkar in their initiative.[25]

The rapidity and ease with which public meetings were organized after Maulana Azad's statement on 24 June suggests that the Dalits had for some time been discussing the implications of the Cabinet Mission Award. Such meetings were held on 26 June in Meerut and 30 June in Saharanpur. The resolution passed in Meerut was later approved by the Dalits of Saharanpur. The close proximity of time and space in the passing of the two resolutions suggests that a great deal of dialogue was taking place among the Harijan leaders of western UP, particularly among the two Harijan organizations. One reason for the Congress-Harijans' difference with the Congress—despite being part of it—could be located in the Dalit agitation taking place in parts of western UP.

II

In its turn, the SCF's rejection of the Cabinet Mission award of 16 May 1946 was not limited to mere statements in the press. It decided to organize satyagrahas throughout India to protest against the Award and the Congress and identified three main issues for the proposed satyagrahas. They demanded a blue-print from the Congress on the position of Dalits in independent India. They also demanded the abrogation of the Poona Pact, which they described as political fraud against the Dalits.[26] They reiterated their demand for separate electorates for the Dalits. Gandhi and his Harijan movement were held responsible for denying rights to the Dalits.

The Dalit movement affected twenty-three districts of UP. Out of these, ten districts witnessed prolonged agitation from June to November 1946.[27] Altogether, the extent and success of the satyagraha speaks remarkably well of a party only four years old. To ensure participation in the proposed satyagraha, leaders of the SCF toured their respective areas. (In the absence of party papers or much reporting in the newspapers, it is difficult to make detailed statements regarding these efforts.) The decision to launch the satyagraha was taken in the first week of June 1946, and by the second week, the leaders of the SCF in UP began to mobilize the Dalits. Dr Manik Chand and Faqir Chand, the Dalit leaders, toured western areas of UP. In Saharanpur, Faqir Chand organized a meeting on 12 June in which he 'threatened to oppose the Congress Government if all the Dalit demands set out in a leaflet distributed at the meeting were not conceded.'[28] Manik Chand organized similar meetings in the district of Ferozabad. Tilak Chand Kureel of Kanpur, the President of the UP SCF, organized the Dalits not only in Kanpur, but also toured Azamgarh and Gorakhpur. At a meeting in Lucknow, Piare Lal Talib reiterated the demands of the SCF, and mobilized volunteers. Similar meetings were also held in Etah and Etawah district by Swami Chhamanand. In some respects organizing Dalits in these areas was not difficult, since the SCF had done considerable political work during the elections of 1945–46.

The agitation began in Lucknow on 16 July when hundreds of achhut satyagrahis marched in a procession towards the Legislative Assembly. The demonstration was led by Tilak Chand Kureel. The satyagrahis carried placards and raised slogans saying: 'Down with British Imperialism'; 'Down-with Congress'; 'Scrap the Poona Pact'. The prominent Dalit leaders—Kureel, Jaiswar, Talib and Shastri— were arrested immediately after their speeches to the satyagrahis. On the first day of the satyagraha, 222 Dalit satyagrahis were arrested. The satyagraha was subsequently held on 17, 18, 22, 24, and 29 July 1946. After a gap of a fortnight, the UP SCF organized another satyagraha on 11 August, when 45 satyagrahis were arrested.[29] The All India SCF suspended the satyagraha in Bombay on 28 July, when the session of the Legislative Assembly in Poona was adjourned. The SCF in UP, however, continued the satyagraha until 15 August when the Legislative Assembly in Lucknow was adjourned.[30] The official statement in the Legislative Assembly put the total number of satyagrahis arrested at 311.[31]

I would like to emphasize two aspects of the Dalit agitation: first, the choice of the Legislative Assembly as the site of protest and second, the appropriation of the Gandhian concept of satyagraha as the mode of protest. The SCF had decided to question the democratic credentials of the UP Legislative Assembly that was in session in Lucknow. It was keen to make a point about the lack of true Dalit representation in the Legislative Assembly, for which the SCF held the Poona Pact responsible. They were eager to highlight this point. The choice of satyagraha was a deliberate political act in the context of the SCF's opposition to the Congress and Gandhi. It was thus more than a mere appropriation, a point noted and commented upon by the Hindi daily *Vartman* in an editorial about the illegitimacy of the choice. The editorial noted that 'the most amusing aspect (of the satyagraha) is that today Dr Ambedkar has to depend on Gandhiji's weapon of protest: satyagraha, the same person against whom his opposition is well known.'[32] That a nationalist Hindi daily would represent the SCF choice of satyagraha as a 'contradiction' suggests that its subversive potential was generally understood.

In his book, Shastri mentions Kanpur (besides Lucknow) as another centre of achhut protest. The SCF organized a satyagraha to mark 'Poona Day' in Kanpur on 15 August by 'hoisting black flags on their houses and holding meetings at which caste-Hindu leaders were denounced.'[33] Meetings and demonstrations were also organized in rural areas. Members of the SCF were particularly active around Etah and Etawah, where meetings and demonstrations were organized in co-ordination with the satyagraha in Lucknow. The objectives of the SCF were reaffirmed at demonstrations organized in other districts as well; Faizabad, Gorakhpur, Fatehgarh, Ferozabad, Agra, Azamgarh and Farrukhabad are some of the places that are mentioned repeatedly in the weekly CID reports. For instance, at the Faizabad meeting, 'the audience was asked to follow Ambedkar' as their leader. At a meeting in Gorakhpur, 'speakers criticized the Congress government with the remark that rather than enjoy Swaraj under Congress, they [will prefer] to live under British rule.'[34] Great emphasis was laid on the unity of the achhuts. Speakers also warned their audience about the 'undemocratic' character of the caste-Hindus and their party, the Congress; the Poona Pact was cited as an example of their undemocratic attitudes. These points were specifically made at the achhut meetings in Etah, Etawah and Farukhabad.[35] The SCF in UP decided to resume its agitation during the next session of the Legislative Assembly.

The second phase of the Dalit agitation which was aimed at enlisting volunteers for the proposed satyagraha, began in Agra from the first week of August. Manik Chand, his wife, and Gopi Chand Pipal, the President of the Agra SCF, had enrolled about 150 satyagrahis by the middle of September.[36] Meetings to mobilize satyagrahis were also organized in Etah, Etawah and Farrukhabad by local leaders of the SCF. At a meeting in Fatehgarh, a Hindi leaflet, *'Alarm Bell Arthath Khatrey Ki Ghanti'* ['Alarm Bell, that is, Danger Signal'], was distributed in which the Dalits were 'warned not to join' the Congress but to 'prepare for a satyagraha'.[37] In this agitation, the status of Ambedkar as the leader of the Dalits was emphasized in conscious opposition to Gandhi, Nehru, and Jagjivan Ram. At their meetings in Hamirpur and Agra, Gandhi was described as 'a traitor and a cheat to the cause of [Dalits]' and accused of 'misleading the [Dalits] into the Congress'.[38] Dalits were urged to follow Bhim—Ambedkar—personifying strength, rather than Ram. At some places symbols of Gandhian politics like khadi clothes and Gandhi caps were also burnt.[39] At a Dalit meeting in Moradabad, a resolution was passed declaring Dr Ambedkar their 'true leader and representative'.[40] Similar resolutions were also passed in Faizabad, Etah, Etawah and Allahabad. Reposing faith in Ambedkar's leadership and declaring him their true representative became a integral feature of the new achhut identity. Efforts along similar lines had also been made during the election to the Primaries in October 1945 and at the General Election in March 1946.[41]

As the Dalit agitation extended into rural areas it provided a new dimension to their efforts. The Anglo-Indian press and official reports noted the involvement of Dalit women in the agitation; Dalit women protested against begari—as we can extrapolate from reports like one in the *Pioneer* which notes that 'the Dalit women of Rampurva village (district Gorakhpur) engaged in the work of cutting umbilical cords are demanding Rs 5 per case.'[42] That this was not a local instance but part of a wider protest is shown by comparable newspaper reports.[43] *Aaj* reported that in many parts of the province, Chamar women were demanding Rs 5 for cutting the umbilical cords of new-born babies. *People's Age* also reported similar events from the district of Jaunpur, where Dalit women were refusing to act as 'dais' or midwives.

Dalit women were required to perform begari not only in the domestic sphere but also in the fields of zamindars, where they worked as labourers, particularly in the reaping and harvesting season. Intelligence reports from Bijnor noted that 'the [Dalits] have stopped their women folk from doing menial work such as removing dung and grinding' in the household of Hindu zamindars.[44] In village Kealowara, district Azamgarh, a Dalit woman, Jhunia, went to the police station and filed a complaint against the zamindars of the village. In the complaint, Jhunia accused zamindars of forcibly demanding begari from the Dalit men and brutally beating them when they asked for wages.[45] Thanks to these newspaper reports, however brief, and the odd question in the Legislative Assembly, Dalit women emerge as visible participants in the agitation. We should take these reports as representative of a wider process of women's participation in the protest. The involvement of Dalit women was geared to the demands of their community, and the issue of achhut identity—for men and women— was thus linked crucially to their right to fair wages, or to start with, any wage at all.

III

The building of an alliance between the SCF and the Muslim League was another significant development in achhut politics during this period. The alliance was an indication of changing times, a conscious move to legitimize Dalit claims to minority status by identifying the similarities of their social conditions with those of the Muslims. From the middle of September 1946, regular interaction between the leaders of the SCF and the League became a distinctive feature of their struggle for achhut identity.[46] The League's participation in the Dalit agitation in UP was symptomatic of similar changes at the national level. The election of Dr Ambedkar to the Constituent Assembly from the Bengal Legislative Assembly as an independent candidate supported by the Muslim League was one such indication.[47]

Early instances of cooperation between the SCF and the Muslim League, in the course of the Dalit agitation, were reported from Kanpur and Farrukhabad.[48] At Kanpur, a Dalit meeting was addressed by two Muslim League leaders. In Farrukhabad, at a Dalit meeting, League leaders compared the position of their community with those of the

Dalits in India. They supported the achhut struggle and reminded them that 'unless they filled the jails, their demand would not be conceded.' Prior to this, in the last week of August, the SCF in its meeting at Kanpur, had supported the demands of the Muslim League, including that of boycotting the Constituent Assembly and Interim Government.[49]

The SCF and League leaders began to emphasize the similarity of their struggles against the Congress. It was not long before ordinary members of the League began to participate in SCF meetings. League members participated in Dalit meetings at Kheri, Lucknow and Kanpur. It was repeatedly stated in Kanpur that 'no scheduled caste movement would be launched in Provinces which have [a] Muslim League government.'[50] At Kanpur, Farrukhabad, Kheri, Lucknow and Mainpuri, 'Jinnah was thanked' for the support the League had extended during Dr Ambedkar's election to the Constituent Assembly. The Muslim League was impressed by the enthusiastic response of the Dalits, and heartened by their criticism of caste-Hindus, the Hindu religion and its scriptures. Their criticism of the Congress, Gandhi, the Poona Pact and their demand for separate electorates strengthened the League's conviction. These two aspects of the achhut agitation may have convinced a few leaders of the League that the Dalits might convert to Islam. In some of their joint meetings they appealed to Dalits to embrace Islam and join the League: a Muslim League leader, Haji Mohammad Saleh, asked his audience in Lucknow to join hands with the League and together embrace Islam.[51] The perception that Dalits might convert *en masse* seems to have acquired a fair amount of credibility, till the SCF denied, in Allahabad, any such intention. The denial may have undercut the very separateness from Hindus which was a major feature of the Dalit struggle.[52]

The alliance between the League and the SCF elicited an immediate response from Hindu organizations like the Arya Samaj and the Hindu Mahasabha which felt especially threatened by this development in Dalit politics. In early November, these organizations took initiatives in Aligarh, Etah, Bareilly, Nanital and Mathura to demonstrate their willingness to consider the demands of the achhuts for social uplift.[53] In these districts, Hindu organizations opened temples and wells for the achhuts, organized meals together and invited them to religious ceremonies in caste-Hindu temples. Subsequently, similar measures were taken in other parts of the province, in Bijnor, Saharanpur, Jalaun and Etawah.[54]

Elite 'Hindu' nationalism had formulated the question of untouchable identity as a 'Hindu' question in the 1910s and 1920s. This was related to the concerns of the Arya Samaj and the Hindu Mahasabha about the numerical strength of the Hindu community and its dominant position in the Indian nation. Hindu organizations went a step further and claimed that untouchability emerged during Muslim rule.[55] The insensitivity of the Hindu organizations in thus offering tired solutions to the issue raised by the achhuts is remarkable. They were unable to respond to changes in Dalit politics, or to negotiate the new agenda put forward by the achhuts, primarily because they did not acknowledge the SCF and its political agenda.

The Congress followed suit: the Mau Mandal Congress Committee organized a meeting on 17 November 1946 and warned Dalits about the nefarious designs of Ambedkar and the League.[56] Similar attempts were also made in meetings at Azamgarh, Unao, Kheri and Agra, which at times turned violent. In Unao two thousand members of the Congress, caste-Hindus at that, made an effort to disrupt the proceedings of an SCF conference. Quick police intervention averted a clash. In a more amiable response, Congressmen in Agra distributed leaflets in which the Dalits were urged to join the Congress.[57] The nature of Congress opposition was very similar to that of the Hindu organizations: they wooed the Dalits and warned them against the Muslim League, describing it as 'separatist', a part of 'communal politics'.[58] It was with this perspective that the Congress and Hindu organizations intervened in Dalit politics when the alliance between the SCF and the League acquired a more stable character in UP from late September. As rumours of Dalit conversion to Islam or their co-option into the League spread, the Congress and the caste-Hindu organizations offered a religious reform carrot. They chose not to address the political demands of the SCF, particularly for separate electorates, which in any case they labelled a communal demand.

At the time of negotiations for the transfer of power, there was thus no space in the Congress perspective to even acknowledge Dalit demands. To erode the legitimacy of their politics further, Dalit leaders were described as agents of feudalism or imperialism, or as urban leaders involved in institutional politics without a mass base among the people. In a Hindi leaflet entitled 'Congress Socialist Party ki Salah', Dr Sheo Shankar Upadhya identified Ambedkar, among others, as a Congress enemy and an 'obstacle to our Independence'.[59] The skewed electoral arrangement worked out under the Poona Pact ensured that Dalits opposed to the Congress would never succeed in the elections. This allowed nationalist historians to create and perpetuate the myth that the Dalits were traditional supporters of the Congress.[60]

In such a scenario, historians too easily see the League as the pre-eminent partner in the alliance with the Dalits, and as encouraging and manipulating Dalit politics to fulfil its own 'communal' aims. In this reading, therefore, there is no alliance, merely a conspiracy hatched by the League to capture the Dalits. Official reports too took a similar view towards the alliance and attributed the increasing strength of Dalit agitation to the intervention of the League.[61] The possibility that Dalits could enter into an alliance with the Muslim League on their own terms was not even considered. Evidence, on the other hand, suggests that the initiative for the alliance was taken by the SCF, in response to changing political circumstances. Moreover, there was nothing 'natural' in the efforts of the SCF to seek an alliance with the League: as late as 1944, the UP SCF in its annual conference had passed a resolution against the demand of Pakistan, describing it as 'anti-national'.[62] Two years later however, the SCF not only initiated an alliance with the League but also supported their demand for Pakistan. The shift was a reflection of the Dalits' new political agenda. In seeking an alliance with the League, the SCF expressed their shared concern about the issue of political justice for members of deprived sections of society—the achhuts and the Muslims. Shankaranand Shastri writes that the Congress 'effort was to suppress our freedom movement by describing it as communal.'[63] This he writes, 'was truly an example of their opposition to the emergence of true citizenship and nationalism.' For him then, the abolition of untouchability was in fact necessary to provide Dalits with a citizenship and nationality. It was a political ideal, not simply a problem of social reform.

IV

On 28 April 1947, the Constituent Assembly unanimously passed a Bill abolishing untouchability and making its practice a criminal offence. It was, perhaps, the first step from the Congress towards rapprochment with the SCF. A more concrete gesture was made on 2 July, when Ambedkar was nominated as the Congress candidate to the Constituent Assembly from the Bombay Legislative Council.[64] (This paved the way for his subsequent appointment as Law Minister in Nehru's cabinet.) Soon after, on 18 July, the UP Government released all the leaders of the UP SCF who had been arrested during the satyagrahas.[65] These initiatives from the Congress were aimed at integrating the SCF into the 'national mainstream'. If these were steps to disarm the Dalit struggle, perhaps the most decisive was Ambedkar's decision to accept the Congress nomination. Predictably, his decision has been celebrated by nationalist historiography as the final triumph of Indian (Congress) nationalism. However these events need to be understood in the context of achhut politics. The initiative on the part of the Congress should not lead us to believe that the SCF had disowned its agenda. I would in fact suggest that Ambedkar's decision reaffirmed the endurance and significance of achhut identity in Indian politics. The fact that the Congress had no option but to negotiate with Ambedkarite politics was a recognition of the power of the Dalit struggle. In the changed realities of 1947—the Congress government and Independence—some kind of cooperation with the Congress was a worthwhile proposition for Ambedkar.[66]

The Congress initiatives were certainly not wholly beneficial to Dalit politics in UP; Ambedkar's decision in particular disrupted the developing cohesion in Dalit politics. There was an indication of the first major division in the SCF when three senior leaders of the UP SCF, Piarelal Talib, R.S. Shyamlal and Nandlal Jaiswar, pledged their cooperation with the policies of the Congress Ministry in UP.[67] These leaders soon joined the Congress, as did Manik Chand, and contested the elections in 1951–52 as official candidates of the Congress. Piarelal Talib and Manik Chand were elected to the Lok Sabha from the Banda district constituency in UP (General and SC) and Bharatpur (Reserved) constituency in Rajasthan respectively, while R.S. Shyamlal was elected to the UP Legislative Assembly as a Congress candidate. Another prominent leader of the SCF, Karan Singh Kane, was appointed a Rehabilitation Officer by the UP government. He, however, remained a loyal Ambedkarite and worked for the SCF.[68] Gopal Singh, a Dalit activist of the SCF from Ludhiana (Punjab), responded differently. He described Ambedkar's move as an opportunistic 'surrender' to the caste-Hindus and their politics, and announced his decision to become a socialist.[69] Gopal Singh's response was certainly shared by many other workers of the SCF, who saw in the 'surrender' to the Congress the loss of what had so far been the ideals of the SCF. This does not mean, however, that they renounced their commitment to these ideals. Rather, Dalit activists found individual solutions to cope with a new political situation, and continued to pursue their objectives.

Ambedkar in turn realised the disorienting impact of his decision, and felt it necessary to clarify his stand so as to reaffirm the ideals of the SCF and its opposition to the Congress. The fifth conference of the UP SCF provided him the opportunity to explain his position to the Dalits. The conference was held in Lucknow on 24 and 25 April 1948 and attended by 7,000 members and delegates.[70] In his speech, Ambedkar denied the rumours that he had joined the Congress. He clarified that his objective was to serve the interests of the Dalits, a cause for which he had fought against the Congress for twenty-five years. 'What I want is power—political power—for my people, for if we have power we will have social status,' reaffirmed Ambedkar in his inaugural address.[71] He particularly emphasized the significance of their separate identity and the need to transform it into a potent political force, under one banner, one slogan, one leader, one party and one programme. He criticized the Premier of UP, who had turned down the legitimate demands of the Dalits because he commanded a majority in the House.

Ambedkar's speech was important in its reaffirmation of the SCF's differences with the Congress. Notions of 'Independence' and 'citizenship' were meaningless for the Dalits unless they had a share in political power, he argued. The point driven home at the Conference was that despite the abolition of untouchability and the promise of citizenship, their struggle were far from over. The SCF was doubtful about implementing these principles through administrative measures. Therefore it thought the Dalits urgently needed to continue their efforts to maintain their separate identity.

Ambedkar's speech was dismissed by the nationalist press in UP as a 'frustrated outburst'.[72] With Partition fresh in collective memory, the editorial in the *Leader* commented, 'Dr Ambedkar has chosen precisely at this moment to tell the Scheduled Castes, "a united nation is all rot". Dr Ambedkar wants the Scheduled Castes to *form a third nation*.'[73] Ambedkar's criticism of the Congress, including his remarks about the disintegration of the Congress, was also considered unacceptable. An editorial in the *National Herald* described his speech as a cynical outburst lacking in wisdom and foresight.[74] The editorial in *Vartman* described the speech as 'reactionary and against the ideals of Indian nationalism. Any hopes of change in the ideas of Ambedkar, when he joined the Cabinet, have been quashed by his speech.'[75] The editorial presented him with two choices: either submit to nationalism or resign from the Cabinet. These newspapers, indeed the UP press in general, were clear that their loyalty lay with the Congress. For the press, the Congress symbolized nationalism and national unity; editors were clear about what constituted nationalism; consequently, they were equally clear about 'Indian' politics, and what was 'anti-national' or 'communal' politics. Ambedkar was described as a potential Qaid-e-Azam, and this despite the fact that he did not raise the SCF's demand for a separate electorate, always the bane of Ambedkarite politics for the nationalist.

After Independence, the nationalist press was certain that there could not be two identities: that of being Dalit or Muslim in addition to that of being 'Indian'. This, they argued, was a necessary precondition to building the new Indian nation-state, and all political parties were exhorted to help Congress achieve this noble aim. Only the Indian state and the Congress possessed the sole right, according to the nationalist press, to constitute the new 'Indian' citizen. Dalits could be thus scarcely be allowed to define their citizenship in ways that would allow them to retain their achhut identity along with their Indianness, even if they attempted, as Owen Lynch has argued 'to make the politically ascribed status of citizen and not the religiously ascribed status of caste, the dominant status.'[76]

Indeed, not only Ambedkar, but Dalits in general in different parts of UP began to make their feelings about post-Independence political realities quite clear. In 1948, the SCF organized a series of demonstrations and meetings in some twenty-one districts of the province.[77] Two concerns came to occupy centre-stage: the first addressed the 'failure' of the Congress government, and the second demanded statutory provisions for Dalits. These points were reiterated at SCF meetings in Allahabad, Etah, Lucknow, Bareilly, Kanpur, Agra, Saharanpur and Meerut.[78] The Congress was described as a caste-Hindu party, and Dalit slogans were anti-Hindu, e.g. 'Hindu Quam ka nash ho', 'Kangress Government ka nash ho', 'Achhuto ke Shattroun ka nash ho' and 'Manu Smriti ka nash ho'.[79]

This was the polarized context in which the Chamars launched an agitation in July 1948 (the movement continued till November before petering out) against begari, an agitation that was not even acknowledged as a legitimate protest by the Congress government in UP.[80] Official reports in fact insisted that the Chamar agitation was harming 'public' interests. A report noted that 'Chamars of Bijnor district have refused to remove the dead bodies of animals and this is causing considerable inconvenience to the public.'[81] Dalits were clearly not considered part of the 'public', the 'public' being constituted by the caste-Hindus, Muslims, Sikhs and so forth, so that 'public life' was seen as being harmed by the Dalits' refusal to work without wages. Particularly revealing is the fact that the Chamars protested not only against their supposed 'duty' to remove dead bodies, either human or animal, in a village, but also refused to perform this task for the police: in the second kind of protest, the Chamars refused 'to perform menial duties including removal of corpses connected with crimes'. This obstructed the functioning of the police.[82] In Jalaun, Kanpur and Hamirpur, reluctant caste-Hindu police constables were compelled to perform the task of removing corpses.

The Chamar protest thus had twin targets: one was caste-Hindus and zamindars, the other the police and state (now represented by the Congress government). The Chamars were of course compelled to provide assistance to the police because they were Chamars, and not because they were appointed to paid posts by the state. The so-called menial duties demanded by the police were thus a form of begari imposed on Dalits. Like caste-Hindus, the police in many areas did not hesitate to apply coercive measures to ensure that the Dalits worked.[83] But this time the Dalits were determined to assert their rights. In Bareilly, a group of a hundred odd Chamars organized a demonstration against the police, and approached the District Magistrate to initiate action against it. Similarly, the Chamars were ready to fight the zamindars, in case they retaliated with violence.[84] Police reports noted that 'in Bijnor and Bulandshahr districts, Chamars are refusing to remove the dead bodies of animals which is naturally causing inconvenience.'[85] The official perception of these protests was similar to that of caste-Hindus: the Chamars were violating the norm—what they owed caste-Hindus—by refusing to 'perform their duties'. In using these terms—'public' and 'duty'—official discourse underlined the distinction between caste-Hindus and Chamars. The Chamars were assumed to have a specific role within the public domain, even as they could make no claims on it. In spite of the commitment of the state to universal principles of modernity and citizenship, Dalits were treated as a group apart, forced to acknowledge customary and discriminatory caste practices.

The SCF was very much involved in these protests, which explains why the protests began in Kanpur and Jalaun where the SCF had a substantial following. The agenda was outlined in the fifth annual conference of UP SCF at Lucknow. In one of the resolutions at the conference, the SCF demanded abolition of begari and criticized the tyranny of zamindars.[86] Tilak Chand Kureel threatened to launch a satyagraha if their demands were not accepted. The criticism of the Congress government and the demand for the abolition of begari was also repeated at the second conference of the Rohilkhand Division of the SCF, held on 16 and 17 June 1948 at Bareilly.[87] That these protests had to take place after Independence confirmed to them that they would need more such struggles to achieve their liberation. It also re-affirmed the continuing necessity of separate achhut identity, and enshrined it as a cardinal principle of their new politics.

V

These new trends in Dalit politics in the 1940s, built upon the rapid expansion of the SCF in UP, were different from earlier forms of Dalit politics which emphasized the need for 'ritual purity' or 'clean' social status. Since many Dalit caste mahasabhas merged their existing net-works with the SCF, a new all-encompassing identity for the achhuts could be imagined. For instance, the Adi-Ravidass Mahasabha of Allahabad in their resolution of 16 February 1946 maintained that the Dalits 'are trying their utmost to gain all their legitimate social, moral and citizen's rights, considering themselves a separate element from the caste-Hindus.'[88] Resolutions along similar lines were passed by the Dalits in various districts of UP in 1946. Shastri too, in his book, points to a shift in Dalit political understanding: 'If Gandhi and Company had done genuine work for their uplift, then the Dalits might not have felt it necessary to raise their own voice.'[89] The failure of the Congress to address the issue of caste-inequality further alienated the Dalits, particularly as the Congress considered untouchability a Hindu religious issue whereas the Dalits considered it a political pro-blem.

Accordingly, Shastri identified two key areas of real social reform for the achhuts: 'special educational facilities—particularly higher studies and twelve per cent reservation in the Government jobs.'[90] He tells us that these programmes were implemented for the first time by

Dr Ambedkar in 1942. In fact, in the 1940s, education had become a kind of panacea to the Dalits for all their problems.[91] Political power and education were seen by the achhuts as a necessary precondition for disrupting the social and occupational discrimination which perpetuated their confinement to menial or low labour. The Dalit intelligentsia and the Adi-Hindu ideologues played a crucial role in propagating these ideas in the Dalit neigbourhoods of major towns in the province.[92] Their vision was one in which the Dalits would occupy influential positions in the Assemblies, government offices and other institutions. This would enable them to provide genuine benefits to the community, and actually *implement* public policy and programmes. Thus, the demand made by the Dalits in 1946 for adequate representation in the Constituent Assembly and Legislative Assembly was really a crucial event in their larger political struggle to acquire an influential role in the state.

The various political mobilizations that led to Independence, particularly the arguments for separate communities and constituencies which ultimately underlay the Partition of the subcontinent, had a generative effect on much political thinking and action, including that of Dalit politics. The conceptions of Dalit communities which existed among them in the 1930s and earlier were moulded in the 1940s into a new notion of a 'unified' and far more inclusive community. If the mahasabhas of the Jatavs, the Chamars and the Ravidassis had earlier represented 'fragmented' communities, split along lines of caste identity, the emergence of the SCF in UP and its articulation and mobilization of new pressing political issues suggested a new conception of achhut community. The recognition of, and insistence upon, Dalit difference led to the abolition of begari and the introduction of safeguards in administrative and educational institutions. The assertion of an achhut identity became the fulcrum of a new Dalit politics. Like other communities, Dalits utilized the conditions created by Partition politics, particularly the legitimation of questions of community identity in constitutional discussions, to mould an awareness and a politics viable in the newly independent nation.

Dalits, more than anyone else, brought into focus the narrowness of the Congress' (caste-Hindu?) commitment to citizenship, rights, and nationalism and pointed to its exclusive character, despite its claims to the contrary. Dalit struggle questioned the democratic structure being implemented in India which tended to grant all powers to the majority—the caste-Hindus—at the cost of minorities like Dalits, Muslims, Sikhs, women and so forth. They demanded a constitutional arrangement to safeguard the minorities against the potential misuse of elected bodies by the majority community. Recent developments in the contemporary politics of India have suggested the importance of such safeguards. This may well be the legacy that these Dalit struggles bequeathed to the politics of independent India; a legacy which continues to play an important role in the democratic governance of the nation.

NOTES AND REFERENCES

1. Shankaranand Shastri, *Poona Pact or Gandhi*, Lucknow: 1994, [1946], p. 76. Translation from Hindi mine.
2. Ibid. Preface (no pagination).
3. Begari is the unequal, unpaid and coercive labour demanded by caste-Hindus as their traditional or religious privilege over lower-castes and Dalits.
4. See Jawaharlal Nehru, *Glimpses of World History*, Allahabad: 1935, 2 vols, pp.1115–26, 1141–55. Also Satyapal and P. Chandra, *Sixty Years of Congress: India Lost; India Regained*, Lahore: 1946.
5. The term achhut or untouchable was used by the Dalits in their struggles and movements in UP to mean 'pure' or 'untouched', giving it a new radical meaning. This point is also noted by Shastri. He further emphasizes that the Dalits should organize under a new separate achhut identity and give up their separate caste identities. I use the term achhut and Dalit interchangeably.
6. The Poona Pact was signed between Dalit and caste-Hindu leaders. The Pact denied separate electorates for the Dalits, which were provided for by the British. Instead they were allotted more reserved seats, where the elections were held separately for Dalits and caste-Hindus. The Pact was signed in good faith, but caste-Hindus betrayed the achhuts by not initiating any pro-Dalit policies.
7. Urvashi Butalia, *The Other Side of Silence: Voices from the Partition of India*, New Delhi: 1998, p. 223.

8. *Aaj* (Hindi daily), 18 February 1947; the civil disobedience movement, which was launched by the Muslim League, continued from February to June 1947 and Dalit participation was highlighted by the newspapers.

9. 'Letter from J.N. Mandal, 10 July 1947, Enclosures I and II: Representations by Western Pakistan SCF, Punjab Ad-Dham Mandal, Punjab Ravidass Sabha, Punjab Depressed Classes League, Punjab Municipal Workers Federation', in Muhammad Sadullah (ed.), *The Partition of Punjab, 1947: A Compilation of Official Documents*, Lahore: 1983, 2 vols, vol. I, pp. 142–9.

10. Sekhar Bandyopadhyay, 'From Alienation to Integration: Changes in the Politics of Caste in Bengal, 1937–47', *IESHR*, vol. 31, no. 3, 1994, p. 391. See also Joya Chatterji, *Bengal Divided: Hindu Communalism and Partition, 1932–1947*, Cambridge: 1996, pp. 191–203.

11. For a more detailed discussion of the elections of 1946, see Chapter 1 of my unpublished M. Phil. thesis, 'The Making of the Scheduled Caste Community in UP: A study of the SCF and the Dalit Politics, 1946–48', submitted to the Department of History, University of Delhi, 1996.

12. Mark Juergensmeyer, *Religion as Social Vision: The Movement Against Untouchability in Twentieth-Century Punjab*, Berkeley: 1982, p. 164.

13. Owen Lynch, *The Politics of Untouchability: Social Mobility and Social Change in a City of India*, New York: 1969, pp. 86–7.

14. Shail Mayaram, *Resisting Regimes: Myth, Memory and the Shaping of a Muslim Identity*, New Delhi: 1997, p. 276.

15. It was also put forward at the Simla Conference in 1945. See B.R. Ambedkar, 'What Congress and Gandhi have done to the Untouchables', in Vasant Moon (ed.), *Dr Balasaheb Ambedkar: Writings and Speeches*, Bombay: 1990, vol. IX, Appendix XI, pp. 345–9.

16. An important speech in which the British formally offered Dominion Status to India. *Speeches by The Marquess of Linlithgow*, vol. II, November 1938–October 1943, Government of India, New Delhi: 1944, pp. 64–8.

17. Moon, *Dr Ambedkar*, vol. X, 'A Critique of the Proposals of the Cabinet Mission', p. 538.

18. *Papers Relating to the Cabinet Mission to India 1946*, Govt. of India, New Delhi: 1946, p. 100.

19. *Dr Ambedkar*, vol. X, 'A Critique of the Proposals of Cabinet Mission', pp. 523–38.

20. *The Pioneer*, 21 February 1946.

21. Shastri also recognizes a shift in Jagjivan Ram's position; *Poona Pact*, p. 50.

22. Nalin Vilochan Sharma, *Jagjivan Ram, A Biography*, Patna, undated, pp. 127–32.

23. This paragraph is based upon reports in *The Pioneer*, 18, 21, 28 and 29 June 1946.

24. File No. 41/4/47-R 'Request from the Scheduled Castes of UP', Secretariat of the Governor-General Reforms, National Archives of India, New Delhi.

25. They further emphasized their relationship with the Congress through the involvement of Chowdhury Jaipal Singh and the Kumar Ashram. Jaipal Singh, a Congress MLA from Faizabad, attended the conference at Meerut. Kumar Ashram was established by a prominent Congressman Algu Rai Shastri in 1924 to undertake an *achhutodhar* programme in the Meerut region.

26. File No. 41/4/47-R, two pamphlets, 'To Boycott Mahatma Gandhi is Justified', and 'The Poona Pact—A Political Fraud'.

27. Based on the reports of Police Abstracts of Intelligence for the United Provinces of Agra and Oudh, Weekly (hereafter PAI) for 1946, CID Office, Lucknow. The districts in question are Meerut, Bareilly, Muzaffarnagar, Aligarh, Etah, Etawah, Kanpur, Azamgarh, Gorakhpur and Kheri.

28. PAI, 21 and 27 June 1946.

29. PAI, 16 August 1946.

30. *The Pioneer*, 17, 18, 19, 23, 25, 29 and 30 July, and 16 August 1946.

31. *Proceedings of the Legislative Assembly UP 1946*, vol. XXIV, Official Report, Allahabad 1947, pp. 7–8.

32. *Vartman* (Hindi daily), 22 July 1946. It was argued in the editorial that the Gandhian satyagraha was used to legitimize a political farce and to satisfy the personal ambitions of Dr Ambedkar.

33. PAI, 26 July and 23 August 1946.

34. PAI, 26 July and 2 August 1946.

35. PAI, 2, 9, and 16 August 1946.

36. PAI, 9 August and 20 September 1946.

37. PAI, 30 August 1946.

38. PAI, 20, 27 September and 18 October 1946.

39. PAI, 8 November 1946.

40. PAI, 20 September 1946 and 25 October 1946. In an apparent cultural attack against the Hindus, the Dalits were asked 'to boycott Ramlila celebrations' in Agra, 27 September 1946.

41. PAI, 22 February and 15 March 1946.

42. *The Pioneer*, 11 June 1946.

43. *Aaj*, 12 August 1946 and *The People's Age*, 29 September 1946.

44. PAI, 18 October 1946.

45. *Proceedings of the Legislative Assembly of UP*, vol. XXXVIII, 25 April 1947.

46. The first reference is noted in PAI, 20 September 1946.

47. Dr Ambedkar was elected on 19 July 1946; cited in R.K. Kshirsagar, *Dalit Movements in India and its Leaders: 1857–1956*, New Delhi, 1994, p. 162.
48. PAI, 20 September 1946.
49. PAI, 30 August 1946.
50. PAI, 18 October 1946.
51. PAI, 27 September 1946.
52. PAI, 6 December 1946.
53. PAI, 8 and 22 November 1946.
54. PAI, 13 December 1946.
55. For a detailed discussion on this issue see Vijay Parshad, 'The Killing of Bala Shah and the Birth of Valmiki', vol. 32, no. 3, *IESHR*, 1995.
56. *Aaj*, 10 November 1946.
57. PAI, 27 September, 8 November, and 13 December 1946.
58. Bandyopadhyay described the politics of the SCF as a 'separatist' strand among the Scheduled Castes which 'appears to have been marginalised in view of the extended franchise' (the results of the 1946 elections). He attributes the separatist posture to 'ambitious urban middle class leadership, which evinced decidedly more interest in institutional politics than in mass mobilisation.' Bandyopadhyay, 'From Alienation to Integration', pp. 367, 373, 377 and 381.
59. PAI, 27 December 1946.
60. I have argued this in Chapter One of my M.Phil. thesis.
61. PAI, 18 and 25 October 1946.
62. PAI, 13 October 1944.
63. Ibid. See also Shastri, *Poona Pact*, p. 116.
64. *The Pioneer*, 2 July 1946.
65. *The Pioneer*, 18 July 1947.
66. There is an unmistakable parallel with the recent decision of the (Dalit) Bahujan Samaj Party to form a government in UP with the support of the caste-Hindu Bharatiya Janata Party. BSP leaders argued that as far as Dalit priorities are concerned, there was no difference between the Congress, the BJP and the Samajwadi Party. I say parallel because both Ambedkar and the BSP made a radical shift in what received opinion understood as their supposedly 'natural' political position. Since there was already a precedent in Ambedkar's decisive departure to claim a position of *power*, the BSP followed this example and formed the Government in UP. The comparison underlines the Dalit point of view about capturing state power.
67. *The Pioneer*, 10 May 1947.
68. R.K. Kshirsagar, *Dalit Movements*, pp. 230–2, 235–8, 253–5 and 372–4.
69. I owe this reference to Saurabh Dube. File No. 108 CF 1f 947, DC Nagpur

Memo No. 521/CC dated Nagpur 20 November 1947 to Chief Secretary to Govt. of Central Provinces (CP) and Berar, CP Govt., Pol. & Mil. Confidential Dept.

70. *The Leader*, 26 April 1948.
71. *National Herald*, 26 April 1948.
72. *The Leader*, 27 April 1948.
73. Ibid.
74. *National Herald*, 27 April 1948.
75. *Vartman*, 27 April 1948, my translation.
76. Owen Lynch, *Politics of Untouchability*, p. 40.
77. Most of these twenty one districts were located in Agra, Rohilkhand, Meerut, Jhansi and Lucknow divisions of the province, mainly in central and western UP. These meetings became a regular feature from April 1948 onwards and were organized almost every week or fortnight. On an average, participation by the Dalits in these meetings varied from 400 to 500 persons although in some meetings their numbers rose to 1500 (Aligarh) and 1000 (Fatehpur). These statements are based on the PAI reports for 1948.
78. PAI, 19 March and 30 July 1948.
79. Roughly translated, these slogans call for the destruction of Hindu society or community, of the Congress government, of the code of Manu, and of the enemies of the achhuts. 'SCF Fatehpur Ka Sandesh'; PAI, 3 and 24 September 1948. Such slogans were also raised in other meetings at Barielly and Fatehpur.
80. The agitation began in Jalaun and involved around twelve districts located mainly in the Western and Central UP. Based on the PAI reports, 1948. There are no official reports available after 1948, especially the detailed PAI reports. The paucity of sources is further compounded by absence of reports in newspapers.
81. PAI, 6 August 1948. According to Intelligence reports, the protest was mainly organized by the Chamar castes, which constitute even today almost sixty per cent of the total Scheduled Caste population in UP. They provided the bulk of agricultural labour to caste-Hindus and zamindars. In the zamindari areas of the Awadh and Saryapur plains they constituted more than ninety per cent of the work force, in eastern UP ninety-six per cent of the work force, and in western UP about seventy per cent. A.B. Mukerji, *The Chamars of Uttar Pradesh: A Study of Social Geography*, Delhi: 1980, pp. 94–7.
82. PAI, 9, 30 July and 13 August and 15 October 1948.
83. In police station Bhutta of Bareilly, 'the police forced four Chamars to take a dead body to the mortuary'. PAI, 13 August 1948.

84. Official reports mention such instances for areas like Bijnor, Bulandshahr, Jaunpur, Etawah, and Jalaun. In Bijnor 'the villagers retaliated by not permitting Chamars to graze cattle in their lands, while in Bulandshahr the zamindars have begun to curtail the privileges enjoyed by the Chamars.' PAI 9, 23 July and 10, 17 September 1948.

85. This kind of protest took place in Bijnor, Bulandshahr, Sultanpur, Etawah, Jhansi, Kanpur, Hardoi, Bareilly, Jaunpur, Jalaun, Basti and Hamirpur. PAI, 23 July to 15 October 1948.

86. *National Herald,* 26 April 1948.

87. PAI, 18 June 1948.

88. Harijan Sahayak Department, File No. 164/1946, Box No. 370, UP State Archives (Lucknow).

89. Shastri, *Poona Pact,* p. 9. This is a major theme in his work.

90. Ibid., p. 41.

91. Dilip Menon makes a similar point in the context of Malabar in his book, *Caste, Nationalism and Communism in South India at Malabar, 1900–1948,* New Delhi: 1994, p. 145.

92. The intelligentsia represented leaders and activists from various caste mahasabhas. Chamars, Jatavs, Ravidassis, Balmikis, Kabir Panthis and the Adi-Hindu ideologues based in urban centres played a crucial role in formulating the new agenda.

Qutb and Modern Memory

SUNIL KUMAR

T HE QUTB MĪNĀR and mosque, Delhi's first masjid-i jâmi', constructed in the last decade of the twelfth century, has drawn the attention of tourists, antiquarians and scholars over the years. The tall minaret with its elaborate balconies and intricate inscriptions has an element of what Gell called 'magic'.[1] How did people in the late twelfth and early thirteenth centuries construct something so enormous, so perfectly symmetrical, and yet so delicate? Our cultural sensibilities, attuned to appreciate uniqueness, size, proportion and the investment of money and labour, savour the immensity and beauty of the structure and marvel at the accomplishment of mortals nearly a millennium ago. The reactions of visitors to the adjoining mosque, constructed out of

This is an abbreviated version of a paper presented at the Indo-French Seminar (sponsored by the University Grants Commission, Indian Council of Historical Research and the Maison des Sciences de l'Homme) held at the School of Social Sciences, Jawaharlal Nehru University, 14–16 February 1994. I am currently revising the paper for publication as a monograph entitled 'Defining and Contesting Territory: The Delhi Masjid-i Jâmi' in the thirteenth century'. The paper has profited from the comments of Anjali Kumar, David Gilmartin, Dilip Menon, Ebba Koch, Gail Minault, Suvir Kaul and Tanika Sarkar, none of whom necessarily share the opinions of the author expressed here.

the rubble of twenty-seven demolished temples, are, however, more ambivalent. The starkness of the mosque is relieved only by the redeployed temple spoils. Temple columns, Hindu and Jain iconic motifs, some complete and many defaced idols, are beautiful in themselves but clearly out of context within the environs of the mosque. They appear to be spoils of war, the evidence of pillage and victory in a conflict fought in the distant past. Most visitors in the mosque today are unaware of the identity of the contestants nor are the events of the conflict any clearer. But since the presence of plundered material from 'Hindu' temples within a 'Muslim' mosque is unmistakeable, the masjid confirms images of Islamic iconoclasm and fanaticism. It resurrects memories of communal distinctions and strife which almost every Indian regards as a part of his country's social history. Unlike the minaret, the mosque impresses visitors with its images of destruction, power and might, but not 'magic'.

The manner in which visitors to the Qutb complex understand and interpret the structures at the site is not simply shaped by their cognitive understanding of what constitutes an object of 'beauty'. It is as much a product of their socialized, historicized, understanding of the intentions of the constructors, and the meanings they presume are encoded into the structure. This paper seeks to study the manner in which the Qutb complex is understood today, and the epistemological assumptions which have supported such an understanding. As I discuss in my paper, both the builders and detractors of the mosque attached a host of meanings to the mosque in the Middle Ages, many of which were reworked in the popular imagination in the early modern period. Yet, today, only one interpretation has survived through the ages.

Historians have played a major role in the construction of this modern memory of the Qutb. They have written extensively on the Qutb itself, and on the political and religious conditions of the time when it was built. Their research on the Qutb has not remained relegated to the pages of arcane tomes; it has received wide circulation in text books and the popular press. Daily, thousands of visitors are guided through the Qutb monuments by the descriptions and interpretations provided by the Archaeological Survey of India at the site of the mosque itself. These narratives were culled from the works of scholars on medieval architecture, Islam, and Indian history. Together they constitute a text through which the experience of visitors to one of the major tourist spots in north India is refracted into authoritative knowledge about the character of Islamic piety and the nature of 'Muslim rule' in medieval India. This paper enlarges on the complex relationship between scholastic interpretations and popular perceptions in the constitution of the Qutb complex as a statement of the 'Might of Islam' in India, an interpretation which unfortunately consolidates the fractured communal realities of a post-Partition subcontinent.

I. The Delhi Masjid-i Jâmi', Its Builders, and Its Main Features[2]

The Delhi masjid-i jâmi' underwent construction on three different occasions. The first mosque, 214 by 149 feet, was a relatively small rectangular structure, with a central courtyard surrounded by colonnaded arcades. The construction of the mosque was begun in 587/ 1191-2 by Qutb al-Dîn Ai-Beg, and relied upon material derived from plundered temples. The temple spoils were used randomly, but very ingeniously. Column shafts, bases, and capitals, of different sizes and forms, with Hindu or Jain sculptures and iconic motifs, were placed one upon the other to attain a uniform height for the roof. The lack of concern for iconic symmetry, with Shaivite, Vaishnavite and Jain motifs placed cheek-by-jowl with each other, conveys the impression of destruction, a temper which is very much a part of the construction of the first mosque. The Archaeological Survey of India helps in the consolidation of this impression. Through its tourist literature it reminds visitors that the better portion of the mosque resides on the plinth of a demolished temple. Together with other evidence of redeployment of plundered material, it is left to be assumed that the 'iron pillar' of the Gupta period was another trophy of conquest placed within the centre of the mosque by Muslim invaders.[3]

Sometime later, perhaps in 595/1199, the huge arched screen was built in front of the west wall of the mosque. The east face of the screen was decorated with Arabic calligraphy, verses from the *Qur'ân* and the traditions of the Prophet, interspersed with floral and geometric patterns.

Perhaps even more dramatically than the reused temple spoils, the screen carries evidence of the handiwork of native artisans, who used familiar traditions of corbelled architecture to satisfy unusual stylistic requirements. It was around this time that work on the ground floor of the minaret was also completed. Although derived from the architectural precedents established in the Ghûrîd minaret of Khwaja Siyah Push in Sistan, the mînâr, in Qutb al-Dîn's reign, was not very tall, and its girth lent it a rather squat appearance. Built out of red sandstone and inscribed with *Qur'ânic* inscriptions and eulogies of conquest, it served as a memorial of victory and a vantage point to call the faithful to prayer.

The second phase of construction within the masjid-i jâmi' occured during the reign of Shams al-Dîn Iltutmish (607-33/1210-36) and was completed sometime around 627/1229-30. Although Iltutmish's additions nearly doubled the width, if not the depth, of the mosque, very little survives today of this construction. New courtyards were added to the north, south and the east, in a form which maintained the overall stylistic symmetry of the mosque. Hence the arches and the additions to the minaret harmonized with the preexisting architecture. Since these additions are largely in ruins today, the final impact of their size and grandeur, their dwarfing of the original masjid, is completely lost upon the modern audience. Only the extended minaret, towering over the environs with three additional storeys, provides a sense of the huge transformation that Iltutmish introduced in the architectural landscape of the masid-i jâmi'. Many historians tend to obscure this intervention by suggesting that rather than altering the mosque, Iltutmish merely 'completed' it.[4]

The changes in the mosque introduced during the third phase of construction, in the reign of 'Alâ' al-Dîn Khalajî (695–715/1296–1316), are also nearly lost today. But for one entrance hall, and an unfinished minaret, there is no visible trace of any Khalajî building activity within the mosque. Archaeological evidence, however, has clarified that 'Alâ' al-Dîn extended the mosque until it was twice the size of Iltutmish's, that the arches on its west wall towered over the older constructions, and if the girth of the unfinished mînâr is any indication, it would also have been twice the size of the old. Other than the size, the entrance hall on the south wall, today called the 'Alâ'î darwaza, stands as a testimony to the quality of construction during this period. Built out of red sandstone, the square silhouette of the 'darwaza' is pierced with evenly spaced rectangular windows and doors. These are outlined with marble trimmings and epigraphs carrying *Qur'ânic* verses and statements commemorating the achievements of the Sultan. The modern visitor needs to imagine, if he or she can, a rite of passage from the bustling world of the medieval city of Delhi, through the ornate 'Alâ'î darwaza into the relative peace of the enormous K̲h̲alajî mosque, with huge arches decorated with *Qur'ânic* verses on the western wall, and a new minaret under construction to balance and dwarf the old one. In sheer size and grandeur it would have been one of the most awe-inspiring mosques of its time in the world.

Since the middle of the nineteenth century, scholars and archaeologists have studied this mosque and attempted to explain its significance to a lay audience. Their writings have over the years assumed 'authoritative dimensions', until most visitors rely upon their guidance to consolidate their own opinions of the structure. The next section attempts to disaggregate this scholarship to understand how changing historical assumption and research methodologies are reflected in the study of the Qutb monuments.

II. Reading the Masjid-i Jâmi' as the · Might of Islam Mosque

The munsif of Delhi, Sayyid Ahmad Khan, was the first scholar to make a detailed study of the epigraphs and architectural form of the Qutb complex in the 1840's. Many of his conclusions were summarized and developed in the reports of the Archaeological Survey of India written in the 1860's, and some years later in the *Epigraphica Indo-Moslemica*, a journal devoted to the study of Persian and Arabic inscriptions. Much of this information was recompiled in the 1920's in the report of the excavations and conservation efforts of the Archaeological Survey of India narrated by J.A. Page. This corpus of information provided the empirical data on the basis of which an early consensual opinion on the nature of the Qutb complex developed.[5] The guides prepared at the turn of the century for English tourists to Delhi also relied upon these scholarly texts for their information and interpretation.

The major subject of interest in the works of all these authors was the redeployment of Hindu and Jain temple material within the masjid structure. Their narrative and line drawings focused upon the details of this aspect of the congregational mosque: what was the extent of the original plinth of the temple upon which the mosque was built; how many temple pillars were in fact used in the making of the cloisters? Alternatively their attention was drawn to the fact that 'Hindu' architectural styles continued to predominate within a 'Muslim' mosque. They noted the absence of the true arch in the great screen of the mosque and the use of a corbelled technique by indigenous craftsmen, together with the *voussoir*, to convey the impression of the 'saracenic' arch. In a similar fashion these scholars also noted the inability of the 'Hindu' craftsmen to construct domes; instead 'domes' which once again followed the corbelled technique were used from despoiled temples. Their discussion of the minaret was again largely restricted to its stylistic origins: was it of a 'Hindu' provenance, or did it have earlier Ghûrid and Ghaznavid antecedents?

Khan, Cunningham and Page's analyses suggested that in the usage of plundered temple material, which was defaced, inverted, or plastered over, the military commander, Qutb al-Dîn Ai-Beg, made a statement of conquest and hegemony over an infidel population in north India, and conducted a ritual cleansing of profane territory. The authors also recognized the presence of temple material in the mosque as evidence of a swift transposition of 'Muslim rule' in 'India' where the 'Turkish cavalry' had outdistanced the 'Muslim artisans'. Architecture in the formal 'Saracenic' tradition, constructed under the supervision of immigrant 'Muslim architects' and craftsmen had to, therefore, await the later years of Iltutmish's reign (607–33/1210–36). Meanwhile the symbolic redeployment of plundered temple rubble in the masjid-i jâmi', did not merely proclaim Quṭb al-Dîn's conquest of Delhi (588/1192), it also served as a statement of Islam's victory over idolators. This point was driven home when Sayyid Ahmad Khan, Horowitz and Page recorded in their respective scholarly publications that the name by which the congregational mosque was known in the past was 'Quwwat al-Islâm', or the 'Might of Islam'. Their self-confident assertion was surprising for the masjid-i jâmi' was not identified as Quwwat al-Islâm by any extant inscription in the mosque or referred to by this name in any Sultanate chronicle.[6] As we will see later it was the corruption of a name sometimes used for Delhi in the thirteenth century. Suffice it to note for now, that for these scholars, it was almost logical that the congregational mosque which celebrated the conquest of Delhi should be called the 'Might of Islam'. After all, the conquest of Delhi, the capital of the Sultanate, was the final, victorious culmination of a preceding series of plunder raids led by 'Muslims' into Sind, Punjab, and 'Hindustan'. In the early narrative of Indian history, where the medieval period was synonymous with the Muslim, it was entirely apposite that Delhi's first masjid-i jâmi' should be named the Quwwat al-Islâm mosque, and symbolize the beginning of a new historical epoch.

In the 1960's when a more 'secular' narration of the South Asian medieval past was attempted, historians like Meister, Mujeeb and later Husain, glossed over the 'Might of Islam' interpretation of the masjid.[7] Their writings focused instead upon the architectural characteristics of the monument where Islamic inspiration was dependent upon indigenous craftsmanship for its ultimate realization. In an effort to mute the episode of plunder and military conquest involved in the capture of Delhi, the 'Hindu' adaptation of the 'saracenic arch', or the corbelled dome, were highlighted as examples of inter-community cooperation and amity. Although these scholars continued to accept the interpretation of the masjid as the Quwwat al-Islâm, their writings suggested that this might have been merely a formal statement not to be taken very seriously. To their mind, the presence of the Hindu hand in designing and constructing the mosque needed to be given greater recognition.

Anthony Welch and Robert Hillenbrand could not disagree more with such 'secular' interpretations of the mosque.[8] Writing in the 1990's, these scholars are strongly influenced by the cultural anthropological emphasis upon semiotics and ideology. Unlike scholars in the past, who were presumably guided by their anachronistic communal or secular assumptions, these scholars sought the 'native's point of view', a potentially more dangerous interpretive move in its assumption that it could capture an indigenous, native perspective. Welch found it significant that the Muslim patrons of the Hindu craftsmen never compromised with the indigenes: the Delhi Sultans forced the Hindu craftsmen in their service to always conform to a 'Muslim aesthetic'. In an important passage he noted that

> the architecture of this early Turkish-dominated period is not eclectic: instead it is obsessed with imposing an aesthetic that carried comforting meaning for the conquerors. The attempt to replicate the familiar from back home is overriding: it ignores north India's established building types and twists indigenous architectural techniques to accommodate it. The resulting torque is obvious, but not surprising: without such mimetic references the [Delhi] Sultanate would have appeared adrift in an all too new and unfamiliar land.[9]

In his study of the epigraphical remains in the congregational mosque, the mînâr, and Iltutmish's tomb, Welch concluded that the inscriptions were carefully located within the masjid-i jâmi' precincts bearing in mind the architectural and functional qualities of the specific structures. Thus, since the mînâr performed the 'symbolic function of marking the *Dâr al-Islâm* (the land of Islam)' newly conquered from the infidels, and the towering structure was 'most visible to believers and non-believers outside the city walls', it carried *Qur'ânic* statements of conquest and warning to the heathen population.[10] The *Qur'ânic* and *hadith* inscriptions on the qiblah screen, the direction all Muslims faced during prayer, stressed 'instead the importance of worship, of adherence to the principles of Islam, and of recognition of the obligations incumbent on believers.' While the mînâr was directed primarily to the 'Hindus' and its epigraphs proclaimed victory over heathens, the inscriptions within the sanctuary of the masjid-i jâmi' were addressed only to the Muslims and expounded 'general religious statements' concerning their conduct.[11]

Welch's analysis of the congregational mosque and its epigraphs was not far removed from that of Khan, Cunningham or Page. While the latter had emphasized the theme of Muslim conquest and victory symbolized by the Qutb monument, Welch developed the idea further and argued that the congregational mosque also reflected the political context in which it was created. The monument was an uncompromising Muslim celebration of conquest, and the building material, architectural forms and epigraphic texts of the congregational mosque asserted the unity and cultural uniqueness of the 'Muslims'. It distanced the conquerors from their 'Hindu' subjects while for Muslims resident in a 'foreign' land it created familiar, reassuring landmarks of Islam's superiority.[12] From a different methodological track, Welch confirmed that the Qutb complex needed to be understood as the 'Might of Islam'.

III. Providing the Political Context

Welch could push his reading of 'the native's point of view' with a great deal of confidence because his arguments coincided with, and were supported by, a larger historiographical interpretation of the nature of early Sultanate society and polity in north India. In the early thirteenth century, according to the author, the Turkic ruling class of the Sultanate was both 'compact and cohesive', and severely threatened by 'Hindu' opposition. The historiographical understanding of the bonds which tied the Delhi Sultan with his military commanders were worked out in the writings of a number of authors which included scholars of the stature of Habibullah, Nizami, and Nigam.[13] In the interpretations of these scholars, despite the occasions when the 'crown and the nobility' were in conflict, an underlying material self-interest, a shared Turkish ethnicity, and the religion of Islam, provided coherence and an exclusive nature to the Turkic ruling oligarchy in the thirteenth century. In this logic, the common background of the ruling elite and their Sultan made them a category apart, and in the absence of any shared affinities with the ruler, the 'Hindus' were a distinct group who were then treated indifferently as subjects. The equation, Muslim rule—Muslim state, was worked out to its full extent in the writings of Habibullah, who completed the juxtaposition by defining resistance to the Sultanate as 'Hindu aggression'.[14] In Welch's analysis this was summed up in his declaration that 'with their victory in 1192 . . . [the Muslim armies] . . . initiated an Islamic state that by the beginning of the fourteenth century encompassed nearly all of the Indian subcontinent.'[15]

In this vision of medieval history it was also argued that by the fourteenth century, the composition of the Muslim ruling elite began to alter until it started to include 'low class' indigenous Muslim converts, a process which one scholar described as the 'plebianization of the nobility.'[16] The presence of these neo-convert indigenes provided the Sultanate with cultural 'roots' in the subcontinent.[17] This was most apparent in art, architecture, literature, and ritual; but it did not affect the great chasm which separated the politically cohesive, rapacious Muslim state from the exploited peasantry. The juxtaposition of the monolithic entities—the rulers and the ruled—was perceived by scholars as an axiomatic reality throughout the middle ages. With regard to the establishment of the Delhi Sultanate, Irfan Habib, perhaps the most influential scholar writing on medieval India, noted:

> The Ghorian conquests of Northern India, leading to the establishment of the Delhi Sultanate (1206–1526) may be said to mark the true beginning of the medieval period in India . . . To begin with, the new conquerors and rulers, who were of a different faith (Islam) from that of their predecessors, established a regime that was in some profound respects different from the old. The Sultans achieved power that was, in terms of both territorial extent and centralisation, unprecedented (except, perhaps, for the Mauryas 1,500 years earlier) . . . [Centralisation] . . . ensured that the

land revenue (*kharaj/mal*) demanded on their behalf should comprehend the bulk, if not the whole, of the peasant's surplus produce; and the King's bureaucracy thereby became the principal exploiting class in society.[18]

Habib shifted the argument of his peers to suggest that the contradiction within the medieval political systems constructed by Muslims in south Asia derived from class and not confessional interests; it was the fundamental divide between the rulers and the ruled which determined the fate of the state. In Habib's argument, the binary relationship between the extractive state and oppressed peasantry was initiated by the Delhi Sultans, but given finesse under the Mughal emperor Akbar (963–1014/1556–1605). 'The peculiar feature of the State in Mughal India—indeed, in Medieval India,' according to Habib, 'was that it served not merely as the protective arm of the exploiting classes, but was itself the principal instrument of exploitation.'[19]

Habib's description of the Mughal state as an instrument of class oppression also led him to define the Mughal manṣabdârî corp as the primary exploitative class. This class was certainly largely Muslim in composition and almost wholly Persianate in its urbanity, and, as Habib argued, 'for the Hindu population in general the imperial services were not something they could aspire to.'[20] In his analysis, the homogeneity within the Mughal ruling class of exploiters was quite exceptional, but this interpretation left the large class of rural zamîndârs quite literally as intermediaries, a group oscillating somewhere between the peasantry and the Mughal elite. 'For the indigenous population' argues Habib, 'in many parts of the sub-continent, the Mughal empire was a machine to extract resources to be consumed or hoarded by a small number of aliens, with a share of the spoils going to the native ruling class.'[21] Despite the zamîndârs' role in the revenue administration of the state, Habib was at pains to point out that zamîndâri interests did not always coincide with that of the Mughal ruling elite. As a result, while these intermediaries were important for the collection of revenue from huge areas of the Mughal empire, zamîndâri conflicts with the state originated over their share of the collected land tax. The ability of the zamîndârs to raise large armies and sometimes withstand Mughal pressure 'always [made them] a thorn in its side. Thus the

statements of [Mughal] official chroniclers frequently reflect an attitude of hostility towards the zamîndârs as a class.'[22]

Originating from a completely different set of epistemes, the implications of Habib's analysis actually left him very close to Habibullah's
(and Welch's) conclusions. Despite differing methodological perspectives, both Habibullah and Habib agreed that the cohesive unity of
the state was never challenged by its participants. Habibullah argued
for a hostile relationship between the Muslim Turkic ruling elite and
the Hindu subject population, and for Habib, a variety of class contradictions notwithstanding, the significant divide remained the one
between the exploiters and the exploited. Although the 'hostile relationships' and 'class contradictions' derived from different reasons, their
implications for the state and the ruling elite were very similar. Just as
Habibullah had suggested that 'dynastic troubles and rebellions'
might have temporarily *weakened* the state during the inter-regnal
years of the early Sultanate, but 'Hindu aggression' *threatened* and
challenged its structure, Habib argued that the Mughal 'Empire never
really faced a serious revolt from within the ranks of its own bureaucracy . . . [and] . . . the major upheavals . . . caused by the wars of
succession . . . did not by themselves endanger the Mughal throne.'[23]
Hence, when the tyranny of the exploitative state resulted in agrarian
distress, peasant forces, sometimes led by zamîndârs, were ranged
against the state mechanism. It was the politically 'disenfranchised',
the outsiders, that endangered the state. In the analysis of the two
authors, at least this aspect of the medieval state system did not alter
dramatically through the Sultanate into the Mughal period.

IV. Positivistic Readings of the Text

In a historiography where the material interests of the monolithic state
were threatened only by the exploited, conquered indigenous population, the discursive assertions of the authority of the state were read as
reaffirmations of the existing [class] solidarity of the ruling elite. What
was lost in reading a text from this perspective was the recognition that
discursive texts, like Delhi's thirteenth century masjid-i jâmi', carried

the authorial voice of their patrons, the Delhi Sultans, and they would have hardly acknowledged the presence of competing centres of power or resistance in a monument that was a public statement of their authority. In a similar fashion it was hardly likely that the court chroniclers of the Delhi Sultans would organize their narratives to suggest that Delhi was not the legitimate centre of power and authority in north India. In the Persian chronicles of Minhâj-i Sirâj Jûzjânî, Ẕiyâ' al-Dîn Baranî or Abû'l-Faẓl, the power of the monarch might be challenged by his subordinates—as it certainly was when rulers were morally incompetent—but the occasional hiatus notwithstanding, there was never any alternative to the authority of Delhi or the Mughal Pâdishâh.

Since the 1960s historians of the medieval period have shown increasing care in the usage of their primary sources, and have stopped taking literally the encomiums paid to their masters by court chroniclers. Such a literalness was largely a result of positivistic emphases of the historian's craft, where greater attention was paid to ascertaining 'facts' from 'unimpeachable sources'. In his 'defence' of Baranî's *Tâ'rîkh-i Firûz Shâhî*, Habib explained his argument: 'first, that Baranî's factual account is correct in all substantive matters; and secondly, that, though the 'analysis' is his (Baranî's) own, it is nevertheless sound. . . .'[24] In the same historiographical tradition, Shireen Moosvi worked out the reasons to believe in Abû'l-Faẓl's veracity:

> Abû'l-Faẓl in his conclusion to the *Â'în* tells us of the way he collected the material for his work. He says that his information was based on the testimony of contemporaries and eyewitnesses, after a critical assessment of whatever they had said . . . for the *Â'în-i Akbarî* he relied practically entirely upon state papers, and his statistical data were, naturally, supplied by government departments. He tells us he revised the text five times. . . .[25]

Most contemporary scholars forget, however, that the medieval documentation used by them, either chronicles or archival, was either produced by or for the state. For them, once we sift the encomia from these texts we remove the obvious elements of bias, and are left with a largely unaltered narrative in which the king and his subordinates, remain the principal actors in the history of the period. In a sense, as in the case of Ranke himself, the search for 'authoritative information' in chronicles and archives privileged the knowledge conveyed by the written word which, for the medieval period, concerned the state and governance. Information from other authors was understood to be biased unless it corroborated the product of the state. In his study of the Sikh sacred text, the *Guru Granth Sahib*, Habib argued that 'my purpose has been to suggest that research for material of historical value in this popular religious literature of medieval times may not altogether be an unfruitful pursuit. But it should be borne in mind at the same time that such research should go hand in hand with a close study of the Persian evidence as well, for only a familiarity with the latter can help us to pick out information that is *really* of significance (my emphasis) in the source-material in local languages.'[26] If research is going to privilege information produced by the state and then look for its corroboration from other sources, Athar Ali's conclusion is hardly surprising: 'fresh explorations of documentary evidence have only tended to confirm and underline the standard proposition about the elements of centralisation and systemisation in the Mughal polity . . .' and 'the picture of the Mughal Empire in its classic phase, as centralised polity, geared to systematisation and creation of an all imperial bureaucracy, . . . still remain[s] unshaken.'[27]

The positivist methodology which exalted documents as the pristine source for the study of the past directed scholars of medieval India to seek in their Persian documentation the secrets of the Middle Ages. But a Rankean epistemology, which elevated the state as the epitome of historical development and the proper subject of historical investigation, also led them to accept the discourse of a unitary dominion, a cohesive ruling elite, and a potentially recalcitrant peasantry, without any critical reflection. It is this epistemology which enables the reading of the Qutb monuments today as the 'Might of Islam'.

There can be no gainsaying the fact that Persian chronicles are the major extant sources available to the historian of the Middle Ages, especially for the Delhi Sultanate. There are, however, other sources of information as well: epigraphs, coins, monuments, and a voluminous literature produced in the 'courts' of the ṣûfî saints. With very few exceptions, these sources lack the coherence and chronology present in the chronicles, and they are, therefore, used as repository of facts useful to substantiate or expand the material provided by the 'histories'. Information which contradicts the 'evidence' of the court chronicles has frequently remained unexplored. The discourse of the monolithic state has therefore remained unquestioned.

It is, however, possible to pluck the seams in this discourse. The texts of the Persian court chronicles themselves are riddled with discrepancies, with niggling inconsistencies which are significant only if the reader approaches the text with the awareness that it carries information deliberately organized to impress specific conclusions upon the reader. These discrepancies in the text are important indicators of fractures in the discourse, dissonances which need to be enlarged with the aid of other source material. But giving space to the internal dissonances within a text is not always an easy task and it certainly does not contribute to the writing of monolithic, linear histories of state systems.

V. Political Competition and the Discourse of the Unitary State

The premise of the unitary Muslim state, and a composite ruling elite owing allegiance to the Sultan of Delhi, would be difficult to question if we followed the obvious conclusions of the Persian chroniclers. Fakhr-i Mudabbir's *Tâ'rîkh-i Fakhr al-Dîn Mubârak Shâh*, a text dedicated to Quṭb al-Dîn Ai-Beg, suggests, for example, that the favourite, competent military slave of Mu'izz al-Dîn, was appointed as the sole authority, the 'viceroy' of his master's dominion in north India.

> This hero and world conqueror of Hind (Quṭb al-Dîn) was addressed as Malik,[28] and was made the heir apparent, *wali 'ahd*, to Hindustan, and the lands from the gates of Peshawar (Parshûr) to the limits of Hind were given to him, and the [authority] to appoint and remove, (literally, 'unfasten and bind, *hall wa 'aqd'*), the remaining commanders was entrusted with him, *ba-dû mufauwaz gardânîd.* [Mu'izz al-Dîn] left [Quṭb al-Dîn] as his deputy and heir in the capital of Hindustan, *qa'im maqâm wa wali 'ahd-i khud ba-dâr al-mulk-i Hindustân ba-guzasht,* and sent him back to Delhi.[29]

The narrative of the near contemporary chronicler Minhâj-i Sirâj Jûzjânî also supported Quṭb al-Dîn's claims to be the Amîr al-Umarâ', the chief of the Mu'izzî military commanders in north India. Writing in the 660's/1260's for the Delhi Sultan, Nâṣir al-Dîn (644–64/1246–66), Jûzjânî arranged his text to suggest that Delhi and its ruler had always been the paramount power in Hindustan.

Jûzjânî's narrative, however, was organised in the more disaggregated *ṭabâqât* form, where each unit of the text studied 'people belonging to one layer or class in the chronological succession of generations.' As a result, the history moved beyond the sharp focus on the ruler and included accounts of social peers or dependents. Thus, the twentieth section, *ṭabâqa*, narrated the history of other important Mu'izzî subordinates in Hindustan without losing sight of his need to emphasize Qutb al-Dîn's overall superiority.[30] In this section Jûzjânî provided a somewhat circumspect account of the independent ability of the Mu'izzî commanders to raise a military retinue, wage war, and sometimes compete with each other over the distribution of spoils. One such military commander was Bahâ' al-Dîn Tughril, the governor of Thangir, in the province of Bayana.

According to Jûzjânî, Bahâ' al-Dîn sought to improve the economy of his appanage by attracting merchants, *tjjar*, and well-known men, *ma' araf-i rûy*, from different parts of Hindustan and Khurasan towards his domain. In an effort to encourage trade within the Bayana region, all merchants were granted accommodation and material support, *jumleh-ra khânah wa asbâb bakhshîd*, by the Mu'izzî subordinate. As a result, Jûzjânî noted, Bahâ' al-Dîn Tughril made his province prosperous, an indication of which was the construction of Sultânkôt, a new capital to go with changed circumstances.[31] From Sultânkôt, Bahâ' al-Dîn commenced periodic raids towards Gwalior and was promised its territory by Mu'izz al-Dîn upon its capitulation. The seizure of Gwalior would have opened up the frontier into northern Rajasthan and Bundelkhand and brought considerable plunder and war material into the Amir's reach. Bahâ' al-Dîn's efforts to enlarge and consolidate his appanage were resisted by Qutb al-Dîn Ai-Beg, who reacted to Bahâ' al-Dîn's increasing influence in the area by seizing Gwalior himself in 597/1200. Jûzjânî, who narrated this incident, concluded rather diplomatically that as a result of the Gwalior episode there was (not?) a little dislike between Tughril and Quṭb al-Dîn, *miyân Malik . . . wa Sulṭân andak ghabârî bûd.*[32]

Although Quṭb al-Dîn Ai-Beg may have believed and proclaimed that he was the supreme Mu'izzî commander in north India, his peers certainly did not share this opinion. Despite the predisposition of the Persian documentation towards Quṭb al-Dîn and the authority of Delhi, the presence of competing autonomous dominions could not be wholly obscured. Even the eulogy of the likes of Fakhr-i Mudabbir wore thin on occasion, and he confessed:

> And although all the victories which God caused him (Quṭb al-Dîn Ai-Beg) to win are clearer than the sun, and well known to all the world: nevertheless it must not be forgotten how much was due to the care and assistance of the *Sipahsâlâr* Ḥusam al-Dîn Aḥmad Ali Shâh, who was the slave and officer of the King of Islam (Mu'izz al-Dîn), and was never absent from his stirrup, and was present at these victories and battles. Indeed all the generals of this court were gifted, brave and noble, and each was distinguished for his courage, and received an ample share of the fortune and prosperity of the King of Islam, who by his patronage and favour made each and all famous. To some he gave high commands, body guards, pavilions, drums, standards and districts, and each performed fine acts of service, and was duly praised . . .[33]

In a political world where all the generals of Mu'izz al-Dîn's court were 'gifted, brave and noble, and each . . . received an ample share of the fortune and prosperity of the King of Islam, who . . . made each and all famous', there was also considerable rivalry and conflict. It is in the context of a factionalized political environment of the 'north Indian Sultanates' (certainly in the plural), rather than a unitary dominion of the Delhi Sultanate, that we need to situate Quṭb al-Dîn Ai-Beg's urgency to appear as the unique Amîr al-Umarâ', the protector of the fortunes of the Muslim community.

The construction of the Delhi masjid-i jâmi' was a part of Quṭb al-Dîn's effort to impress the Muslim congregation of his military and pious virtues. The inscriptions on the main entrance to the mosque remarked on his unique prowess and piety as a military commander destroying infidel temples. But again, given the nature of the political competition of the age, Quṭb al-Dîn was hardly unique in making statements of this nature. His rival in Bayana, Bahâ' al-Dîn Tughril, also constructed congregational mosques which were architecturally similar in form and conception to the Delhi masjid-i jâmi'. The Bayana mosques also eulogized Bahâ' al-Dîn as the conqueror of infidels and the creator of havens for Muslim congregations. But if Quṭb al-Dîn Ai-Beg's inscriptions in the Delhi masjid-i jâmi' drew the attention of the visitor to his military and moral accomplishments as the 'viceroy' of Mu'izz al-Dîn G̲h̲ûrî, the visitor to the mosques in Bayana saw evidence of the same virtues in Bahâ' al-Dîn's constructions. The only difference was that the inscriptions in the Bayana mosque went beyond Quṭb al-Dîn's claims and introduced Bahâ' al-Dîn as *Pâdishâh* and *Sulṭân*.[34]

Divorced from their assumed political context of a unitary dominion and a composite ruling elite, the discursive statements carried in texts like Delhi's masjid-i jâmi' need to be oriented to audiences beyond just the infidels. Indeed, the probity of the military commander as the paradigmatic Muslim leader, God's choice of a shepherd for his flock, was an important theme in the epigraphs in the mosque, but these statements seem to have been directed to the Muslims who visited the congregational mosques, and were aimed at displacing rival claims made by Mu'izzî peers.

VI. The Congregational Mosque and the 'Hindus'

The Delhi masjid-i jâmi', like other congregational mosques, differed from ordinary mosques in its size and function. Where the latter served purpose of performing prayer for a limited number of people, the Delhi masjid-i jâmi' was a huge public monument created for the purposes of a congregational gathering of Muslims. Through the performance of prayer in congregation, Muslims acknowledged the fact that they were one united community who had submitted to the will of Allah. In the normal course of events, unbelievers, especially profane idolaters, would not have been allowed within the precincts of the

Delhi masjid-i jâmi' and, as a result they may have only possessed a general sense of the manner in which temple spoils were redeployed within the mosque. The architectural composition of the mosque, however, would have impressed the congregation of believers, who would have seen in it the evidence of their Amir's ability to defeat infidels and provide a sanctuary for Islam.

Despite their ignorance of the precise architectural forms in the interior of the Delhi masjid-i jâmi', it would be naive to assume that the 'idolators' were unmoved by the destruction of their places of worship. But certainly within Delhi itself, there is no epigraphic record of rancour or sorrow at the destruction of temples, not even in the devnagiri graffiti inscribed by Hindu artisans in the nooks and crannies of Quṭb al-Dîn's mosque.[35] Instead, one early inscription in a local dialect identifies the minaret as 'the pillar of Malikdin. May it bring good fortune.' Another anonymous artisan in 'Alâ' al-Dîn's reign (695–715/1296–1316) had no hesitation in recognizing the minaret as Shrî Sultan Alâvadî Vijayasthamb, the Sultan's pillar of victory. In Muḥammad Shâh Tughluq's reign (725–52/1325–51) the architects Nânâ and Sâlhâ recorded their contribution to the repairs of the minaret in an inscription which also celebrated the completion of their work 'by the grace of Sri Visvakarma'.[36]

Sultanate court chronicles and the inscriptions on the masjid-i jâmi' seek to create the impression that the righteous Muslim Sultans of Delhi obliterated all evidence of temples and Hindu habitation in the vicinity of Delhi. Historians who have conscientiously followed these narratives have ignored evidence to the contrary just eight hundred metres away from the Qutb. A stone's throw from the site of iconoclastic destruction was a large garden, known as the bâgh-i Jasrath. Jasrath's garden was described by Niẓâm al-Dîn Awliyâ' as a landmark, and the memory of its owner was fresh even at the turn of the thirteenth century. Adjoining the garden was a reservoir which was built by a 'Hindu' queen prior to the capture of Delhi. Not merely was the reservoir the site of several court ceremonies in the thirteenth century, but the memory of the original infidel constructor was preserved in its name: the Queen's reservoir, *ḥauz-i Rânî*, an interesting admixture of languages (Arabic>Persian: *ḥauẓ*, Sanskrit>vernacular: *Rânî*) which passed quite unremarked in the literature of the period. In other words, in the immediate vicinity of iconoclastic destruction, there were other important areas built and patronized by 'Hindus', some large enough to be major landmarks in the city, others which were sites of public congregation.[37] Unlike the destruction and reconstruction within the Qutb complex, 'Muslim' conquest of Delhi left these areas undisturbed. In fact, their original 'profane' identities were preserved in public memory in their names. The extent of the rupture caused by 'Muslim' conquest in 'Hindu' society certainly deserves to be recontextualised more carefully.

Although the destruction, desecration, and appropriation of temple artifacts was an unexceptional event during conflict between rival 'Hindu' kingdoms in the Middle Ages (and it is perfectly possible that Qutb al-Dîn's conduct drew a reaction from the local population quite dissimilar from ours today), we need to nevertheless remember that the actions of the Mu'izzî commanders differed from those of the precedents set by the 'Hindu' rulers. When 'Hindu' rajas pillaged each other's temples, the authority of the vanquished lord was either appropriated or reconstituted within the temple shrine of the conqueror. The statements of conquest embodied in the process of destruction and reconstruction of imperial temples, was carried out within ritually homologous forms of Hindu kingship.[38] By contrast, Qutb al-Dîn's statements of conquest in the masjid-i jâmi' redeployed temple spoils, but there was no sense of appropriation of authority. It signified instead the arrival of alternate traditions of governance in Delhi. This carried larger social and moral implications for the constitution of authority in Delhi since the royal temples were also the sites of redistributive and transactional relationships between the king, his subordinate chieftains and the larger subject population. Qutb al-Dîn's conquest, the destruction of temples and the construction of a mosque in their stead, fractured the relationship between the king and his subordinate chieftains. This development need not necessarily imply, however, a concomitant distancing of the subordinate echelon of rural chieftains from newly emerging structures of Sultanate authority. It is certainly worth querying whether the Mu'izzî governors constructed new, but different, relationships with these local political regimes in the countryside.[39]

The discourse of the Persian chronicles and the nature of the masjid-i jâmi' would suggest that this was not the case; political authority remained the exclusive preserve of the new Muslim Turkish elite and 'Hindus' were hunted, not recruited, in the new political order. Stray references within the same chronicles, however, would suggest that this was hardly universally true. The author of an early Muslim epic of conquest, Fakhr-i Mudabbir, mentioned that *râtkan wa tâkran/ rautagân wa thakurân*, petty ['Hindu'] chieftains and their military subordinates, were present within the ranks of the pillaging armies of Quṭb al-Dîn Ai-Beg.[40] We lack a sense of numbers and roles occupied by these subordinates within the new dispensation, but their sheer presence forces us to reevaluate the relationships between the different ruling elites in ways more complicated than those suggested by a simple confessional divide.

The efforts of Quṭb al-Dîn, and other Mu'izzî commanders, towards consolidating relationships with 'Hindu' chieftains only becomes clearer when we turn to other source material. In their ability to reach a far larger audience, the coinage of the Mu'izzî governors, even more than the masjid-i jâmi' in Delhi (or Bayana), served as effective discursive statements of conquest. Unlike the congregational mosque, however, the coinage carried statements of both conquest and reassurance to the conquered people. To begin with, the coins were unequivocal in their announcement of a new political order, and they introduced the new masters, the Mu'izzî Amîrs, as Shrî Hammirah; the Persian titles of the new lords stamped in the locally comprehensible devnagiri script.

The presence of the new political order, however, did not seem to suggest any evidence of material change. The conquerors made no effort to alter the weight and purity of the precious metals in their coins which harmonized perfectly with existing circulating mediums. Deliberate attempts seem to have been made to emphasize continuity with the older patterns of fiscal and commercial exchange. Perhaps even more impressive was the confessional ambiguity in the sigilla of the Mu'izzî coins of this period. Emblems of a previous political regime, the image of God Shiva's vehicle, the *nandî* bull and the 'Chauhan horseman' were stamped on the coins together with the title of Shrî Hammirah. Even more significant were the gold coins which carried both the outline of Lakshmi, the Hindu Goddess of wealth, and the Sultan's title in the devnagiri script. As discursive statements, these coins made deliberate attempts to incorporate the conquered people within the newly established political and economic systems, not through pillage and mayhem, but through reassuring measures and symbols that suggested continuity with a preceding regime. These statements would suggest that 'Muslim conquest' did not seek to traumatize the subject population and it certainly did not wish to create any major disjunctions in their material life. As the hoard evidence from north India confirms, Mu'izzî coins were valued as much as the earlier Rajput currencies and were fully assimilated within an economic world unimpressed with transitions in the political realm.[41]

Without devaluing the statement of plunder and conquest conveyed by the Delhi masjid-i jâmi', it should not be forgotten that it is the Persian chronicles and the epigraphs in the mosque that make much of the episode of temple destruction. It is these texts which saw in the mosque proof of the incumbent ruler's piety, a statement directed to the Muslim congregation in the mosque. From a different aspect, the destruction of the temple of the 'Hindu' Raja was also necessary to break the social and political networks which sustained the old regimes. The ideology of iconoclasm, even within a 'Hindu' context, carried the familiar sense of conquest and valour, but the construction of the masjid-i jâmi' denied a reconstitution of authority along old 'familiar' lines. Within the new Sultanate regimes, 'Hindu' subordinates might have been ritually distanced, but the sigilla on the coinage points to the presence of discourses—different 'non-monumental' structures—which eased the political transition and sought to construct new, stable, productive relationships with the *rautagân wa thakurân*. The trauma of the political change was assuaged somewhat by the remarkably restrained and confessionally ambiguous ways in which the new regime intruded into the life of a second rung of 'Hindu' political commanders. Within the context of their own discursive statements, this was a fact that the Persian chronicles and the Delhi masjid-i jâmi' would not wish to recognize.

VII. Pietistic Muslim Responses to the Mosque

The main audience of the Delhi masjid-i jâmi' was the Muslim residents of the town. This community of Muslims increased in both size and heterogenous complexity during the 620s/1220s. Because of the destruction and havoc caused by the Mongol invasions, people from different regions in Afghanistan, eastern Iran, Transoxania and the central Asian steppes, immigrants of varied ethnic backgrounds, speaking distinct regional dialects, and with separate customary usages, had made their way into the sanctuary of north India. It is doubtful if they automatically felt any sense of solidarity with each other purely because they were denominationally Muslim. Many of them possessed artisanal skills which made a material difference to the regional economy of the fledgling Sultanate. Whether the presence of a greater number of 'Muslims' contributed to any sense of an integrated community is a different question altogether. Jûzjânî's history was sensitive to the appearance of such large numbers of immigrants but, to his mind, integration was not a problem since the confessional solidarity of Islam overcame all distinctions between Muslims. Jûzjânî claimed that Iltutmish (607–33/1210–36) collected people from all parts of the world in Delhi,

> (which is) the capital of Hindustan, *dâr al-mulk*, the centre of Islam, *dâira'i Islâm*, the cradle of the commands and prohibitions of the *Sharî'at*, *mahbit-i awâmir wa nuwâhi-yi Sharî'at*, the keeper of the Muslim faith, *hauz-i din-i Muhammadi*, the dais of the Muslim community, *manassa'i millat-i Ahmadî*, the sanctuary of Islam in the eastern world, *Qubba'i Islâm mashâriq-i gîtî.* . . .[42]

The author's description of Delhi as the *qubba'i Islâm*, the sanctuary, the dome of Islam, conveyed to the reader the new identity of the capital in its axial role of representing the fortunes of the larger collectivity of Muslims. This was accurate enough in the context of Delhi's emerging military influence in north India; by 625/1228 Iltutmish had managed to defeat and annex the territories of the remnant Mu'izzî and Quṭbî commanders. Jûzjânî's representation of this political transformation, however, went much further. The chronicler's narrative suggested that just as Iltutmish's sultanate was a monolith, Islam was also a unitary, homogeneous entity without any internal dissonances or complexities, at peace with itself, especially since the Delhi Sultan was its great protector.

Doubts about the degree of confessional coherence within the Muslim population of the Delhi Sultanate, however, emerge rather ironically from Jûzjânî's history itself. Towards the end of Iltutmish's reign, sometime around, or after 634/1236, Jûzjânî mentioned that a 'sort' of learned man, *shakhsî-yi danishmand gûna*, by the name of Nûr Turk collected a large following near Delhi. According to the chronicler, this was a congregation of common people, *khalq-i 'awâmm*, who collected from distant areas like Gujarat, Sindh, the environs of Delhi and the banks of the Ganga and Jumna. They were strongly moved by Nûr Turk's exhortations, *tazkir*, where the preacher referred to the 'ulamâ' of the majority community, *'ulamâ'i ahl-i sunnat wa jamâ'at*, as those who had wronged the cause of 'Alî. According to Jûzjânî, Nûr Turk specifically condemned the 'ulamâ' of the *Shâfiî* and *Ḥanafî* legal schools of interpretation, and instigated his followers to conspire against Islam, *qasd Islâm kardand*. This group of people attacked the Delhi masjid-i jâmi', an action which led Jûzjânî to describe the group as Shî'i Qarmatians and heretics, *mulâhida wa qarâmiṭa*.[43]

Jûzjânî sought to obscure the significance of the 'Muslim' attack on the Qutb mosque by suggesting that it was the conspiracy of 'heretics', a people who were outside the pale of the Sunni community. As a result, the attack on the masjid-i jâmi' would have remained one of the many curious details of a challenge which the 'Muslim' Sultanate had withstood successfully. A thorough vindication of the main protagonist in this story, however, by no less a person than the widely revered and respected ṣûfî saint Niẓâm al-Dîn Awliyâ', makes it impossible to accept Jûzjânî's gloss of the incident.

On the 13th of Sh'aban, 718/October 10, 1318, during one of his daily meetings with the congregation who visited his hospice in Delhi, the ṣûfî was queried about Nûr Turk and Jûzjânî's description of the derwish's beliefs and actions. Contrary to Jûzjânî's evaluation, Niẓâm al-Dîn Awliyâ' made it a point to clarify that Nûr Turk's faith was free from any heresy and absolved him of all Shî'i Qaramaṭi links. According to Niẓâm al-Dîn Awliyâ', Nûr Turk had publicly criticized the 'ulamâ' because he had seen how polluted they had become by the material world of the capital, *ishân-râ âluda'i duniyâ dîdî*. It was for this reason that the 'ulamâ' had fabricated all kinds of offensive charges (of the kind reported by Jûzjânî, no doubt) against the pious derwish, *u-râ badân chîzha mansûb kardand.*[44] In Niẓâm al-Dîn Awliyâ's recounting of the tale, Jûzjânî's appraisal of Nûr Turk coincided with the biased opinions of the 'ulamâ' in Delhi. The wheel had come full circle; for Niẓâm al-Dîn Awliyâ' the sharî'a minded 'ulamâ' were certainly not paragons of virtue or comportment.

The renewed discussion of Nûr Turk's beliefs, his animosity towards the Delhi 'ulamâ', and Jûzjânî's account of the incident may well have cropped up accidentally during the course of Niẓâm al-Dîn Awliyâ's discourse. In the manner of his discussion of the Nûr Turk episode however, the ṣûfî saint's arguments did not merely rework Juzjani's report, it also sought to foreclose all options for independent analysis on this subject. If Nûr Turk's piety was unimpeachable, the conduct of the 'ulamâ' offensive, and Jûzjânî's history biased, then, without so much as actually articulating the thought, Niẓâm al-Dîn Awliyâ's narrative suggested that Nûr Turk's righteous moral indignation exonerated the derwish's attack on the masjid-i jâmi' and its corrupt 'ulamâ'. Hidden as a sub-text in this discussion was a comment on the sacred character of the Delhi masjid-i jâmi' if its 'ulamâ' misrepresented Islam.

These contrasting evaluations of Nûr Turk are important because they were made by two not entirely dissimilar people. Both Niẓâm al-Dîn Awliyâ' and Jûzjânî were members of the sunni-jama'a community, and both were popular preachers, respected for their piety. Yet, even within the sunni-jama'a community there were obviously wide differences in their ideal of the virtuous, especially amongst mystics and sharî'a-minded scholars. Some of these differences were explained by Niẓâm al-Dîn Awliyâ'.

> The 'ulamâ' are the people of intellect *ahl-i aql*, the *derwishes* are the people of love *ahl-i 'ishq*, the intellect of the 'ulamâ' overpowers, *ghâlib*, [their sentiment] of love, [whereas] the [emotion] of [divine] love of these mystics triumphs over [their] intellect.[45]

Intellect in the thirteenth century, carried with it the associated meaning of a prescriptive, scholastic method of 'knowing' a mortal's subordinate relationship with God. Conduct and belief for the individual Muslim was carefully worked out in its details in authoritative texts by the 'ulamâ', with the intention of securing social conformity and the ideal of a unity within the Muslim community. This sharply reduced the opportunities for independent speculation, and contrasted with the emotion of divine love. In the ṣûfî understanding of Islam far greater importance was given to an inner, intuitive understanding of ritual. The faith of the believer could lead him to experience aspects of God's bounty and love, foreign to the cognition of the 'ulamâ'. As a result the ṣûfî could believe that

> a preacher . . . was so transported by his own eloquence that he flew away from the pulpit (*minbar*) to a neighbouring wall; . . . [that] meetings . . . [took place] . . . in deserted places with Khwaja Khizr who has everlasting life; . . . [that there were] various 'fairy people'—. . . *abdals* who physically fl[ew] above the territories which they protect from harm, . . . [that] a holy man [circled] around the [*miḥrab* of the Delhi masjid] through the night till the dawn, . . . [that] the *mardân-i ghaib*, men of the unseen, . . . appear[ed] and disappear[ed], and sometimes call[ed] away a mortal to join them.[46]

Whereas reason and intellect would regard these as patently fraudulent experiences, for many people in the early thirteenth century these were real events, evidence of God's intervention in an insecure mortal world. The mystic's interpretation of the individual's relationship with God resisted the authoritarian intervention of the intellect; the *nûr-i bâtin* of the ṣûfî, his internal, hidden emotions, provided him with the space to contravene the 'ulamâ's understanding of the social dictates of the sharî'a.

This independence, the freedom to negotiate one's piety through a variety of prescriptive norms, was abhorrent to the 'ulamâ' who regarded the ṣûfî ability to mobilize huge congregations to their way of thinking as positively dangerous to the unity of Islam. The Delhi Sultans, nervous about the popular charismatic appeal of the saints, could not have agreed more with the conclusions of the 'ulamâ'. Although the Sultans lacked the ability to interfere and discipline the conduct of the ṣûfî, they could encourage a homogeneity of conduct by constructing and patronizing institutions which supported the sharî'a. Both Iltutmish and 'Alâ' al-Dîn Khalajî, two Sultans who added to and reconstructed the Qutb mosque, took their roles as the 'preservers of the sharî'a' very seriously. 'Alâ' al-Dîn's inscription in the mosque explained the Delhi Sultan's contribution:

> When God Almighty, whose greatness is sublime and whose names are exalted, for the revival of the laws of the [Muslim] community, *ihyâ'yi marâsim-i millat*,[47] and the elevation of the banners of the sharî'at, chose the lord of the Caliphs of the world, *khudaygân-i Khulafâ'i jahânrâ*, so that every moment the foundations of the Muslim religion, *asâs-i dîn-i Muḥammadî*, and the roots, *binâ-yi*, of the Muslim sharî'a are strengthening, *istihkâm mîpazîrad/qawi mîgardad*, and for preserving the state and consolidating the Sultanate, *dawâm-i mamlikat wa niẓâm-i Sulṭanat* [the lord of the Caliphs] built mosques in accordance with the commands of Him beside whom there is no God, (*Qur'ân* IX: 18). 'But he only shall visit the mosque who believes in God.'[48]

Other than acknowledging the divine dispensation of authority to 'Alâ' al-Dîn, the Khalajî inscriptions linked 'reviving', 'protecting' and 'strengthening' the sharî'a to the construction of mosques. 'Alâ' al-Dîn's constructions created the material conditions in which Muslims could cleanse themselves of sin, and it is for this reason that another inscription implored: 'may God perpetuate his kingdom (so that he may continue) to build mosques, and preserve till eternity his sovereignty (so as to protect) the lustre of the places of worship.'[49]

Iltutmish's inscription quoted the Qur'an, *sûra* 62: 9–10, to clarify the importance of performing the obligatory rituals of prayer in the midst of one's daily activity:

> O' believers, when proclamation is made for prayer on Friday, hasten to God's remembrance and leave trafficking aside; that is better for you, did you but know. Then when the prayer is finished, scatter in the land and seek God's bounty, and remember God frequently; haply you will prosper.[50]

Another inscription cited the traditions of the Prophet Muhammad to emphasize the connections between individual and congregational worship:

> The Prophet . . . said, 'whoever offered his morning prayer in congregation got his (worldly) troubles removed by Allah; and whoever offered his afternoon prayer (in congregation) got his living made plentiful by Allah; and whoever offered his late afternoon prayer (in congregation) became (as pure) as on the day he was born; and whoever offered his evening prayer in congregation is considered as if he has given away his wealth and (even) his life (in the way of Allah), and whoever offered his bed-time prayer in congregation received Allah's blessing.' (The Prophet) . . . said 'whoever observed these five prayers in congregation would have his way (to Heaven) widened by Allah.'[51]

As a part of their 'administrative' repertory aimed at controlling their Muslim subjects, the Delhi Sultans needed the 'ulamâ' in their supervisory role of enforcing obedience to the sharî'a. The construction of mosque and schools proclaimed the Sultan's pietistic intentions while providing the 'ulamâ' with the monumental sites where the Muslims could be socialized into following the prescriptive codes of the sharî'a. It was the fractionalized social world of the Muslims that the Delhi Sultans sought to cohere within one community, governed by one law, under the authority of a morally upright monarch. The Delhi masjid-i jâmi' was extremely important in disseminating this sentiment, and 'Alâ' al-Dîn Khalajî was very direct in developing its sacred significance. His inscription on the left pier of the south door to the mosque argued:

he ('Alâ' al-Dîn) built this mosque, which is the mosque of paradise, for saints and . . . men of piety and a place of assembly of the eminent angels, and an edifice inhabited by the souls of the chief prophets.[52]

'Alâ' al-Dîn did not question the spiritual authority of the saints of God, *awliyâ'*, instead he argued that together with angels and prophets, their presence in his masjid-i jâmi' was on account of the sacredness of the mosque. It was the Delhi Sultan's special relationship with God and His blessings which had transformed the mosque into a hallowed precinct. Rather than the congregation lending significance to the mosque, the pious congregated in the masjid because of its holy character and willingly accepted the dictates of the sharî'a which it represented.

As we have already seen, Nûr Turk was far from impressed by similar claims made by Iltutmish. Although he had chosen a more direct military recourse in challenging the sharî'at order constructed by the Delhi Sultan, Niẓâm al-Dîn relied upon his teachings to counter the coercion of the 'ulamâ'. In establishing an alternative disciplinary formation, the teachings of the ṣûfî were as threatening to Sultanate 'order' as an armed attack. There was no mincing of words in his inversion of 'Alâ' al-Dîn's claims regarding the sacredness of the Delhi masjid-i jâmi':

[Niẓâm al-Dîn] asserted: 'Whatever place there might be, it is scented by the blessed feet [of the ṣûfî saints]. Take, for example, the Delhi masjid-i jâmi'. The feet of so many saints and pious have trod there, which is why that place has so much tranquility.'[53]

In other words, 'Alâ' al-Dîn's masjid-i jâmi' would have remained a spiritless place, a pile of stones and mortar, had the ṣûfî saints not transformed it. It was important to make this point in case visitors to the mosque attributed the pious environment of the mosque to its constructors, the Delhi Sultans. Niẓâm al-Dîn wanted to make sure that his audience realised that the 'tranquility' of the place originated from the blessings of the saints of God and not from the efforts of the Delhi Sultans.

VIII. Conclusion: 'Objective' History and the Memory of the Qutb

At the time of its construction, the Delhi masjid-i jâmi' left a variety of different impressions upon visitors. For many it was a symbol of a flourishing Muslim community abiding by the tenets of the sharî'a, triumphant over its idolatorous opponents, secured by the energetic, armed interventions of its Sultans. For others, it was a haven for 'scholars', who were concerned less with the spiritual fate of their congregations and more with a coercive regimen of rituals, pecuniary gain and their own authority. These claims and counter-claims were very much a part of the history of Delhi's first masjid-i jâmi' in the thirteenth and fourteenth centuries. Events after the thirteenth century consolidated rival interpretations of the congregational mosque and the modern memory of the Qutb was strongly impressed with these conflicting images.

For over three centuries after 'Alâ' al-Dîn Khalajî's death (715/1316), the old masjid-i jâmi' was sporadically associated with the authority of the rulers of Delhi. But this was not at the expense of the ṣûfîs whose influence remained undiminished during this period. In the fourteenth century itself, the tomb of Niẓâm al-Dîn Awliyâ' emerged as the most venerated shrine in the region of Delhi, completely eclipsing the Delhi masjid-i jâmi'. The area around his shrine was blessed by the grace of the saint and his disciples chose to be buried in the proximately of their pîr, their intercessor with God on the day of judgement. Amongst many others buried in this necropolis was the Mughal emperor Humayun (died 963/1556). A pilgrimage to the dargâh, or the 'court' of Niẓâm al-Dîn Awliyâ', was a part of the Mughal itinerary whenever the rulers of the dynasty visited Delhi.[54] Mughal patronage to the shrine, paradoxically, 'controlled' the saint's discourse against the inadequacies of temporal government. The Mughals did not hesitate to appear as disciples of mystic saints and incorporated strains of mysticism within the ideological baggage explaining their rites of kingship.

The example of Niẓâm al-Dîn Awliyâ' notwithstanding, not all ṣûfî shrines were equally hegemonized by the Mughals. To the south of Delhi, near the old masjid-i jâmi', the dargâh of Quṭb al-Dîn Bakhtiyâr Kâkî (died 634/1236) was also an important ṣûfî shrine. Although he was not an unusually influential saint in his own life time, Bakhtiyâr Kâkî was the pîr of Bâbâ Farîd, Niẓâm al-Dîn Awliyâ's spiritual master, and the renown of the student had certainly accrued to his teachers as well.[55] The record of royal visitations to the dargâh suggests that Bakhtiyâr Kâkî's shrine emerged as a pilgrimage site as early as the late fourteenth and early fifteenth centuries.[56] In 932/1526 it was included in Babar's tour of significant areas worthy of a visit in Delhi and in the mid 1150s/early 1740s Dargâh Qulî Khân commenced his account of Delhi's ṣûfî shrines with a narration of Bakhtiyâr Kâkî's dargâh.[57] Bakhtiyâr Kâkî may have lacked the popularity of Niẓâm al-Dîn Awliyâ', but in the eighteenth and nineteenth centuries, his mystical powers were considered so commanding that the Mughal emperors Shâh 'Âlam Bahâdur Shâh (1119–24/1707–12), Jalâl al-Dîn Shâh 'Âlam (1173–1221/1760–1806) and Mu'în al-Dîn Akbar (1221–53/ 1806–37) chose to be buried near the dargâh. The wish of the last Mughal ruler, Bahâdur Shâh 'Zafar' (1253–74/1837–58), to be buried near the saint remained unfulfilled; he was deported to Rangoon by the British where he died.[58]

Unlike Niẓâm al-Dîn's dargâh, Bakhtiyâr Kâkî's charisma did not materially alter the prestige of the Mughal emperors. This was not because of any shortcoming in the saint's popularity. By the end of the eighteenth century, Mughal might had not survived the onslaught of the Afghan, Maratha and British incursions and its capacity to command obedience was in obvious decline. The Mughal ability to access the increasing popularity of Bakhtiyâr Kâkî's shrine for its own ends was also severely limited. In the eighteenth century many people in Delhi regarded Quṭb al-Dîn Bakhtiyâr Kâkî as seniormost in the 'hierarchy of saints', the Quṭb al-aqṭâb, specially chosen by God to maintain order in the world. The actual extent of his influence is uncertain, but at least within a local, popular cosmology evident in Delhi in the late eighteenth, early nineteenth century, Bakhtiyâr Kâkî was regarded as the Quṭb, the axis, around whom the world revolved. This interpretation was also provided an iconic representation when the mînâr of the neighbouring, thirteenth century masjid-i jâmi', was described as *Qutb sâhib kî lâth*. In other words, the minaret was believed to represent the staff of Qutb al-Dîn Bakhtiyâr Kâkî which pierced the sky, and like the pîr himself, connected heaven with earth, providing stability and shelter to mortals on earth.[59] In this reworked popular cosmology, it was the saint who was the *qubbat al-Islâm*, the 'sanctuary of Islam' and not the congregational mosque. It was in acknowledgement of the pîr's charisma, that the minaret of the mosque was christened the Qutb mînâr, the name which it still carries today.

The reason why we have any information at all about the later developments in the meaning of the masjid-i jâmi' is because of attempts made in the nineteenth and twentieth centuries to correct some 'errors'. In 1263/1846–47 the judge (munsif) employed with the British East India Company, Sayyid Ahmad Khan, wrote his famous topographical monograph on Delhi, the *Âsâr al-Sanâdîd*. At that stage in his life, Sayyid Ahmad was strongly influenced by the emerging positivistic historiographical methodologies gaining currency in the west. In his research on Delhi's monuments, the scholar was extremely careful in citing his literary and archaeological evidence, and in ascertaining chronological, geographical and lexicographical details. Subsequent to the *Âsâr al-Sanâdîd*, Sayyid Ahmad Khan published critical editions of Abû'l-Fazl's *Â'în-i Akbarî*, Ziyâ' al-Dîn Baranî' *T'ârîkh-i Fîruz Shâhî*, and Jahangir's *Tûzuk-i Jahângîrî*, all medieval Persian chronicles on which he had started work several years before. The course of his research was charted by his belief that 'only a correct and sober presentation of the facts can convey a true sense of direction in history and enable the Indians to arrive at a realistic assessment of their situation.'[60] The documentary record of the court chronicles was an important source for the historian, and Sayyid Ahmad Khan carefully selected texts which were, in his opinion, repositories of reliable, objective information.

His concern to recount the 'correct facts' about the capital of the great Sultans and the Mughals motivated Sayyid Ahmad Khan to write the most comprehensive text on the monuments of Delhi. In his account of Delhi's old congregational mosque, he did mention that one of the names for the minaret was 'Qutb sâhib kî lâth', and, amongst other names, the masjid was also called Quwwat al-Islâm.[61] Presumably, because these names belonged to the realm of an oral, popular culture, and not to an 'objective', 'scientific', verifiable, documentary record, there was no discussion of why the mosque and the mînâr were ascribed such intriguing names. Sayyid Ahmad Khan's text led the reader away from these names towards the more 'relevant' subject of the architectural and epigraphical content of the monument and each Sultan's contribution to its construction.

In its own turn, the *Âsâr al-Sanâdîd* was regarded as an 'authoritative' text because it carried all the evidence of sound historical research. Archaeologists and historians of a later generation were dependent upon Sayyid Ahmad Khan's collection of data, his readings of the epigraphs, bibliography of sources, and discussion of the authorship and architectural significance of the mosque. The major development in the early twentieth century occured when the analysis of the congregational mosque was further elaborated by an emerging consensus about the history of the Delhi Sultanate. Ironically, in their research in this area as well, scholars continued to be dependent upon Sayyid Ahmad Khan's scholarship. It was his editions of the Persian chronicles which became the staple diet for most medievalists, because their 'factual account[s]', scholars in the twentieth century noted, were 'correct in all substantive matters'.

There is no doubt that the scholarship on the medieval period today bears little resemblance to that of Sayyid Ahmad's time. Irfan Habib's work in itself has inspired research into questions concerning material culture, agricultural production and the structures of the state. These developments notwithstanding, historians are still wary of examining medieval Persian texts as discursive constructions of evidence, or as images which sought to shape reality. In the absence of such interrogation, a circular logic which first locates 'authoritative' sources, and then reconstructs a 'definitive' history of the Middle Ages, has led to the writing of histories which have in different ways remained congruent with the fortunes of the state.

This methodology has left little space for the presence of local histories, popular memories or contesting discourses in the history of medieval India.[62] For the Qutb mosque, it led to the 'clarification' that the minaret was not named after the ṣûfî saint Quṭb al-Dîn Baḵẖtiyâr Kâkî, but the military commander Quṭb al-Dîn Ai-Beg. The term *Qubbat al-Islâm*, or the 'sanctuary of Islam', which was at first ambiguously used by Jûzjânî for Iltutmish's Delhi and later applied to define the spiritual domain of Baḵẖtiyâr Kâkî, was transformed into *Quwwat al-Islâm*, or the 'Might of Islam' and used for Quṭb al-Dîn's mosque. This name coincided more closely with the military persona of the first constructor of the mosque and his proclamation of a new political order built out of the rubble of temples. Despite all the other developments in research on medieval Indian history, this interpretation of the mosque has remained unquestioned. In that sense, the problem before us today is not a simple one of reinterpreting the significance of the Qutb monuments. We need to be aware that it is the epistemologies dominant in the study of medieval Indian history that enable the interpretation of the Qutb monuments as the 'Quwwat al-Islâm' mosque.

As purveyors of 'information', historians shape the contours of India's past, in history text-books, school and college syllabi and the popular media. Despite the best intentions of many of these practitioners, their work only serves to consolidate popular misconceptions concerning the monolithic character of Hindu and Muslim social structures in the medieval period. Historians may no longer use the term 'Muslim period' to refer to the subcontinent's Middle Ages, but their histories still consider the Delhi Sultans and the Mughal pâdishâhs as the principal actors in the history of medieval India. The different rulers and their structures of administration, revenue and diplomatic policies are studied as the agencies which introduced social and economic change in the subcontinent. Marxist analyses of relations of exploitation and dominance in Sultanate and Mughal society, confirm the image of a monolithic ruling elite, predominantly Muslim and obsessed with 'a' Persian culture. This static and undifferentiated account is disturbed only occasionally by the bhaktî, sometimes the ṣûfî, perhaps even by groups such as the Mahdawîs. But these are often discussed as dissenting groups, 'non-conformist movements', related to, but outside the pale of two well contoured religions. During this entire period 'Muslims' remained the politically dominant group within the subcontinent. The relationship of these historiographies to the memory of the Qutb is extremely important. The events and individuals—Qutb al-Dîn Ai-Beg or Qutb al-Dîn Bakhtiyâr Kâkî, for example—are not terribly significant in themselves, but once situated within larger contextual frames of signification they recall a host of memories. The Qutb is one of those historic sites which can extend beyond its own historical moment to carry a much larger symbolic statement.

Part of its importance lies in the manner in which it has been preserved and 'done up' into a national and world heritage monument. In one of its advertisement campaigns, the *Hindustan Times*, a national newspaper, asked its readers the rhetorical question: 'Can you imagine Delhi without the Qutb?' Its ruins are presented today as a part of 'Indian' antiquity, a part of each citizen's inheritance which he or she can cherish. One mosque out of several from the twelfth century has gained this doubtful honour. Indians are asked to take pride in 'their' mînâr—we are told that it is one of the tallest free standing minarets built out of stone and mortar. Nationalist pride, however, is short-lived and the Qutb monuments lead to a host of ambivalent reactions.

If the minaret is wonderful, what of the mosque? Responses vary. For many, especially children, the monument is an incredibly beautiful and grandiose palace or a larger congregational hall. That it is a mosque escapes most of them. Other, more 'discerning' visitors, remain disconcerted by the statues, pillars, and elaborate carvings, so obviously of a Hindu/Jain provenance situated within a congregational mosque. Still others may see in the mosque evidence of the might and dominance of 'their community' in the affairs of the subcontinent in the near past.

Since it is a major tourist site, the Archaeological Survey of India has placed short descriptions inscribed on stone near the several monuments to 'guide' visitors through the Qutb complex. These inscriptions provide the name, the physical properties, functions and significance of the respective monuments. These are facts; there is no hint of doubt, speculation or debate concerning the multiple interpretations of these sites or the changing historical contexts in which they were built. Instead, the self-confident recounting of undisputed information is in itself reassuring to the visitors. It is presented as the wisdom of the professional body of historians and archaeologists, the 'authorities' whose knowledge should be above doubt.

Once armed with the crucial information that the Quwwat al-Islâm masjid celebrates the conquest of Hindustan by the Muslim Sultans of Delhi, the nature of the monument itself leaves little space to visitors for doubt. Even as they function as historians themselves, the 'evidence' of plunder before them is 'proof' sufficient of Muslim iconoclasm and a bigoted hatred of Hindus and their religious beliefs. Their empirical conclusions are not very far from a seamless historiography of medieval Indian history which has provided little to contest the overriding impression of the hegemony of the Muslim state.[63] As a result, the Qutb serves as a catalyst which resurrects a host of memories about Muslims and their governance: from casual stories concerning Muslim fanaticism and violence, to history lessons where Muslim rulers and their subordinates monopolized power and exploited Hindu subjects. Within the mosque the visitor is struck by the juxtaposition of the great monolithic communities, a divide which the Qutb suggests commenced from the very intrusion of Islam into India. A Partition which from its very first encounter was remarkable for its violence.

More than any large tome or pedagogical instruction, the Qutb provides an opportunity to educate visitors about the complex, fragmented political and religious world of India's Middle Ages, a time when there was considerable disunity and contestation within the groups defined as 'Hindus' and 'Muslims'. It is this frame of reference which should also guide us to reflect upon the manner in which discursive constructions of knowledge were formed in the Middle Ages. The Quwwat al-Islâm mosque was built to represent a unity of belief and conduct to a Muslim congregation who not only remained quite unimpressed with Sultanate statements of piety and power but also produced their own contesting discursive texts. The spoils of the Hindu and Jain temples are only a small part of the story of the Qutb;

Mu'izzî *Amîrs* such as Bahâ' al-Dîn Tughril, ṣûfî derwishes like Nûri Turk, *shaykhs* like Niẓâm al-Dîn Awliyâ', the popular veneration of Quṭb al-Dîn Bakhtiyâr Kâkî and the historiography of Sayyid Ahmad Khan and his successors are all ingredients that should be used to explain the multi-levelled history of the mosque and minaret to visitors. Instead it is the extreme nationalist ideologies prevalent in India which filter our understanding of the Qutb. This unfortunately also burdens visitors with unequivocal evidence of wrongs inflicted in the past upon the Hindu community, wrongs that are in need of correction today. As a result, the Qutb stands as an icon, encapsulating the trauma of 1947 and acting as a historical exoneration for the acts of December 1992. What is tragic is the manner in which historians of medieval India have provided 'proof' and 'evidence' supporting the readings of this icon.

NOTES AND REFERENCES

1. Alfred Gell, 'The Technology of Enchantment and the Enchantment of Technology', in *Anthropology, Art and Aesthetics*, eds. J. Coote and Anthony Shelton, Oxford: Oxford University Press, 1992, pp. 40–63.

2. For details on the spatial, architectural and epigraphic information, other than my own field surveys, I am reliant on the research of Sayyid Ahmad Khan, Alexander Cunningham, J. Horowitz, J.A. Page, A.B.M. Husain, M.A. Husain, and Ebba Koch. The full bibliographical citations are given below.

3. Although there is absolutely no evidence to warrant such an assumption, all historians and archaeologists have concluded that it was the Muslims who placed the iron pillar within the Qutb mosque. Their conclusions might have been guided by the fact that later rulers like Firûz Shâh Tughluq and Akbar transported Asokan pillars and placed them as trophies in Delhi and Allahabad respectively. As Richard H. Davis has pointed out, ('Indian Art Objects as Loot', *Journal of Asian Studies*, 52 (1993): 22–48) however, temples were also plundered by Hindu rulers, and their idols were frequently treated as war trophies and publicly displayed as statements of conquest. A similar effort at embellishing his own authority may well have guided the Tomara ruler Anangpal sometime around 1052: at least according to popular legend, it was this ruler who placed the fourth century iron pillar at its current site. See

Alexander Cunningham, 'Four Reports made during the years 1862–63–64–65', *Archaeological Survey of India Reports,* Simla: Archaeological Survey of India, Government Press, 1871, vol. 1, pp. 171–5.

4. See, for example, the opinion of H.C. Fanshawe, *Shah Jahan's Delhi—Past and Present,* Delhi: Sumit Publications, 1979 [1902], p. 257.

5. See Sayyid Ahmad Khan, *Âsâr al-Sanâdîd,* ed., Khaliq Anjum, Delhi: Urdu Academy Delhi, 1990 [1847]; Alexander Cunningham, 'Four Reports'; J. Horowitz, 'The Inscriptions of Muhammad ibn Sam, Qutbuddin Aibeg and Iltutmish', *Epigraphia Indo-Moslemica* (1911–12); 12–34; J. Yazdani, 'Inscriptions of the Khaljî Sultans of Delhi and their contemporaries in Bengal' *Epigraphia Indo-Moslemica,* 1917–18, pp. 23–30; J.A. Page, *An Historical Memoir on the Qutb,* Calcutta: Memoirs of the Archaeological Survey of India, no. 22, Government of India Central Publication Branch, 1926.

6. As far as I have been able to date it, Sayyid Ahmad Khan was the first author to refer to the Delhi Masjid-i Jâmi' as the 'Quwwat al-Islâm' mosque. S.A. Khan, *Âsâr al-Sanâdîd,* vol. 1, p. 310, provided three names for the mosque; *Masjid-i Adîna Dehlî ya* (or) *Masjid-i jâmi' Dehli ya* (or) *Quwwat al-Islâm.* Cunningham (1871) either misread Quwwat al-Islâm in Khan's text as *Quṭb al-Islâm* or, as is more likely (see below), he relied upon a locally current source for his reading. Literature on Delhi produced for English tourists at the turn of the century always referred to the mosque as Quwwat al-Islâm. See H.C. Fanshawe, *Delhi—Past and Present,* p. 258, and Gordon Risley Hearn, *The Seven Cities of Delhi,* New Delhi: SBW Publishers, 1986 [1906], pp. 51, 54, 94. Some years later, the widely cited Horowitz, 'Inscriptions', 1911–12 and J.A. Page, *A Historical Memoir on the Qutb,* 1926, informed scholars that Quwwat al-Islâm was the name of this mosque. It was a fateful christening for it was to eventually become the 'official' name of the mosque. For two edges of the historiographical spectrum where this is used for the masjid-i jâmi', see: J. Burton Page, 'Dihli', *Encyclopaedia of Islam,* eds. C.E. Bosworth *et al.,* Leiden: E.J. Brill, second edition, 1956, vol. 2, pp. 225–6, as representing the 'Islamicist' tradition, and Y.D. Sharma, *Delhi and Its Neighbourhood,* New Delhi: Director General Archaeological Survey of India, 1982 rpt., pp. 17–19, 52–9, amongst the better tourist guide literature.

7. Michael W. Meister, 'The Two-and-a-half day Mosque', *Oriental Art* 18 n.s., 1972, pp. 57–63; Mohammad Mujeeb, 'The Qutb Complex as a Social Document', in *Islamic Influence on Indian Society,* Delhi: Meenakshi Prakashan, 1972, pp. 114–27; and A.B.M. Husain, *The Manara in Indo-Muslim Architecture,* Dhaka: Asiatic Society of Pakistan, Publication no. 25, 1970.

8. Robert Hillenbrand, 'Political Symbolism in Early Indo-Islamic Mosque

Architecture: The Case of Ajmir', *Iran* 26 (1988), pp, 105–17. Anthony Welch, 'Architectural Patronage and the Past: The Tughluq Sultans of India', *Muqarnas* 10 (1993), pp. 311–22.

9. Welch, 'Architectural Patronage . . .', p. 314.

10. Anthony Welch, '*Qur'ān* and Tomb: the Religious Epigraphs of Two Early Sultanate Tombs in Delhi' in *Indian Epigraphy: Its Bearings on the History of Art,* eds. Frederick M. Asher and G.S. Ghai, New Delhi: Oxford and IBH Publishing Co., American Institute of Indian Studies, 1985, pp. 260, 257. Welch summarized here arguments which he presented in another, apparently still unpublished article: 'Islamic Architecture and Epigraphs in Sultanate India' in *Studies in South Asian Art and Architecture,* ed., A.K. Narain, forthcoming.

11. Ibid, p. 257.

12. Welch, 'Architectural Patronage . . .'. pp. 311, 312–14. Welch also Suggests that: 'Building types—mosques, tombs, madrasas, and mînârs—as well as forms are also at the same time assertively alien to the Hindu majority, and in their strident distinctiveness from indigenous buildings, they proclaim Islam's universal aspirations and its distance from the polytheism of the subject population', pp. 312–13.

13. A.B.M. Habibullah, *The Foundation of Muslim Rule in India,* Allahabad: Central Book Depot, 1976 rpt., Khaliq Ahmad Nizaji, *Some Aspects of Religion and Politics in the Thirteenth Century,* Delhi: Idarah-i Adabiyat-i Delhi, 1974 rpt., S.B.P. Nigam, *Nobility Under the Sultans of Delhi, AD 1206–1398,* Delhi: Munshiram Manoharlal, 1968.

14. Habibullah, *Foundation of Muslim Rule,* ch. VI, pp. 120–34.

15. Welch, 'Architectural Patronage . . .', p. 311.

16. 'The plebianization of the nobility', a clumsy formulation at best, has several proponents but was first suggested by Muhammad Habib, 'The Governing Class', in *The Political Theory of the Delhi Sultanate,* Allahabad: Ketab Mahal, n.d., pp. 144–51, and later developed by Irfan Habib, 'Barani's Theory of the Delhi Sultanate', *Indian Historical Review* 7 (1980–81), p. 109.

17. For the architectural consequences of this development see Welch, 'Architectural Patronage and the Past', pp. 314–15. Here the author argues that since the Tughluqs were [more?] secular rulers, governing a pan-Indian state, their architecture was also less 'saracenic' and more eclectic.

18. Irfan Habib, 'The Social Distribution of Landed Property in Pre-British India: A Historical Survey', *Enquiry* n.s. 2 (1965), p. 45.

19. Irfan Habib, *The Agrarian System of Mughal India,* Bombay: Asia Publishing House, 1963, p. 257.

20. Irfan Habib, 'The State and the Economy', in the *Cambridge Economic History of India*, eds. Tapan Raychandhuri and Irfan Habib, Cambridge: University Press, 1982, vol. 1, p. 184.

21. Ibid.

22. Habib, *Agrarian System of the Mughal Empire*, p. 334.

23. Habibullah, *Foundation of Muslim Rule*, chs V–VI, pp. 96–134; Habib, *Agrarian System of Mughal India*, p. 318.

24. Irfan Habib, 'The Price Regulations of 'Alâ'uddin Khalji—A defence of Zia' Baranî', *IESHR*, 21 (1984), p. 393.

25. Shireen Moosvi, *The Economy of the Mughal Empire, c. 1595: A Statistical Study*, Delhi: Oxford University Press, 1987, p. 4.

26. Irfan Habib, 'Evidence for Sixteenth-Century Agrarian Conditions in the Guru Granth Sahib', *IESHR* (1963–64), p. 70.

27. Athar Ali, 'The Mughal Polity—A Critique of "Revisionist" Approaches', *Proceedings of the Indian History Congress* 52 (1991–92), pp. 308, 310.

28. '*In pahwân (?) wa jahândâr-1 Hind-ra Malik khiṭab farmûd*'. '*Pahwân*', in the Persian edition of the *Tâ'rîkh* must be a mistake for '*pahalwan*'.

29. Fakhr-i Mudabbir, *Tâ'rîkh-i Fakhr al-Dîn Mubârak Shâh*, ed., E.D. Ross, London: Royal Asiatic Society, 1927, pp. 28–9.

30. On the ṭabaqât form as a historical genre of writing see Franz Rosenthal, *History of Muslim Historiography*, Leiden: E.J. Brill, 1969, pp. 93–5 and Louise Marlow, *Hierarchy and Egalitarianism in Islamic Thought*, Cambridge: Cambridge University Press, 1997, pp. 9–10. For the Mu'izzî subordinates in Hindustan, see Minhâj-i Sirâj Jûzjânî, *Ṭabaqât-i Nâṣirî*, ed., Abdul Hayy Habibi, Kabul: Anjuman-i Târîkh-i Afghanistan, 1963–64, vol. 1, pp. 415–38.

31. Jûzjânî, *Ṭabaqât. . .*, vol. 1, p. 421.

32. Ibid., vol. 1, p. 421. Notice also the titulature and Jûzjânî's attempt to communicate his sense of the hierarchical relationship: Malik was used for Bahâ' al-Dîn and Sulṭan for Quṭb al-Dîn.

33. Fakhr-i Mudabbir, *Tâ'rîkh-i Fakhr al-Dîn Mubârak Shâh*, pp. 25–6. I have used the translation of E.D. Ross, 'The genealogies of *Fakhr al-Dîn Mubârak Shâh*', in '*Ajab Namah: A Volume of Oriental Studies presented to E.G. Browne on his Sixtieth Birthday*, eds. T.W. Arnold and R.A. Nicholson, Cambridge: Cambridge University Press, 1922, p. 399.

34. For Bahâ' al-Dîn's inscription in the 'Chaurasi Khamba' mosque in Kaman, see Mehrdad and Natalie H. Shokoohy, 'The Architecture of Bahâ' al-Dîn Tughrul [*sic*] in the Region of Bayana, Rajasthan', *Muqarnas* 4, 1987, p. 115.

35. But note the graffiti on the right-hand jamb of the eleventh slit window on the stairway in the minaret: 'May your mother be ravished by a donkey!' See

Page, *The Qutb . . .*, p. 40. This may have been a response to the destruction of temples, but at least equally, if not more likely, a venting of frustrated resentment by an artisan at a personal injury caused by an aggressive supervisor at work.

36. See Page, *The Qutb . . .*, pp. 39–40, 41, 43. I have followed the revised and edited translation of Pushpa Prasad, *Sanskrit Inscriptions of Delhi Sultanate 1191–1526*, Delhi: Oxford University Press, 1990, pp. 3, 19, 35. I concur with Pushpa Prasad's reading of the inscription from Muḥammad Shâh Tughluq's reign. But for an alternate reading see Carl W. Ernst, *Eternal Garden; Mysticism, History and Politics at a South Asian Ṣûfî Center*, Albany: State University of New York, 1992, pp. 32–3.

37. On the bâgh-i Jasrath, see Amîr Ḥasan Sijzî, *Fawâ'id al-Fu'âd*, ed., Hazan Sani Nizami Dihlawi, Delhi: Urdu Academy, 1990, p. 242. On the ḥauz-i Rânî, see ibid.; Amîr Khurd, *Siyar al-Awliyâ'*, ed., S.M. Ghuri, Lahore: Marqaz-i Tahqiqat-i Farsi Iran wa Pakistan, 1978, p. 120; and Jûzjânî, *Ṭabaqât-i Nâṣirî*, vol. 1, p. 469, vol. 2, p. 27. For a fuller description see Sunil Kumar, 'Perceiving 'your' Land: Neighbourhood Settlements and the Hauz-i Rânî', eds. Peter J. Ucko and Robert Layton, *The Archaeology and Anthropology of Landscape*, London: Routledge, 1999, p. 159; and idem, 'Names, Meanings and a History of Delhi's Neighbourhoods', forthcoming.

38. See Davis, 'Indian Art Objects as Loot', pp. 22–48.

39. Peter Hardy, 'Growth of Authority Over a Conquered Political Elite: Early Delhi Sultanate as a Possible Case Study', in *Kingship and Authority in South Asia*, ed., J.F. Richards, Delhi: Oxford University Press, 1998 rpt., pp. 216–41, had studied a similar set of questions years ago without much success. Significantly his research was based primarily on the textual evidence of the thirteenth and fourteenth centuries.

40. Fakhr-i Mudabbir, *Tâ'rîkh . . .*, p. 33; Hardy, 'Authority Over a Conquered Political Elite', p. 238.

41. See John S. Deyell, *Living Without Silver*, Delhi: Oxford University Press, 1990, pp. 193–206, 318.

42. Jûzjânî, *Ṭabaqât . . .*, vol. 1, pp. 440–1.

43. Jûzjânî, *Ṭabaqât . . .*, vol. 1, p. 461.

44. Sijzî, *Fawâ'id al-Fu'âd*, p. 334.

45. Sijzî, *Fawa'id al-Fu'ad*, p. 226.

46. Simon Digby, 'The Ṣûfî Shaikh as a Source of Authority in Medieval India', *Purusartha, Islam et Societe en Asie du Sud* 9, 1986, p. 62.

47. The picture of the Delhi Sultan as the 'reviver of the forgotten commandments, *muhai'yî âsâr-i ahkâm*', recurs on an inscription on the right pier, east door. Yazdani, 'Inscriptions of the Khalji Sultans . . .', p. 24.

48. Inscription on the right pier, west door, ibid., p. 28.

49. Inscription on the left pier, east door, ibid., p. 25.

50. Transcribed and translated by Maulvi Muhammad Ashraf Hussain, *A Record of All the Qur'ânic and Non-Historical Epigraphs on the Protected Monuments in the Delhi Province*, Calcutta: Memoirs of the Archaeological Survey of India, no. 47 (1936), p. 105.

51. Ibid., pp. 109–10.

52. Inscription on the south door, left pier. '*banâ farmûd in masjid kî masjid-i jannât zumreh-yi awliyâ' wa . . . tabaqah-ij atqiyâ' wa majma' malâ'ik-i kirâm wa mahzar-i arwâh-i anbiyâ'-yi 'uzzâm ast.*' I have followed the epigraph as it was transcribed and translated by Page, *Qutb . . .*, p. 37. In this case, Page's reading was less ambitious, but clearer than Yazdani, 'Inscriptions of the Khaljî Sultans . . .', p. 27, and plate VIII.

53. Sijzî, *Fawâ'id al-Fu'âd*, pp. 18–19: *sakhan dar barkat-i qadam-i nîk mardân uftâd: farmûd keh har mauzâ' keh hast, ba-yamn-i aqdâm-i ishan murauwah ast, chunâncheh masjid-i jâmi' Dehli. B'ad az ân farmûd keh, aqdâm-i chand awliyâ' wa buzurgân ânjah rasidah bâshad keh ân maqâm chunâr râhat dârad.*

54. See Ebba Koch, 'The Delhi of the Mughals Prior to Shahjahanabad as Reflected in the Patterns of Imperial Visits', in *Art and Culture*, eds. A.J. Qaisar and S.P. Verma, Jaipur: Publication Scheme Press, 1993.

55. In contrast to the very full account of Bâbâ Farîd, the *Fawa'id al-Fu'ad* provides occasional references to Bakhtiyâr Kâkî's life and teachings: pp. 42–3, 87–8, 104–5, 132, 184–5, 212–13, 246, 268, 315–16, 336, 407, 420. It was in Amîr Khwurd's *Siyar al-Awliyâ'*, ed., Sayyid Mahdi Ghuri, Lahore: Markaz-i Tahqiqat-i Farsi Iran wa Pakistan, no. 23, Mu'assi-yi Intisharat-i Islami, 1978, pp. 48–56, a late fourteenth century biographical compendium, that the spiritual genealogy of the Chistî mystical order was clearly worked out, and Bakhtiyâr Kâkî's position in the descent of Chishtî saints confirmed.

56. According to Ibu Battuta's evidence, Bakhtiyâr Kâkî's grave had already become a place of pilgrimage when he visited it in the mid or late 730s/1330s. Ibu Battuta, *The Travels of Ibn Battuta*, trans. H.A.R. Gibb, Cambridge: Cambridge University Press, Hakluyt Society, second series, no. 141, 1971, vol. 3, pp. 625–6. In 800/1398 the agreement between Mallu Iqbâl Khân and Sultan Nâṣir al-Dîn Maḥmâd Shâh (795–801/1393–99) was reached in the dargâh of Bakhtiyâr Kâkî: see Yahyâ Sîhrindî, *Tâ'rîkh-i Mubârak Shâhî*, ed., M. Hidayat Hosain, Calcutta: Bibliotheca Indica, 1931, p. 163. Faced with the threat of Ḥusain Shâh Sharqî's invasions in 883/1478, Bahlul Lôdî prayed at the dargâh of the saint. See Shaikh Rizqullâh Mushtâqî, *Waqî'at-i Mushtâqî*, trans. and ed., I.H. Siddiqui, New Delhi: Indian Council of Historical Research, 1993, p. 11.

57. Babar, *Babar nâmah*, vol. 2, p. 474. Dargâh Qulî Khân, *Muraqqa'-i Dihlî*, ed. and trans. Nurul Hasan Ansari, Delhi: Urdu Department, University of Delhi Press, 1982, pp. 23–5, 119–21. The description of Bakhtiyâr Kâkî's dargâh followed accounts of shrines venerating the Prophet's and Ali's footprints and it preceded an account of Nizâm al-Dîn Awliyâ's tomb.

58. Mughal construction within the dargâh is in evidence from the eighteenth century during the reigns of Shâh 'Âlam Bahâdur Shâh (1119–24/1707–12), and Farrukh Siyar (1124–31/1713–19). See Sayyid Ahmad Khan, *Âsâr al-Sanâdîd*, vol. 1, p. 335. The author makes no mention of the floral multi-coloured tiles presumed to have been fixed in the shrine by Aurangzeb, for which see Y.D. Sharma, *Delhi and Its Neighbourhood*, pp. 62–3.

59. Sayyid Ahmad Khan, *Âsâr al-Sanâdîd*, ed., Khaliq Anjum, Delhi: Urdu Board, 1990 rpt., vol. 1, p. 312.

60. Christian W. Troll, *Sayyid Ahmad Khan: A Reinterpretation of Muslim Theology*, Karachi: Oxford University Press, 1978–79, p. 105, and for his scholarship in the context of the *Âsâr al-Sanâdîd* see Troll, 'A Note on an Early Topographical Work of Saiyid Ahmad Khan: Athar as-Sanadid', *Journal of the Royal Asiatic Society*, 1972, pp. 135–46.

61. Sayyid Ahmad Khan, *Âsâr al-Sanâdîd*, vol. 1, pp. 310–12.

62. It is also one of the reasons why medieval Indian history is so weak in social as well as women's history.

63. This is not to suggest that no historian has questioned the interpretation of the monolithic state and its ruling elite in the medieval period. The writings of scholars such as Muzaffar Alam and Sanjay Subrahmanyam are, however, restricted to the Mughals. For their most recent contribution see Muzaffar Alam and Sanjay Subrahmanyam, eds. *The Mughal State*, Delhi: Oxford University Press, 1998. The writings of Alam, Subrahmanyam and others, however, have not received the circulation they deserve. Their fate seems to be determined by what Peter Hardy described as 'a kind of Gresham's Law' (which continues to operate for the Sultanate period) where 'one or two text-books of political history . . . drive out of intellectual circulation many articles on cultural history in learned periodicals'. Peter Hardy, *Historians of Medieval India: Studies in Indo-Muslim Historical Writing*, London: Luzac and Company, 1966 rpt., pp. 4–5.

Performing Partition in Lahore

RICHARD McGILL MURPHY

Introduction: The Mirror Stage of National Difference

PARTITION LIVES EACH day at sunset at the Wagah border crossing between Pakistan and India, a few kilometres east of Lahore. The Wagah crossing is actually used only by foreigners travelling overland and by official Pakistani and Indian delegations. Ordinary citizens and goods cross by train at a point down the border, or by air.[1] The main daily event at Wagah is the sunset flag lowering ceremony, for which the Pakistani and Indian army detachments who guard their respective sides of the frontier have developed a precisely coordinated ceremonial choreography.

The commanders of the two border-guard detachments meet monthly to discuss the flag ceremony and other joint responsibilities. According to the Pakistani army captain in command of the Wagah post in 1993, cross-border relations were generally cordial. 'We send them sweets for their festivals, and they send us sweets for our 'Eids,'

This paper is mainly based on dissertation fieldwork conducted in Lahore between 1992 and 1994. My fieldwork was made possible by a Fulbright scholarship, a Dissertation Fellowship from the Social Science Research Council (U.S.), and a Senior Scholarship from Wadham College, Oxford.

he said. This harmony has been ruptured in the past, however, notably during the 1971 war when Indian troops stormed through the crossing, attacked the Pakistani troops and, in the captain's words, 'butchered them like hell.' In the 1980s an electrified wire fence was built along this stretch of the border. The fence is about eight feet high, with searchlights every hundred feet or so, and guard towers more widely spaced. At night the lights are visible from Pakistan Airlines flights between Karachi and Lahore. Before 1971 Indian farmers used to cross into Pakistan in the daytime to cultivate a few border fields to which they held pre-Partition title. Since then this stretch of the border has officially been sealed, although Wagah is well-known as a smuggler's village. Evidently people still find ways through the fence.

There are other gates apart from the one at Wagah where the ceremonial border guard detachments are stationed, but they are normally locked. Apparently the Indians have the only keys to these gates. The captain advanced this as proof that Pakistan could not possibly be sending secret agents to ferment political turmoil in east Punjab, as the Indians often claim. He dismissed the suggestion that secret agents might travel by train. 'It's impossible. The Indians have one hundred checkpoints between here and Delhi. This is rubbish what they are saying.'

The flag lowering ceremony is a popular attraction for local Indians and Pakistanis. Shortly before sunset, sizeable crowds gather on both sides of the border, providing a neat study in national difference. There is more veiling among women on the Pakistani or Muslim side. Most of the Indian spectators are Sikhs, reflecting the post-Partition demographics of east Punjab. The Pakistani border guards are army Rangers, with a prescribed minimum height of six feet. Their Indian counterparts are mostly bearded, turbanned Sikhs, of about the same stature.

The nightly ritual begins just before sunset and lasts for about five minutes. Each side performs the mirror image of the other's actions. One Pakistani and one Indian soldier goose-steps towards the other from points thirty yards across the border. A few yards short of it they stop and perform in unison one quarter turn. Both now stand at attention, bodies perpendicular to the border, staring fixedly at one another over their near shoulders. They maintain ferocious scowls on their faces. The Pakistani soldier and the Indian soldier are then joined by several colleagues, and the ritual proceeds towards its conclusion with much symmetrical stamping, wheeling, shouted commands and saluting. Buglers on each side play in perfect unison as the two flags come down.

These flags are effectively curtains marking closure to a daily performance of nationalist theatre. The different costumes of the principal actors (soldiers) and extras (civilians) on each side, the different flags, the stylized mirror play of the Indian and Pakistani soldiers, all dramatize the political contention that India and Pakistan are two distinct and mutually antagonistic states. The ritual quality of the scene is enhanced by the fact that the Wagah border is rarely crossed by ordinary Indians or Pakistanis. This is a pure theatre of difference, divorced from everyday life just as the Indian and Pakistani states are divorced from one another.

The mirror effect is achieved by a logic of binary opposition: the Indian and Pakistani border detachments distinguish themselves and the larger wholes they represent using a common symbolic language of uniforms, music, and military drill inherited from the British Raj. The value assigned to the terms in each pair is arbitrary: because the symbols wielded on the Indian and Pakistani sides are essentially identical, they could be reversed without affecting the import of the ritual. On the other hand, Pakistani national discourse construes this difference as 'real'. Nationalists from Mohammed Iqbal and Jinnah onwards have argued that Pakistan must exist because of a primordial incompatibility, hardening at times to antagonism, between two communities who by definition were never one. The mirror stage at Wagah is a dramatic illustration of the corollary, that Pakistan is defined as that which India is not.

On close examination, this definition collapses into a dance of similitude: while the border ritual enacts difference, it also illustrates the fundamental similarities that Pakistani nationalist discourse seeks to deny. This ambiguous blurring of self and other is reminiscent of post-Freudian theories of child development. In Lacanian psychoanalytic terminology, 'mirror stage' denotes an early stage of identity formation in which the infant attains phenomenological understanding of her distinct ego status by seeing herself literally reflected in a mirror or metaphorically reflected in another human being, typically a parent.[2] But while based on a logic of binary differentiation, Lacan's argument also stresses the impossibility of clearly differentiating the child-self from the mother. In a similar way, the Wagah border ritual is a dance of identical opposites, each poised in the mirror of the other.

According to Pakistani nationalist discourse, Pakistan must exist because Hindus and Muslims are so radically different that they cannot live together in peace. Discourse meets practice in the mirror-play of Wagah and in the Pakistani social studies curriculum, which tells schoolchildren that Pakistan was pre-ordained because 'Muslim culture' was always superior to 'Hindu culture'. Discourse met practice in particularly dramatic fashion during the aftermath of the 6 December 1992 destruction of the Babri Masjid at Ayodhya by militant Hindu nationalists. In cities throughout Pakistan, angry mobs retaliated by tearing down (mostly) disused Hindu temples, thus erasing evidence that could challenge the nationalist rejection of the region's multi-communal past. And discourse drives practice in Lahori celebrations of Basant, an originally Hindu festival that modern Lahoris have re-invented as the sign of an imagined past authenticity that Basant celebrations project into the countryside.

In all these cases, we are not simply pointing out a gap between nationalist theory and empirical reality. Because human dreams of purity rarely match the untidy complexities of human existence, similar gaps exist in all modern nation states. The purpose of this discussion is rather to describe the rhetorical construction of reality in a particular nation state, Pakistan. Relationships between language and the world are rarely simple: as an ethnographer in Lahore, I was often struck by the complicated ways in which rhetoric and reality reflected, determined, and subverted one another. As with any mirror, what you saw depended very much on where you were standing.

Nationalism and Social Distinction

Pakistan's two-nation theory allows for little classificatory ambiguity. At virtually every level, it stresses racial and cultural differences between Hindus and Muslims while deprecating elements of commonality. The general normative asymmetry between Hindus and Muslims is constructed out of several value-laden binary oppositions (see Fig. 1). Thus Hindus are conventionally described as small, dark, feeble people who worship many gods. Muslims, on the other hand, are tall, fair, warlike monotheists. The possible existence of tall, fair, martial Hindus is not acknowledged at the level of official Pakistani nationalism. The caste Hindu claim to descent from Central Asian Aryan invaders who are supposed to have brought the Hindu scriptures to the subcontinent is not acknowledged either.[3] From a Pakistani nationalist point of view, Muslims are quintessentially northern invaders, while Hindus are quintessentially an indigenous southern people. The fact that the two communities were never distributed with anything like this degree of tidiness (had they been so distributed, there would have been no need for population exchanges at Partition) has no effect on their conceptual identification with opposite points of the compass. All evidence that contradicts this tenet is left out of the two-nation theory's version of South Asian history.

Muslims	Value	Hindus	Value
Tall	+	Short	−
Fair	+	Dark	−
Northern	+	Southern	−
Invaders	+	Invaded	−
Monotheistic	+	Polytheistic	−
Brave/honest	+	Cowardly/dishonest	−
Meat-eaters	+	Vegetarians	−
Women wear salwar kameez (modest)	+	Women wear sari (immodest)	−
Main literary language is Urdu	+	Main literary language is Hindi	−
Pure (pak)	+	Impure	−

Fig. 1: The normative construction of Pakistani Muslim nationalism.

This value system extends into dress, language and diet, where meat-eating is a popular rationalization for the presumed martial superiority of Muslims. The female sari is classified as 'Hindu' dress in contrast to the 'Muslim' salwar kameez and dupatta. Even though upper-class urban Pakistani women are occasionally seen in midriff-baring saris, this is a risqué fashion on patriotic grounds as well as grounds of modesty. And while modern Hindi and Urdu are mutually comprehensible though written in different alphabets (Pakistanis watch Indian films in Hindi with no need for subtitles), Pakistani textbooks describe Urdu without reference to its relationship with Hindi. In the jingoistic terms of one Urdu-medium text for Class 9 students in Sindh:

> Gradually Urdu has developed to a stage where now it is considered one of the more developed languages of the world. Not only that, but next to Arabic, Urdu is the only language which has no equal in the world. The fact is that even English and French languages [*sic*] are losing their popularity and importance before the Urdu language.[4]

Hindi, which is Urdu in another script from the point of view of everyday communication, disappears into the mass of undistinguished tongues over which Urdu is said to hold sway.

This historiography projects the idea of Pakistan into the indefinite past, matching the more general tenet that Hindus and Muslims have always been separate and mutually-antagonistic communities.[5] Since Partition, Pakistani hostility towards Hindus has been focused through the lens of Indian (in Pakistani rhetoric, 'Indian Occupied') Kashmir, where separatist Muslim militants have been fighting a guerrilla war against the Indian government with moral and, perhaps, financial and military support from neighbouring Pakistan since 1990.[6] In Pakistan, the Kashmir revolt is conceived in religious terms, as an Islamic struggle (jihad). The militants are invariably referred to as mujahedin (the agent form of jihad) in Urdu and 'freedom fighters' in English, while the Indian soldiers are often characterized by epithets that deny them rationality and even humanity. This headline from the Urdu press is not atypical of popular Pakistani discourse on Kashmir: 'Kashmiri mujahedin exploded a bomb in an Indian army camp. In the clashes eleven savage beasts [*darande*, i.e. Indian soldiers] went to the valley of death.'[7]

The rhetorical contrast between Muslim mujahedin and their sub-human, non-Muslim Indian opponents subordinates the latter to the former in the very terms of its discourse. The two nations are not mere-ly opposed to one another: they are also ranked. This conforms to a centuries-old pattern according to which the Muslims of the subconti-nent have seen themselves as a morally superior conquering class, ruling over non-Muslim subjects by might and religious right. In Indo-Persian poetry, for example, 'Hindu' has been a metaphor of subordination since at least the thirteenth century, when the Muslim poet Amir Hasan Sijzi of Delhi (1255–1337) addressed his beloved as follows: 'However much I . . . [act like] your Hindu, you station Tur-kish sharpshooters to ambush me when I [try to] steal sugar from your ruby lips.'[8] In other words, 'however much I abase myself in your pre-sence, you still rebuff me when I try to kiss you.'

The modern history curriculum tends to describe the era of Muslim predominance as a golden age of benevolent Turko-Persian Muslims ruling over ungrateful, unscrupulous, and definitely subordinate Hin-dus. Moreover, Pakistani schoolchildren are taught that the entire history of Hindu-Muslim relations on the subcontinent can be ex-plained in terms of an exclusive and primordial Muslim nationalism. The textbooks tend to argue that the differences between Muslims and Hindus were either absolute, or that 'Muslim culture' and religion were so superior that the Hindus rapidly adopted Muslim ways after coming into contact with the invaders.

As one Social Studies text for Class 8 students in Sindh province put it: 'The advent of Islam in India reformed Hindu society.'[9] A Punjab Pakistan Studies textbook for classes 9–10 makes the same point while introducing the association of Muslim nationalism with moral purity embedded in the word 'Pakistan' ('Land of the Pure'[10]) itself: '. . . the Muslims came to this country bringing with them a clean and elegant culture and civilization. The Hindus were influenced by the Islamic civilization. The Hindus are indebted to Muslim culture and civilization today.'[11] The British conquest of India, meanwhile, is generally presented as the result of a Hindu-British conspiracy against Muslim rule. According to an Urdu-medium Social Studies (*mo'ashrati 'ulum*) textbook for Class 4 students in the Northwest Frontier Province: 'The Muslims treated the non-Muslims very well [when they ruled northwest India]. Yet the non-Muslims nursed in their hearts an enmity against the Muslims. When the British invaded the area ['*ilaaqa'*] the non-Muslims sided with them and against the Muslims. So the British conquered the whole country ['*mulk'*]'[12]

This history is pressed into service as evidence bolstering the two-nation theory. It also sets up a complex hierarchy in which Muslims are conceived as having historically held the balance of both power and moral virtue in South Asia. The eclipse of Muslim power that resulted from Britain's colonization of the subcontinent, meanwhile, is glossed as a moral victory: the Muslims were supplanted not because they were physically weak or morally inadequate, but as the result of an alien conspiracy.

There appears to be no felt contradiction between the purifying racial imagination of Pakistani Muslim nationalism and the eclectic linguistic, racial, and religious narratives through which modern Pakistanis structure their relations with the past. For example, various Punjabi Muslim communities, such as the Rajputs, trace their descent from Hindu converts to Islam,[13] but this does not affect the nationalist tenet that the Muslims are essentially an endogamous community who came from elsewhere. The strongly syncretic tendencies of north Indian popular religion are likewise not acknowledged in this discourse. To cite only two examples, Hindus in eighteenth century Shia-dominated Awadh reportedly assimilated the Prophet Mohammed's martyred grandson Hussain into the Hindu pantheon.[14] Shia women, meanwhile, prayed to the Hindu goddess Kali Durga [*sic*] in secret when their children fell ill.[15] And one of Lahore's great Sufi culture heroes, Madho Lal Hussain, is said to be a conflation of two historical figures: a sixteenth-century Muslim *pir* named Lal Hussain and his Hindu disciple Madho.[16]

This is precisely the sort of evidence that is left out of the two-nation theory's history of Hindu-Muslim relations. The physical, economic and social separation of the two states supports this conceptual polarization. There is little tourism or trade between the two countries, hence no web of *jajmani*-style connections through which to conceive Pakistan-Indian relations in complementary rather than oppositional terms. In the purified world of Pakistani nationalist theory, the extreme cultural and religious pluralism of north India is flattened into a simple contrast between two distinct nations who, like the Pakistani and Indian troops at Wagah, constitute one another's negation.

The issue of rank, meanwhile, emerges according to context. Where classical Indo-Persian poetic imagery and modern Pakistani history textbooks subordinate Hindus to Muslims, the flag ceremony at Wagah allows Pakistan and India to distinguish themselves non-hierarchically, in the terms provided by a common language of military drill inherited from the British Raj. Pre-Partition speeches by Jinnah and other Muslim League leaders, similarly, differentiate Hindus from Muslims in specular rather than hierarchical terms. In all these cases, the relationship between hierarchy and equality is not simply paradoxical, or even segmentary. They are two sides of an argument, conversations in history.

Erasing the Sacred: Architecture and Textuality

Lahore's religious diversity was gutted by the population exchanges of 1947, when nearly all the city's Hindu and Sikh population left for India, replaced by Muslim families from east Punjab, Delhi, the United Provinces and other areas. There were a very few outcaste Hindu sweeper families living in the Old City and other areas in the mid-1990s, but most of the younger generation had adopted Christian names and religious observances, at least in public, due to pressure from the Muslim majority. One local journalist wrote in a feature article about this tiny community:

> While the new generation have learned to be flexible and to adapt to their hostile environment, the older Hindus cling tenaciously to their traditional roles. 'Yes, I am a Hindu,' said Kako, the old man in whose house we were sitting. 'I do my *puja*, offer *prasad* at the *mandir* and bathe in the

river Ravi. I have also asked to be cremated when I die.' 'He can admit that because he doesn't have to deal with the world outside,' his nephew inter-jected bitterly. 'We have to earn a living out there.'[17]

In the absence of Hindus with whom to compete or riot, Muslim communalism in modern Lahore is normally a somewhat abstract phenomenon. It was expressed most concretely in a wave of attacks on Hindu, Sikh and Jain temples after the 6 December destruction of the Babri Mosque in Ayodhya, India, allegedly by militant Hindu nation-alists of the Bharatiya Janata Party (BJP). The BJP and their supporters claimed that the Emperor Babur, founder of the Mughal dynasty, built his sixteenth-century mosque over the precise birthplace of the Hindu god Ram (whose son Loh, according to urban legend, was the eponym-ous founder of Lahore). This particular claim relates to a broader context of Hindu nationalist resurgence in India that is often expressed in the form of attempts to deny or denigrate Muslim contributions to the architectural history of the subcontinent.[18]

There were Hindu-Muslim riots across India in the days following the destruction of the Babri Mosque.[19] In Pakistan, with its tiny Hindu minority, there were some assaults on Hindus by Muslims in Sindh and Baluchistan. In Lahore, sacred Hindu architecture replaced live opponents.[20] According to local press reports, forty-one temples were attacked in Lahore in the two days following the Ayodhya inci-dent. All the city bazaars observed a two-day strike. On the Mall and in the Old City tyres burned on street corners, and crowds gathered to watch men with ropes and crowbars swarming over the facades of the shrines. For days there were processions of small children, beating drums and chanting slogans about the 'Hindu dogs' (*kuttai*). These demonstrations were trivial compared to the Partition riots, when Lahore was ravaged by the communal carnage that claimed perhaps a million lives in Punjab and Bengal.[21] But they do show that Muslim communalism is alive and well in Lahore, even in the absence of a significant Hindu minority.

Since Partition the temples had been empty or inhabited by squatter families. Some were also used for shop space, and at least one housed a primary school. The temples were officially owned by the federal government's Awqaf Department, which administers most religious property in Pakistan. Many of them occupied immensely valuable plots of urban real estate in the central commercial and residential districts of Lahore.[22] Local journalists argued that the destruction of the temples was the result of complicity between well-connected real estate developers and political authorities, who paid lip service to the idea of protecting minority shrines but did nothing practical to stop their destruction. The Jain Mandir was actually flattened by a municipal bulldozer while the mayor of Lahore stood by watching, according to local press reports.[23] Another temple, the Moti Mandir in Shah Alami Bazaar, had been occupied by a squatter family. There were also six shops in its courtyard. According to a grimly ironic report in *The Friday Times* of Lahore:

> The owner of the shops was a well-to-do trader who had been trying, allegedly, for the last few years to evict the family from the *mandir* and extend his little empire. According to witnesses, when the thousand strong mob converged on Moti Mandir, this trader was in its forefront. Though the temple was razed to the ground, surprisingly, his six shops were left intact.[24]

This economic conspiracy theory represents an intra-Lahori scale of discourse. From a more broadly modernist point of view, Pakistan's secular intelligentsia also read Ayodhya and its Pakistani backlash through the lens of Western-style liberalism. By failing to protect the shrines, liberal journalists and other argued, their government had yet again sold out Jinnah's vision of a tolerant, secular homeland for Muslims and religious minorities. As one Lahore editorialist put it:

> . . . tens of thousands of Pakistani Muslims need to seriously reflect upon their own savage behavior last week. In mindless retaliation against the outrage at Ayodhya, hysterical, rampaging gangs have destroyed scores of Hindu temples and shrines in Pakistan. While the fanatics were targeting innocent lives and gutting property, the government of Nawaz Sharif stood by and twiddled its thumbs.[25]

The terms 'savage', 'mindless' and 'fanatic' are keyed to the ubiquitous local rank metaphor of 'education', according to which improper behaviour of all kinds can be dismissed as a consequence of ignorance. In this sort of commentary, Pakistani liberals adopt the voice of an intellectual vanguard chastizing less 'advanced' fellow countrymen.[26] By implication, the temples would still be standing if the rest of Pakistani society were only as civilized as its liberal critics. Nationalist and local class hierarchies thus mirror one another internally just as Pakistan and India mirror one another's anxieties internationally. In other words, Pakistani nationalism is one moment in a broader cultural discourse. Lahoris tend to rank one another on a continuum of rationality in the same way that they rank themselves collectively in relation to India.

The Ayodhya affair and its aftermath in Pakistan followed a double logic of erasure. The destruction of the Babri Mosque was motivated by the desire of certain militant Hindu nationalists to remove the Muslim layer of an historical palimpsest. According to this logic, the Muslim building was erased to reveal the birthplace of the Hindu god Ram. The retaliatory destruction of Hindu temples in a city founded by Ram's son was, likewise, a politically motivated editorial intervention in a complex historical record. Erasing temples from the landscape of modern Lahore altered the city's history by selectively removing some of the traces through which it is read. The erasure of sacred architecture was a material act that sparked (or in the Lahore case, replaced) communal riots. Both relate to a modern context of political rivalry between Indian Hindus and Muslims at one level and between majority Hindu India and majority Muslim Pakistan at another. In the absence of Lahori Hindus, the material context of the destruction of temples was provided by a background narrative of property speculation and development. From the secular liberal stance that permeated press analysis of the temple destructions in Pakistan, finally, both the mosque and the temples were destroyed by 'uneducated' fanatics.

In Pakistan as in many other countries today, notions of education, rationality, and social development are keyed to a progressive theory of history derived ultimately from the Enlightenment, according to which the present takes moral as well as chronological precedence over the past. The Pakistani English term 'educated' incorporates a theory of time according to which living people are relegated to a value-laden metaphorical ('backward', 'primitive') past insofar as their behaviour violates moral standards set by more 'educated' peers. In this perspective Lahore's architectural history was edited by historical figures, men of the past who acted in the present. Not at all coincidentally, the 'educated' class is substantially identical, from a Pakistani point of view, with the economic and political ruling class.

Basant in Lahore

Lahore's ambiguous relationship with its multi-communal past is vividly apparent during the spring festival of Basant. Originally a Hindu celebration, Basant is closely associated with the central Punjabi cities of Lahore and Kasur in Pakistan and Amritsar in India. Apart from the festival itself, the word 'Basant' also refers to the vernal season, which in the Hindu calendar includes the months of Chaith and Baisakh (mid-March until mid-May), to the putting forth of yellow blossoms (particularly those of the mustard plant), and to a raga associated with springtime. Punjabi women traditionally don yellow clothes for Basant, which since the late 1980s has developed from a festive but essentially family-oriented holiday revolving around food and kite flying into a media event celebrated, at the upper class level, at huge semi-public parties attended by socialites from all over Pakistan.

In Lahore, Basant is usually celebrated on the first Friday in February, although the district administration moves the date in years when it falls during the Islamic fasting month of Ramzan or the mourning month of Moharram. In the Hindu tradition, Basant has normally been celebrated on the fifth day of the month Maagh. This dating relates to the Bikrami luni-solar calendar, formerly used in most parts of northern India, in which the lunar months are fitted into the annual progression of seasons by a mathematical system of 'intercalation and suppression'.[27] Interestingly, Lahoris refer to this Hindu calendar as the desi maahinai or 'local months', even though the extent to which they are morally 'local' is questioned by the discourse of Pakistani nationalism. Practically speaking, also, this 'local' calendar is not very relevant to the social construction of time in Lahore. While the Bikrami calendar is commonly used in the Punjabi countryside, most Lahoris only refer to its existence in the context of Basant.

The association between Basant and the Hindu calendar was apparently more pronounced before Partition, when there were still Lahori Hindus to celebrate the festival. According to the Lahore memorialist Younis Abid: 'The celebration of Basant was fixed on calendrical principles, with particular reference to the local calendar (desi maahinai).'[28] Today, most Lahoris reckon the passage of time according to the Western Gregorian calendar cross-cut with the Islamic or Hejira calendar, which determines the yearly schedule of religious observance. Because the Hejira calendar is calculated exclusively by reference to lunar cycles, it moves back ten days each year in relation to the relatively more fixed Western and desi calendars. English newspapers print either the Gregorian and Hejira dates below the masthead or the Gregorian date alone, while Urdu papers such as the daily *Jang*, Pakistan's most widely circulated publication, print the Gregorian, Hejira and Bikrami dates together.

Time is thus complex in Pakistan: the various calendrical discourses available for time-reckoning are also subject to the dialectic of sacred and secular, traditional and modern, 'backward' and 'advanced', that structures so much moral and political debate. To the extent that urban Punjabis think about the Bikrami calendar at all, it tends to be identified as an element in traditional, rural Punjabi culture. As such it can be described as either 'authentic' or 'backward', depending on the context. Calling it the 'local' (desi) calendar rather than the Hindu calendar is in itself a revisionist act of national appropriation. For a militantly anti-clerical newspaper such as *The Friday Times*, omitting Hejira dates from the masthead makes a clear statement about the relevance of Islam to contemporary political debate.[29] *Jang's* use of all three calendars, on the other hand, could be described as an ecumenical approach to time-reckoning, appropriate for a mass-circulation newspaper whose readership spans a broad range of political and religious opinion.

Younis Adib claims that in the days when Hindus, Muslims and

Sikhs all celebrated Basant in Lahore, the festival was not particularly identified with Hinduism: 'Lahoris did not celebrate Basant as Hindus or Muslims, because Basant was simply a seasonal celebration. It marked the end of the cold weather.'[30] While most modern Lahoris seem only vaguely conscious of Basant's Hindu associations, some attempt to incorporate the festival into the Muslim historical tradition by arguing that Muslims celebrated Basant with fervour in the distant past. In 1992, for example, one of the Lahore's leading kite-makers, Ustad Altaf Hussain, was interviewed about the history of Basant by a re-porter from the Karachi-based English daily *Dawn*. Asked whether Basant was in fact a Hindu festival, Ustad Altaf replied: 'Not in Lahore . . .' According to him, the festival was celebrated and kites flown in pre-Independence Lahore more by 'the . . . [Muslim] residents of the city than [by] Hindus. They dominated Basant and kite flying.'[31]

To bolster the argument that Muslims had co-opted Basant centuries before, the reporter then narrates a tradition concerning the thirteenth-century Delhi Muslim poet, musician and culture hero Amir Khusro (1253–1325), who apparently appropriated Basant for the Muslims after admiring the yellow flowers draped on Hindu idols in a temple:

> One day Hazrat Amir Khusro heard groups of people singing Hindu religious songs. . . . He followed them to a temple and saw deities laden with flowers of mustard and marigold. Returning, he placed a mustard flower in his turban and narrated the experience to his *Murshid* [in the Sufi Muslim tradition, a *pir* or spiritual guide], Khwaja Nizamuddin, who decided that Muslims should also celebrate the change of season.[32]

This syncretic charter notwithstanding, there is a lively local debate about the morality of celebrating a Hindu festival in a Muslim country. The projection of Pakistani nationalism into the indefinite past in order to create an impression of a distinct Muslim culture separate at every level from the Hindu world is of course complicated by Basant, certainly the most important event in the secular calendar of Lahore. This would appear to explain why many Pakistani Muslim preachers view it with unambiguous hostility.

This, again, is not a new trend. Adib remarks: 'Although in those days also the mullahs used to call Basant a *kafir* [infidel] festival and describe kite-flying as a Satanic activity, on this colorful day nobody listened to mullahs, and all celebrated Basant with the most utmost enthusiasm.'[33] Just before Basant in 1993, the Old City politician Mian Yusuf Salahuddin, who very much represents the regeneration of Basant in the local imagination, appeared on a Pakistan Television panel discussion arguing in favour of Basant against a local cleric who opposed it on Islamic nationalist grounds. And in 1993, as in past years, a case was lodged with the Lahore High Court petitioning that Basant be banned on the grounds that it is un-Islamic and injurious to life and property.[34]

Mian Yusuf first began holding large Basant parties in his family's Old City *haveli* (traditional, court-yarded urban mansion) in the late 1980s. Particularly at the upper level, Lahori perceptions of Basant as an annual performance of ethnic tradition appear to have sharpened during this period. In its 1993 post-Basant coverage, *The Friday Times* gushed:

> Basant madness seized Lahore this year as never before. Brought to life for high society by the inner city aristocrat and hard-core hedonist,[35] Mian Yusuf Salahuddin, Basant has become as much a celebration of ethnic chic as an observance of spring. Mian Yusuf's Haveli Barud Khana has been the venue, five years running, of the most riotous assembly of the trendy multitudes, politicians and film stars. The Haveli itself has attained a sort of cult status with its recent restoration. And Mian Yusuf and Begum Yusuf Salahuddin combine in their persons the bohemian appeal of old money and ethnic regeneration.[36]

In contrast to the negative Islamist view of Basant, Lahore Society tends to include the festival in its nostalgically mediated representations of 'ethnic' Punjabi tradition. Basant is thus a stage on which affluent, upper-class Lahoris can demonstrate that despite being as 'modern' as the next person, they are also firmly in touch with their own culture.

Since ambivalently 'ethnic' self-consciousness is mainly restricted to Society, however, these performances also enact class distinction. Like the other major Lahore Society Basant parties, Mian Yusuf's was theoretically on open-house event. News of the party circulated by word of mouth: Mian Yusuf neither announced it officially nor sent written invitations to anyone apart from foreign dignitaries such as the American Ambassador, who would not have come without an invitation and whose presence enhanced the general prestige of the event. But the party's theoretically public status was belied by practical barriers placed in the way of would-be guests who did not conform to Lahore Society's uncodified standards of social eligibility. In practice, the Barud Khana Basant party was a semi-public affair, attended only by people with sufficient social confidence to brave the intimidating array of armed guards at the haveli door, who scrutinized entrants and occasionally turned away people who did not appear to belong.[37]

Judging from Adib's account of Basant in pre-Partition Lahore, the notion that normal privacy conventions are partially relaxed on Basant appears rooted in the history of the event. Adib describes groups of young men entering empty houses 'without ceremony' (*bai-takkaluf se*) in order to snare downed kites from their rooftops. But he also notes variation in the reactions of different Old City communities to this annual expansion of public space. Because Hindu women were not subject to Muslim purdah restrictions, they used to appear on their rooftops during the festival, while Muslim women were conspicuously absent: '. . . Muslim mothers used to chase their daughters off the rooftops during Basant.'[38] In the Old City, the rooftop is mainly female space, or at least equally open to men and women: only on Basant, when Lahore's public life moved to its rooftops, would the physical boundaries of purdah have contracted to exclude the roof.

At the rooftop level, Basant integrates the communities and classes of Lahore in that its defining characteristic is the kite-filled sky. Just as the realm of public interaction shifts to the rooftop only on Basant, it is also the only day on which the sky is the focus of social activity in the city. The kites in the sky and the people on the rooftops are all connected via kite duels (*paich lara'i*),[39] which unite spatially distant strangers in a mutuality of competition and noise. Adib remarks: 'If not for Basant it's doubtful whether Lahoris would ever feel the need to open their souls and lift their eyes towards the sky.'[40] But this rhetoric of cosmic integration must be distinguished from social levelling: while Lahoris enact their commonality in the mass celebration of

Basant, they do so fairly strictly according to family, community, and class.

Metaphorically speaking, kite fighting might be compared to a *jajmani*-style division of labour, at least as idealized in classical Western Indology. As with economic or ritual relations in the Hindu caste model, people who relate via kite-fighting can remain socially distant in every other way. Thus the mainly Urdu- and English-speaking socialites on Mian Yusuf Salahuddin's rooftop flew kites that were engaged in battle by kites launched from the rooftops of the mainly Punjabi-speaking, working class households surrounding Haveli Barud Khana. The contestants never met because working class people were not welcome at Mian Yusuf's party. Most of his guests, meanwhile, only visited the Old City on the day of Basant.

People in the Old City (*puraana shehr*) tended to meet this annual high society invasion with a certain ironic reserve. In 1994, for example, Muslim children greeted the fashionable yellow-clad women emerging from the 'Ali family's party with mocking [Hindu] namastes. They were probably using religion as an idiom in which to express class antagonism, given that Basant is celebrated with particular enthusiasm by the overwhelmingly Muslim, working class population of the Old City. Certain older shehris grumbled that Mian Yusuf only welcomed 'movie stars and diplomats' while ignoring his own neighbours, many of whom were his family's traditional political supporters. Mian Yusuf responded that he didn't encourage Pakistan People's Party workers to attend the party because there were too many of them. Rather than inviting some and slighting others, it was therefore better to invite none. He also argued that the prestige derived from throwing a glamorous, celebrity-filled party, with attendant media coverage, outweighed the criticism that he was being too elitist.

Like other Basant party-givers in Lahore Society, Mian Yusuf and his wife had definite ideas about the people they wished to see at their spontaneous and open gathering. After Basant in 1994, for example, they were unhappy that the well-known film actress Reema had attended their party. The reason was simple: like many actresses in the *filmi* world her roots were in the Kanjar dancing girl community of Hira Mandi Bazaar, down the street from Mian Yusuf's Haveli. Begum Salahuddin stressed, however, that Reema had not been refused entrance: 'We were just cold to her, so that she wouldn't come back next year.' Mian Yusuf added, gesturing in the direction of Hira Mandi. 'She's a dancing girl, from that community! If I invite her then I have to invite all of Hira Mandi, all my supporters.'[41]

Mian Yusuf's Basant party is one of several on the Lahore Society circuit. Many of the estimated 400 guests in 1993, and the estimated 1000 in 1994, also visited the Shia industrialist 'Ali's family party at their restored (but unoccupied) Old City haveli in Bhatti Gate. Other major parties included an event hosted in a haveli rented for the purpose by the Pakistan Burma Shell Corporation and attended mainly by wealthy industrialists from Karachi. Perhaps the most dramatic performance of ethnic theatre was the Basant theme party thrown by the manager of the luxury Pearl Continental Hotel on the Mall. In its 1994 Basant spread, *The Friday Times* commented approvingly on the Pearl Continental's detailed evocation of an imagined rural Punjabi tradition:

> . . . [it was] a très ethnic event with *bhangra* dancers in brocade *lachas* and colourful turbans, *dhol walas* [drummers] and even an ancient box photographer complete with colorful backdrop. . . . Lunch was an extravagant meal served in the hotel grounds where an entire village had been constructed, complete with the odd cow wandering about.[42]

The cultural coherence associated with 'tradition' is projected onto the countryside, even though Basant itself has come to be identified as a quintessentially urban Punjabi celebration. Hence the anomaly of building an artificial village, complete with imported livestock, near the centre of Pakistan's second largest city. The more Basant is identified as an aspect of Lahore's 'traditional' culture, the more its celebration becomes mediated by representations of what Basant ought to be. Like tradition in general, these representations are associated with the imagined past as well as the countryside.

Yet it seems doubtful that the idea of Basant as high society theatre existed in Lahore before the late 1980s, when Mian Yusuf Salahuddin and other upper class socialites began hosting ambiguously 'open' Basant parties for the Pakistani elite. The article just quoted, meanwhile, epitomizes the nostalgia that began creeping into Lahore Society's representations of Basant in the early 1990s. Written by *The Friday Times'* Moni Mohsin under the male pseudonym Aslam Hussein, which Mohsin adopted so as not to offend those among her friends and close relatives who had hosted large Basant parties that year, it concludes by lamenting the congestion and high-pitched social tone of modern-day, high society Basant:

> At a big Basant 'do' now you can't loaf about in the sunshine, can't enjoy the glorious weather, can't sprawl on a *charpai* and stuff your face with parathas and kebabs, can't learn or teach kite-flying, can't even sit and chat with your friends. The spontaneity, the mellowness, the fun are all things of the past. As Basant grows more glitzy, more glamorous, it also becomes more 'made-to-order'.[43]

Mohsin's phrase 'made-to-order' is apt, given that Lahore Society's celebration of Basant looks increasingly like the performance of a manufactured tradition. Not everyone builds a fake Punjabi village in which to serve Basant lunch. But the increasing tendency of Anglophone, upper class Lahoris to describe Basant as an 'ethnic' festival is another indication that from their point of view Basant is becoming a simulacrum, to use Baudrillard's term,[44] the self-conscious performance of a tradition whose authentic moments are projected away from the city and into the past.

If Lahore Society sees Basant as ethnic theatre, many in Pakistan's Muslim clerical establishment tend rather to interpret the festival as an alien threat to the integrity of Islam and the Islamic Republic of Pakistan. Pakistani nationalism is predicated on the assumption that South Asian Hindus and Muslims constitute two discrete, sealed universes of thought and action. Accepting Basant as an 'authentic' part of Punjabi Muslim culture, however, implies that Hindus have indeed influenced that culture. Like the Wagah border ritual, this paradox enacts the complex moral dilemmas with which all Pakistanis are confronted as they reckon with modernity in relation to themselves.

NOTES AND REFERENCES

1. Under the terms of the February 1999 Lahore agreement between Indian Prime Minister Atal Bihari Vajpayee and Pakistani Prime Minister Nawaz Sharif, the Wagah border was opened to civilian traffic for the first time. However, the temporary bonhomie of Lahore was followed, later that year, by an Indo-Pak military confrontation in Kargil, Kashmir, a military coup in Pakistan, and the terrorist hijacking of an Indian airliner by Kashmiri militants, which the Indian government claimed was orchestrated by Pakistan. At the time of writing, relations between the two countries were frosty and the Wagah border was once again closed to civilian traffic.

2. In English translation, though not in the French original, Lacan's argument plays on the dramatic/developmental ambiguity of the word 'stage'. See Jacques Lacan, *Écritis*, trans. A. Sheridan, New York: Norton, 1977, pp. 1–7; see also J.P. Muller and W.J. Richardson, *Lacan and Language: A Reader's Guide to Écrits*, New York: International Universities Press, 1982, pp. 26–41. In a slightly different way, our discussion uses 'stage' to connote both the site of the dramatic performance and the historical moment in which it takes place. 'History' here denotes an unfolding, non-predictable array of events and meanings constructed by historical actors: we do not wish to suggest that the construction of Pakistani national identity can be explained using Western psychoanalytic stage models of individual development.

3. See Edmund Leach, 'Aryan Invasions Over Four Millenia', in Emiko Ohnuki-Tierny (ed.), *Culture Through Time: Anthropological Perspectives*, Stanford: Stanford University Press, 1999, pp. 227–45, for a trenchant essay on the dubious historicity of the Aryan invasion hypothesis as promulgated by successive generations of Indo-European language scholars and Indologists beginning with William Jones and Max Muller.

4. K.K. Aziz, *The Murder of History: A Critique of History Textbooks Used in Pakistan*, Lahore: Vanguard Books, 1993.

5. Romila Thapar reminds us that the term 'Hindu' was originally an ascription, used in Achaemenid Persian inscriptions and later by Arab geographers to describe the diverse populations living around and to the east of the Indus river. In the first instance, the Achaemenid 'Hindu' and the Arabic al-hind were thus general geographical terms rather than words denoting a unitary religious doctrine and/or community. Romila Thapar, 'Communalism and the historical legacy'. In K.N. Panikkar (ed.), *Communalism in India:*

History, Politics and Culture, New Delhi: Manohar Publications, 1991, pp. 17–33, p. 23.

6. Pakistan and India have fought two of their three wars (1948 and 1965) over Kashmir, a Muslim majority Himalayan province whose Hindu ruler opted for India at Partition. Pakistan currently controls one-third and India two-thirds of the pre-Partition state of Jammu and Kashmir. Approximately 20,000 Kashmiris have died so far in the anti-Indian uprising that began in 1990. There is a gigantic literature on the Kashmir dispute, mostly from an international relations/political science perspective. See, e.g., Virinder Grover, *The Story of Kashmir: Yesterday and Today*, 3 vols, New Delhi: Deep and Deep; 1995. Sisir Gupta, *Kashmir: A Study in India-Pakistan Relations*, Bombay: Asia Books: 1966; Iftikhar Malik, *The Continuing Conflict in Kashmir: Regional Detente in Jeopardy*, London: R.I.S.T.C. Conflict Studies No. 259, 1993; Robert G. Wirsing, *India, Pakistan and the Kashmir Dispute: On Regional Conflict and Its Resolution*, London: Macmillan, 1995.

7. '*Kashmiri mujahedin ne Bharti fauji "camp" "bomb" se ura diya hai. Chharpon mein giyaara darande maut ki vadi mein pahunch ga'ai hain'*, i.e. 'Kashmiri mujahedin blew up an Indian military camp. Eleven savage beasts reached the valley of death', *Daily Pakistan*, 28.2.1993, p. 3.

8. '*Har chand Hindu-ye tu-am chun dozdam laylat shikar/Dar har kamin beneshaandi Turkaan-e-tir-andaaz-ra'*, Wheeler M. Thackston, *A Millennium of Classical Persian Poetry*, Bethesda: Iranbooks, 1994, p. 53, my translation. In poetry, 'Turk' and 'Hindu' can also suggest pale and dark skin respectively.

9. Aziz, *The Murder of History*, p. 69.

10. The word 'Pakistan' is an acronym, coined in a 1933 pamphlet by an Emmanuel College, Cambridge student named Rahmat Ali in response to the Punjabi poet-philosopher Iqbal's call for a Muslim majority state in north-west India, within an all-India federation. The acronym incorporates letters from the names of all the provinces in the proposed state: 'P' for Punjab, 'A' for 'Afghania (the Northwest Frontier Province,) populated by Pukhtuns or 'Afghans'), 'K' for Kashmir, 'S' for Sindh and the suffix 'tan' ('land of') from 'Baluchistan'. Choudhury Rahmat Ali, *Pakistan: The Fatherland of the Pak Nation*, Lahore: Book Traders, 1947 [1933].

11. Ibid., p. 76.

12. Ibid., p. 12, trans. Aziz.

13. The following passage from the Imperial Gazetteer notes this syncretism while serving as a good example of the Raj's classificatory imagination at work: 'Akbar's policy of religious toleration lessened the gulf between the two creeds, but many Muhammadan tribes ascribe their conversion to the zeal of Aurangzeb. Islam in the Punjab is as a rule free from fanaticism, but among

the more ignorant classes it has retained many Hindu ideas and superstitions. Though the great mass of its followers profess the orthodox Sunni creed, the reverence paid to Sayyids as descendants of Ali, the Prophet's son-in-law, is unusually great, and popularly Islam consists in the abandonment of many Hindu usages and the substitution of a Muhammadan saint's shrine for a Hindu temple.' See H.A. Rose, Imperial Gazetteer of India, Punjab, vols 1-2, Lahore: Aziz Publishers, 1976, p. 50.

14. Juan Cole, 'Roots of North Indian Shi'ism in Iran and Iraq', *Religion and State in Awadh, 1722–1859*, Berkeley: University of California Press, 1988.

15. Ibid., p. 225.

16. According to Latif's account, Madho was a Brahmin boy from Shahdara, an area on the west side of the river Ravi, opposite the royal fort. Lal Hussain became enamoured of him, and added the name Madho to his own as a mark of his attachment: 'Madho became a convert to Mahommedanism, and his tomb is situated close to that of his religious preceptor.' Syad Mohammad Latif, *Lahore: Architectural Remains*, Lahore: New Imperial Books, 1892, p. 145. The *pir* and his disciple are honoured each year in one of Lahore's great religious festivals, the *Mela-e-Chiraghan* (festival of lights), which is celebrated around Madho Lal Hussain's shrine in the working class suburb of Baghbanpura.

17. 'The Last of the Balmikis', by Aliya Inam, *The Friday Times*, 6.16.1994, pp. 14–15.

18. A considerable body of revisionist literature to this effect has been published in India. In the back of a slender volume by P.N. Oak entitled, *The Taj Mahal is Tejo Mahalaya*, for example, we find an advertisement for the author's Institute for Rewriting Indian History, based in New Delhi. An appended list of the Institute's other publications includes the following titles, all by Oak: *Lucknow's Imambaras are Hindu Palaces, Delhi's Red Fort is Hindu Lalkot, Fatehpur Sikri is a Hindu City,* and *Agra Red Fort is a Hindu Building*, along with *Who Says Akbar was Great?* P.N. Oak, *The Taj Mahal is Tejo Mahalaya*: A Shiva Temple, New Delhi: Institute for Rewriting Indian History, 1978, pp. 26–7. Elsewhere Oak contends that 'All historic structures in India . . . currently ascribed to Muslim sultans and courtiers . . . are pre-Muslim Hindu constructions', ibid., 29.

19. According to Indian press reports, in the latter part of December over 1000 deaths resulted from Hindu-Muslim rioting in various (mainly urban) parts of the country; 'Bloody Aftermath', *India Today*, 31.12.1992, pp. 40–3.

20. The relationship between symbol (sacred building) and referent (religious community) is thus complex in the Lahori case. The building can be said to stand for the religious community by whom it was built. Equally, it signifies

identity in relation to the other community insofar as it is a site on which communalism is played out. The distinction can be described as a contrast between two modes of signification. The building-sign denotes a social group just as words denote objects in an Augustinian model of language. (See Ludwig Wittgenstein, *Philosophical Investigations*, trans. G.E.M. Anscombe, Oxford: Basil Blackwell, 1989, pp. 1ff). Yet it also stands as the symbolic opposite of the other group's building, taking its place (from a Pakistani point of view) in the general logic of opposition through which the two nation theory distinguishes Muslims from Hindus.

21. Stanley Wolpert, *A New History of India*, third edn., New York: Oxford, University Press, 1989.

22. According to a useful recent study of housing finance in Lahore by Tariq Habib Malik, property values in these areas rose by as much as 1500 per cent between 1983 and 1993. Tariq Habib Malik, *Housing Finance in the Developing Countries: A Case Study of Lahore, Pakistan*, Unpublished Ph.D thesis, University of Central England in Birmingham, 1994, p. 172.

23. In one of the routine ironies of South Asian politics, Indian Jains had nothing whatever to do with the destruction of the Babri Mosque.

24. 'For God's Sake', by Khalid Hussain and Moni Mohsin, *The Friday Times*, 12.17.1992, p. 15.

25. 'Killing Fields of Fundamentalism', by Najam Sethi, *The Friday Times*, 12.17.1992, p. 1.

26. Quite explicitly so: the author of the editorial just quoted, for example, is the founder and chief editor of a Lahore publishing house called Vanguard Books.

27. Robert Sewell, 'Indian Chronography', London: George Allen and Co., 1912, p. 6. See also J.N. Bagga, *Hundred Years Calendar: 1901–2000*, Allahabad: J.N. Bagga, 1970, pp. 3–4.

28. Younis Adib, *Mera Sehr Lahore*, Lahore: Atish Fishan Publishers, 1991, p. 127.

29. As the voice of Lahore Society, *The Friday Times* very much reproduced the tendency of Anglophone, upper class Pakistanis to despise Muslim preachers, who are disdainfully referred to as 'bearded gentlemen', 'beards', or 'fundamentalists'. One 1993 article about Pakistan's Islamic political parties appeared under the optimistically flippant headline: 'Grand fundo alliance may not take off', Adnan Adil, *The Friday Times*, 29.7.1993, p. 7.

30. Adib, *Mera Sehr Lahore*, p. 127.

31. 'A Festival of Kites and Colour', by Zazar Samdani, *Dawn Tuesday Review*, 11.2.1992, p. 11.

32. Ibid.

33. Adib, *Mera Sehr Lahore*, p. 128.
34. The first argument relates to religious nationalism; the latter to damage associated with kite-flying in densely populated urban areas. Every year a few people fall off rooftops while flying kites, and there is also the risk of power cuts and electrocution from kite strings tangled in high tension wires. Perhaps the greatest danger of Basant derives from the local practice of firing Kalashnikov bursts to celebrate the downing of a rival's kite. Before the 1980s people used firecrackers, but as a result of the massive arms trade associated with the war in Afghanistan, automatic weapons now permeate Pakistani society. According to local press reports, two people were killed by falling bullets in the Old City on the day of Basant in 1993.
35. In the morally censorious Pakistani context, this is a rather daring characterization.
36. 'Basant Bonanza', by Jugnu Mohsin and Rina Saeed Khan, *The Friday Times*, 18.24.1993, pp. 14–15.
37. Due to the sharp distinction between private and public space that normally prevails in local society, open house parties are unusual in Lahore: the only other common instance is the gathering held after a family death, when the doors of the home are open to anyone who wishes to come and condole, or 'do sorrow' (*afsos karna*). As with Basant, however, this opening of domestic space is not intended to include strangers. Regeneration and death are thus related in that both their ceremonial observances are marked by an ambiguous blurring of the distinction between public and private space.
38. Adib, *Mera Sehr Lahore*, p. 129.
39. The word *paich* has the general sense of spiralling or twisting. Here it refers to a manoeuvre in which rival flyers manipulate their kites so that they spiral tightly around each other, each trying to cut the other's string.
40. Adib, *Mera Sehr Lahore*, p. 128.
41. In the early 1990s the Kanjars were a vote bank of about 10,000, according to the estimates of Lahori politicians.
42. 'And now—power Basant!' by Aslam Hussein [a pseudonym], *The Friday Times*, 10.16.1994, pp. 16–17.
43. Ibid.
44. Jean Baudrillard, *Simulacres et simulation*, Paris: Galilée, 1981.

An Archive with a Difference:
Partition Letters

URVASHI BUTALIA

Introduction

T HE PARTITION OF India into two countries, India and Pakistan, in 1947 is without doubt the most cataclysmic event to have taken place in the country's contemporary history. In terms of its scale, its wide-ranging impact, and its many resonances and ramifications in the lives of Indians today, Partition remains singularly important. Just the bare statistics are staggering: roughly ten to twelve million people are said to have moved, within the space of a few months, between the new, truncated India and the newly-created Pakistan. Between 500,000 to one million people are believed to have died, hundreds of thousands of children lost and abandoned, between 75,000 to 100,000 women raped and abducted. There is no real record of the number of families separated, the fields of crops left to rot, the homes destroyed, nor of the perilous journeys people made as they fled to their new homelands by train, car, lorry and on foot. This long and painful movement was accompanied, and often prompted, by slaughter and violence, as people who till then had lived, despite their differences (or perhaps because of their differences), in some kind of social contract, suddenly began to see each other as enemies. The grief of leaving home and hearth, friends, wives, children, husbands, was compounded by the inhospitable conditions in which people travelled, the virtual penury that dogged them, and the violence and danger lurking at every corner. Nor did the destination promise certain safety—for without money and resources, it was far from easy to arrive in a new and possibly hostile environment and try to make a life there.

For a half century now, historians have argued about whether or not Partition could have been avoided and about who was primarily responsible not only for the event itself, but for its tragic and horrifying consequences. A great deal of research has gone into the political aspects of Partition and into profiling its principal actors (Nehru, Gandhi, Patel, Jinnah, Mountbatten) as well as the organizations they were part of (the Congress, the Muslim League, the British Empire).

This wealth of writing on the political aspects of Partition however, hides other aspects of its history on which historians and others have long remained silent. These are the experiences of the people— women, children, men, people differentiated by caste and class, by religion—who lived through the time. Until recently, we have known little about what the experience of Partition meant for those who lived through it, how they put their lives back together again, how they coped with the loss, the trauma, the grief. This silence about what I call the 'underside' of the history of Partition, that is, its human dimensions, its many hidden histories, is not a silence of simple historiographical neglect. Rather, it is, to my mind, a silence because Partition represents, for historians as well as others, a trauma of such deep dimensions, that it has needed nearly a half century for Indians to acquire some distance, and begin the process of coming to terms with it. The historical explorations of Partition we are seeing now are deeply rooted in contemporary political realities, in the kinds of polarizations along lines of religious identity that have become a part of the realities of people's lives in India today. It is these that have forced people's attention to Partition and to the stories of its victims and survivors.[1]

A Personal Beginning

My own work on Partition began several years ago. The initial impetus came as a result of my involvement with feminism and secularism. Like many Punjabis of my generation I come from a family of Partition refugees. Stories of Partition and its many horrors have formed the staple of my childhood and like many others of my generation, I listened to them without really taking them in. But it was the experience of living in Delhi in 1984 and watching the brutal and senseless massacre of thousands of Sikhs after the death of Mrs Gandhi, that brought home to me the violence of Partition. For many people who lost homes and families in the violence of that time, the experience was 'like Partition again'. Listening to the survivors talk about how 'this time' was similar to 'that time' I began to understand, at first only partially, how deeply Partition had touched and scarred those who had lived through it. And how little we, who had not lived through that time, understood this because often we simply did not have the patience, or indeed the time, to listen to the stories we had grown up with. I realized too, the inadequacy of my secularism: I had grown up in an atmosphere of relative calm and prosperity and with the assumption that religious differences did not count for much. Yet across the River Jamuna, barely a few miles from where I lived, people had killed each other for no apparent reason other than that they belonged to a different religion. Men were the main targets, but it was the women who were left behind to take on the business of putting lives together again. I began to feel that we needed to understand these realities if we were to make any difference with our work as secular Indians.

If 'secularism' (a much maligned and contested word today) drew me into this work, it was my involvement with feminism that turned my attention to women, children and others marginalized by society. I began a slow, painful and eventually rewarding process of collecting testimonies from Partition survivors. It was through this process that, gradually, I began to understand that even in my own family—where the history had not been one of violence and bloodshed—Partition was not a closed chapter of history. I decided therefore to begin the process by exploring my own family history.

Partition divided our family as it did hundreds of thousands of others. Although we did not have to face any physical violence, the trauma of the division remained with my mother and her family. At Partition, my mother's younger brother, Rana, stayed back in Lahore and chose to convert to Islam after marrying a Muslim. My mother, her sisters and their other brother, Billo (who has since died), saw this as an act of betrayal—not only because Rana had converted to another religion but also because he had held on to the family property and so no one was able to claim compensation for it on the Indian side. Much worse, however, was the fact that he had kept my grandmother back mainly because—my mother and her sisters felt—the property was in her name and she, a devout Hindu and Arya Samaji, had been forced to convert to Islam. Although we—my sister, my brothers and I—had heard about Rana and our grandmother all our lives, we had not paid much attention to their stories. It was only when I began working on Partition that I started to re-explore his story.

Forty years after he had been separated from his family I went to see Rana. The family had had no contact with him in the meanwhile. I arrived at his home without warning and then spent a fair amount of time with him on that and subsequent visits, talking and trying to find out his side of the story. Although my mother had not attempted to stop me on this journey, I was aware of her sense of unease about it. I have described this journey in detail in my book. *The Other Side of Silence*.[2] Here, I'd like to draw attention to two details—my mother's sense of betrayal where Rana was concerned came, first, from his re-fusal to allow my grandmother to leave, and second, from what she saw as his desire to hold on to the family property. In her mind, the two were closely connected. Rana had not, she felt, kept my grandmother back out of any special love for her, but because she was the owner of a substantial piece of land and a house. He had had no qualms about 'forcing' her to convert to another religion. She saw her brother as mercenary and scheming. This belief was confirmed when, just before Partition, she went to Lahore to try and bring her mother away and she came across a letter from one of her uncles to Rana, which advised him to hold on to his mother, and not let her, my mother Subhadra, take her away. If the mother went with Subhadra to India, the letter said, then that would be the end of the property—Rana would not be able to lay claim to it.

It was this letter that, in many ways, put the seal on Rana's betrayal, and acted to separate him from his family. Years later, after I had visit-ed Rana and re-established contact, it was once again a letter which brought him back in contact with, and into the hearts of, his remaining family. Rana wrote to his sisters, describing his life in Pakistan, and I carried the letter across for him to India. At first my mother and my aunts were suspicious of this letter and they sat around, fearful of open-ing it, touching it gingerly, carefully. Then someone unfolded it and they began reading, tentatively and then with growing absorption. Within minutes it was being passed from hand-to-hand, touched, smelt, laughed and wept over—suddenly my mother and her sisters had acquired a family across the border.

Rana's letter was the first of many such communications our fami-lies exchanged. At the time, I did not pay it much attention—it was only later that I began to realize its importance. In order to explain this, however, I shall have to tell another story. Together, these two stories prove for me that the process of arriving at a different understanding of events and processes of history is often half random, half deliberate. By this I mean that I did not set out specifically to look at letters as an archive that might lead to a more complex understanding of the under-side of the history of Partition. But having come across letters more or less by accident, my attention was drawn to them as an important source for the kind of historical exploration that focuses not on the grand narratives but on the small, intimate stories that make up the history of a time, an event. The story I tell below illustrates this point.

Bedi and Latif: Crossing Borders

One day, an article in a Pakistani newspaper, *The News*,[3] told a moving story about a school teacher from Lahore, Harkishan Singh Bedi. Bedi was one among the many millions who were forced to leave for India as the communal situation worsened. He left, without any warning or preparation, leaving behind everything, but particularly his treasured books and papers. His house in Lahore was then allotted to a refugee from India, Chaudhry Latif. In December 1947, shortly after Chaudhry Latif had settled into his new home, he received a letter from Jullundar addressed simply to The Occupant. Opening it, he read, in Urdu: 'I hope you will not mind me writing to you. I write to you not as a Hindu but as a human being. We are human beings first and Hindus and Muslims only after that.' The letter spoke of Bedi's love for his home of many years, it described each nook and cranny, each box in which Bedi had left his precious books and papers, and asked 'The Occupant' to not destroy these. Chaudhry Latif responded by following Bedi's careful instructions, locating the things he mentioned, making them up into small packets and sending them to Bedi in Jullundar. For many years afterwards the two men wrote regularly to each other. Their correspondence, their long friendship by letter, came to light after Chaudhry Latif's death, when his daughter-in-law found all Bedi's letters neatly tied in a bundle and stored inside an almirah, a valuable record, not of violence and loot, but instead of the bonds of humanity and friendship stretching across borders.

Hitherto, my work on Partition had consisted of interviewing people who had lived through Partition in order to bring their experiences to bear on the way the history of this time had been written. It was in their stories that, I felt, the voices of Partition could be heard. In many ways, they were the voices of history, the voices that gave this major event the manifold and complex meanings it has in our lives. Over time, I began to realize that the voices I was attempting to hear and interpret resided in many places and these were not necessarily egalitarian: for example, a major part of the discourse on Partition is framed in the voice of the State. There were a number of oppositional voices to be heard too, for instance those of people who were opposed to Partition, who believed it should not have happened. Then, there were the voices of ordinary people—of men, of women and children, of minorities, of scheduled caste women and men, of others such as mental patients and so on—which had had to struggle against the more powerful voices to be heard, and who had, more often than not, been ignored. If these voices were to be heard, I felt, it was important that I turn my attention to the sources in which they could be located: oral histories, testimonies, diaries, memoirs. I had, however, not considered letters as one such source.

A Different Archive

It was the story of Bedi and Latif that turned my attention to letters written during and after Partition. I did not expect to find much—Bedi and Latif had been exceptions I thought—for in times of such dramatic upheaval, it seems unlikely that people would actually write letters. And in some ways this was what had happened: the archive that might contain personal letters, people's reflections, at the time, on what they saw around them, on the loss of homeland, family, friends—this was an archive that seemed to me to be lost to us. Not only did it seem that people had not written letters, as they might do in more 'normal' times, but those who had, had not preserved them. Life after Partition took on a different turn, and many people felt it unnecessary to keep memories that they felt were best put away. But if personal letters were unavailable, perhaps there were other sources that might yield other kinds of letters. I turned therefore to another archive, official files and documents, to see what they would yield. And it was here that I came across a rich resource of letters written, not to friends and relatives but to different figures of authority, to political leaders, the government, expressing a wide range of concerns. People were anxious to know what exactly Partition would mean for them, in terms of their homes, their jobs; they wanted to understand why political leaders had agreed to Partition: had they even considered what this would mean for their—the people's—lives? They asked about resettlement, about property, about their rights as citizens, they made offers of help, they expressed reproach and betrayal. I was excited by both the potential and the limitations of this archive: the potential because it allowed for an understanding of what it was that occupied and concerned people as Partition became imminent, and then, as that history played itself out in their lives; and the limitations because the glimpse it allowed was, after all, only partial and related to those who could write, and more especially, those who felt confident of writing to people in authority.

Through all the letters I looked at, notwithstanding their sense of reproach, and sometimes alienation, ran a thread of commitment to the new nation, and to the newly-forming state. As people made more and more complaints to the state, and addressed their grievances to it, it was almost as if they were addressing themselves to a parent, expressing their sense of rejection, bewilderment, betrayal, and, at a deeper level, loyalty. We have been loyal to you, the letters seemed to say, why have you let us down? If you continue to do so, they sometimes threatened, we will give you up, we'll stay on in Pakistan, we will convert to the other religion—the ultimate rejection. This sense of the state as *mai-baap*, both mother and father rolled into one, has been noted by various historians.[4] In many ways, it was a sense the state itself cultivated: the whole relief and rehabilitation operation of the Indian state had as its basis a kind of charity, a sort of looking-after-its-children role that the state extended towards its citizens. Like a child who has been deprived, the refugee was a victim of circumstance. He (and in most cases it was a 'he'—women refugees called up different responses) was wounded, hurt and needed healing. An account of the genesis and development of the Ministry of Relief and Rehabilitation describes the horror and devastation of Partition and then goes on to say: 'That is the first part of the saga. The second revolves round the indefatigable effort to bring healing to these bruised masses of humanity, to wipe away their tears, apply balm to their wounds, assuage their hunger and thirst, clothe their nakedness.'[5] If the refugee, then, looked upon the state as its parent, the state equally looked upon the refugee as its child. This relationship was to change over time, as refugees began to mobilize on questions of their rights as citizens and began to make demands of the state. For the moment, however, the letters expressed principally a sense of reproach and betrayal.

The state-as-parent relationship had, I believe, to do with other issues as well. The post-1947 Indian state was no longer a foreign state. Born of a difficult birth, beset with more than its fair share of problems, the fledgling India nonetheless belonged to its citizens. Because of the kind of mobilization the nationalist movement had achieved, the sense of identification, perhaps even the sympathy, with the new, emerging state was significant. Equally, people's expectations were vast, and the sense of betrayal they felt when these were not fulfilled, also greater. This was perhaps the reason so many letters expressed a sense of reproach when people felt the state had failed them. All sorts of complaints and demands—for small sums of money, for help with a job, for help with setting up a shop, for reinstating a particular officer—were addressed to the state in the form of letters. To me, these letters became very important: they spoke of people's immediate concerns at the time, concerns that, in retrospect, were not so sharply articulated when people narrated their stories several decades later. Perhaps because of the time that had elapsed between the actual occurrence and the recounting of people's stories, the sort of concerns that we see reflected in the letters, did not figure, by and large, in the longer narratives of the interviews. Some of them had been resolved—for example the need for jobs, housing etc.—while others had been replaced by different concerns.

The letters also turned my attention to the fact that there are differences in the way memory structures events, and the way they are recounted at the time they take place. By the time I came to doing my first interview, forty years had elapsed after Partition. The spirit of involvement in the new nation that marks many of the letters, the sense almost of belonging and ownership, was not in evidence in any of the interviews that I conducted then, and in the years that followed. The relationship with the state seemed to have undergone a shift: no longer was it one of the parent and its children. Indeed, the state itself had changed in character; it had become somewhat authoritarian, it had taken on a distance and remoteness, and many people saw it as an institution from which they could perhaps hope to gain little, but to which they could nonetheless address specific demands as a matter of right. 'You are filling all these tapes,' Manmohan Singh of Thamali told me, 'do you think they will make any difference to anyone?' In other words, could I expect the state to take any account of what I was doing? Did the state even care?[6] This sense of resignation, acceptance and disillusionment was much more in evidence in the interviews conducted several decades after Partition.

Traumatic though Partition was, it retained, in many ways, the imbalances of society. For all those who had the access, and the education, to write these letters (and perhaps have their complaints attended to), there were thousands who did not, whose complaints, grievances, and sense of betrayal were never able to find this kind of expression. Very few of the letters that I looked at, for example, were by women. And when they were, none that I looked at expressed concerns specific to women: perhaps these were not 'legitimate' enough, or could not be easily expressed, or perhaps it is, as Sherna Gluck and Daphne Patai say, that women's voices often express those things that women feel others want to hear.[7] And if there are few letters by women, there are none from those who could not read or write, or from those whose identities were perhaps not 'legitimate' enough for them to make claims on the state. By this I mean, for example, the many prisoners who were exchanged by the two countries, or real life mental patients such as the ones we meet in fiction about Partition, or people such as eunuchs, who live on the fringes of society, or indeed the thousands of abandoned or destitute children of whom I have spoken elsewhere. As another kind of voice then, these letters are both important, and limited.

I

The first group of letters I would like to look at includes those that offer help and support to the state. Refugees—and indeed others—with money, time, or labour to offer, wrote to those in power, asking what they could do. On 29 May 1948 Thakur Phool Singh, M.L.A. from Meerut, wrote to the All India Congress Committee. His letter said:

Poojya Pant ji

I think one of the greatest needs of the refugees is the housing problem. Next comes that of making them self-supporting. Even amongst the refugees the cases of those women who have nobody left to support them or those unfortunate ladies who are being recovered from Pakistan and are not being readily accepted by the relations and the orphans, deserve special attention. An industrial home for these persons is greatly in need. It is proposed to build one such house in Meerut district where we have about 3 lakhs of rupees at our disposal at present, some of which is likely to be spent in building houses. I wonder whether this amount will be enough for the purpose. In any case, finances will be forthcoming in case this is not enough.

But the main difficulty is that none of us has any idea as to what an industrial home will be like? Please suggest somebody who can be of help in
the matter. It will also be of use to know the name of any such institution
whether within or outside the province'which can serve as a model.[8]

I was struck by this letter for the many resonances it has with the kinds
of citizens' responses we see in civil society today. In times of crisis, for
example during the anti-Sikh riots in Delhi in 1984, or in the wake of
the destruction of the Babri mosque, concerned groups of citizens
came forward with all kinds of offers of help. The difficulty, for many
who wanted to help, was to know what form such help should take,
of where and how to direct their initiative. How, they asked, could
they show their solidarity with those who were affected? Thakur Phool
Singh's letter, asking advice about how to run a women's home, seems
to me to be part of the same kind of response. In this, as with other
letters that follow, I was unable to trace whether or not the state had
actually provided the kind of information that Thakur Phool Singh
was asking for. The chances are that such information was not forthcoming. One of the continuing ironies that this letter points to is the
gap between what is needed on the ground for those who are affected,
and what the state is able to provide, or indeed what citizens are able
to do, given their limited resources.

Although Partition is often characterized only by the violence that
formed part of it there are many other aspects to it that need examining. We are aware, because of the way existing histories have been
written, of the massive rehabilitation effort mounted by the Indian
state to provide relief and help settle the many millions of refugees who
flowed in. But what the above letter highlights is that there must have
been many hundreds or thousands of ordinary citizens who took on
the task of helping to settle refugees. Partition histories have not traced
the involvement of such people—how did the experiences of working
in camps, of trying to collaborate with the state, of helping people in
need, impact on them? How far were they able to carry on the work
they had begun? How did such close interaction with refugees affect
those who worked with them?

If there were people like Thakur Phool Singh who were seeking ways to help, there were also those who had actually been involved in some kind of social and/or political work, and now found themselves at a loss for something to do. Things were in a state of flux. There were no easy slots into which people could fit their work. They wrote asking for advice of the kind the following letter requests:

Jai Hind

I am coming from Frontier Province (Pakistan) where I worked in the Congress for about 26 years. I was an organizer and worker of Frontier Congress and my work was appreciated by the Provincial Congress as well as our great leader, Pandit Jawaharlal. I remained in jail several times in connection with the civil disobedience movement. I spent a high portion of my properties in Congress work [many people donated their property to the Congress, as this writer claims to have done] and what [I] saved [was] lost in Pakistan. I came here with bare head and three clothes on my body.

I am seeking the way to serve my motherland under Congress discipline but regret to say that still I could not find way to start.

No body knows me here and my work done in the Congress fold in my dear Province. Here in UP [where] I want to pass my further life the Congress organisations and as well as administration are ignoring me. They won't . . . take me as an ordinary member even. My previous time of life [was] spent in the national movements to [for] which I have pride . . . now I am of 56 and forcibly exiled from my home I am wandering disappointed. Will you kindly advise me what to do and where to do in this critical moment of my life. I have also extreme heart still to serve my national country. Jai Hind.[9]

The backbone of political parties is made up of rank and file members. Their commitment and sense of belonging, however, is not necessarily appreciated by those in power. In times of dislocation and upheaval such as Partition, political leaders might have been able to carve new niches for themselves, but for the cadres things were not so easy. They were not known in their new homes and communities, and were often reliant on the largesse and tolerance of others around them.

The kind of plea contained in the letter above, however, was less common than the large number of complaints several of the letters contain. Many bore a sense of grievance: we have been faithful citizens, they said, working for the Congress Party, helping to control communal violence, committed to the new nation, and now that we have been dislodged, and our lives thrown out of gear, the government, in particular the Congress Party, has discarded us. It has no time for us, it is too busy making its own power base. This enormous sense of grievance was only compounded by the kinds of expectations people had of the state. Looking to it as the only authority capable of intervening to set their lives back on an even keel, people appealed to the state for all manner of redress. In June 1948 a woman who identified herself as the 'wife of Mehta Ram' wrote to the Minister for Relief and Rehabilitation:

Sir

My husband Mehta Raja Ram was a Political Worker in the Pind Dadan Khan Tehsil Chakwal. His views were in distinct conflict with those of Muslim League, which stood for creating a poisonous atmosphere against the Hindus in general and Congress in particular.

The activities of my husband drew upon him the wrath of the League-minded official of the District and he had to abscond from the place all alone, or else he would . . . have been exterminated without any trace being left.

After he had successfully reached this side of the border he made repeated attempts to get us evacuated and ultimately 'Free Air Passage' was granted to the Petitioner and her children. This would be apparent from the Register and other documents showing allotment of air passages relating to the evacuation of Evacuees from Chakwal on 5 November 1947

After, however, the undersigned had boarded the plane, the undersigned was told by the Conductor-in-charge that she must pay Rs 264 as fare or get out. To ask a person to [get] out in the circumstances then existing, was tantamount to pushing him or her on the knife of the assassin, more especially as the aerodrome is 5 miles away from the town with hardly any reliable means of conveyance.

The undersigned was penniless and this sudden and unexpected demand would have resulted in the massacre of her self and her children, but for the fact that one Pir Santokh Raj Jogi, then present, took pity on her and lent her the amount.

The undersigned and her husband have brought absolutely nothing from Pakistan, and have no property. In spite of their best efforts, they have not been able to pay off their debt. They have a large family to support.

It is inconceivable as to why the undersigned should have been coerced into paying when free passage had been sanctioned.

It is humbly requested that a sum of Rs 264 be paid to the undersigned as passage be refunded to her and the previous intimation [an earlier application for a refund of this amount had been refused] turning down her request be reviewed and cancelled.[10]

Mehta Raja Ram was a worker with the Provincial Congress Committee, Ajmeri Gate, Lahore. His membership of the Congress, and the fact that he had been supporting of its policies and had fought the Muslim League—for which reason he was forced to flee at short notice—is seen to legitimize the claim his wife is making on the state. This sense, that something was owed to those who had been loyal and supportive, runs through many of the letters written by refugees that fill the files of the All India Congress Committee. There is no evidence—or none that I have been able to trace—that the state actually responded to such appeals from its citizens.

II

For the Indian state, as indeed for the Pakistani, it was not easy to keep track of refugees. Sheer numbers made this impossible. Although attempts were made to regulate the flow and to house people in specific areas, this did not always work. And yet, some kind of record had to be kept in order that relief could be provided, and, at a later stage, housing and other forms of compensation made available. Keeping a record was also important so that relief and compensation—in whatever form—went to those who were 'bonafide' refugees. But this presented the state with particular difficulties. Often, families were scattered—some had come away, others had stayed on or been killed or were simply missing, lost somewhere along the way. How could the authorities determine whether a person claiming compensation on the Indian side had actually lost his/her property on the other side, that one or other member of the family had not stayed back out of choice, in which case the other's claim to property would not be valid? One way of ensuring that this did not happen was to ask refugees to register themselves. But this brought its own problems. How could the state ensure that people were actually who they said they were? In several cases they had no papers, nothing to prove their claim to a particular identity. How, then, could a legitimate identity be assumed for the purposes of relief? The legislation that empowered the police to register each refugee, also required that the police note down the identification marks on each refugee's person as proof that that person was indeed who they said they were. Yet, how could police do this unless they examined the person? A further difficulty arose with the requirement of a physical examination of women and girl children: male police could not, under any circumstances, do this. Under pressure to remove this clause, the government yielded, but brought in an equally problematic requirement. The police were granted exemption from recording identification marks on women and children if the head of the family (assumed to be male) stated that he did not know of any such marks.

Concerned at this, Hiranand Karamchand, an editor from Karachi, wrote the following letter to various newspaper editors and political leaders in June 1948:

Dear Sir

I am surprised that the Director of Information Bombay in his Press Note, published in your issue of the 15th instant, states that the Refugees were under wrong impression that the presence of every member of the family at the Police Station is required under the Act, for the purpose of registration. But will the Director deny that the authorities of at least some Police Stations, did require every member of the family to be brought before the Police Station, before accepting their registration. If under the Act the presence of women and children is not essential, what steps have been taken against the Police officials responsible for the order that all members of the family must be brought before them, before certificate of Registration could be issued to them. In any case, how are the Refugees to be blamed if they are asked by the Police officials that Registration could be effective only if all members of the families are brought before them.

But how can even the Police Authorities be blamed for putting the interpretation on the Act as it is specifically laid down in the Registration certificate given in the appendix, that identification marks of every person registered are to be noted down in the Registration Certificate, and how can these identification marks to be noted down, by the Police officials, without sc[r]eening every individual concerned. The Director now naively says that the recording of these identification marks is not to be insisted upon, though no such clarification is given in the Act anywhere. It is obvious that the Government has seen fit to modify its attitude with respect to this clause, after realising the strength of public feeling in the matter. But even instead of gracefully withdrawing the entire clause, it has thought fit to retain the clause, but has only instructed the Police authorities to grant exemption to recording of identification marks of women and children, if the head of the family states that he does not know them. It is absurd to say that the head of the family is not likely to know the identification marks of his wife, children, or ward. But the government wants them to speak untruth, to get exemption from recording the identification marks of women and children. The Refugees, however, object in principle to the very recording of identification marks, as it reduces them to the position of criminals.

It should not however be understood that these minor modifications make the Act unacceptable to Refugees. There are still features in the Act, which are offensive to the self-respect of Free Citizens, e.g. reporting to Police station, every time, any change in the address etc. Those who seem to applaud the Act, will realize its obnoxious nature, if the Act were suddenly applied to the non-refugee population as well.[11]

Defining the refugee as a refugee was important for the state. Else how could rehabilitation be set in motion? Registration was one part of the process of definition: it could enable state functionaries to keep track of people, to estimate the size of the problem. Legislation played an important part in this process: each act of the state had to receive legislative sanction. Thus, when abducted women had to be recovered, the state needed to enact an enabling legislation that allowed it to do so; when the children of abducted women became a problem, the definition of an abducted person had to be constructed in such a way that it could incorporate children. So also, when refugees had to be provided relief or rehabilitated, legislation had to be enacted that could allow the state to establish the credentials of those claiming relief. But for the refugees, such measures were like rubbing salt in their wounds. As the writer of this letter pointed out, some of the measures that were being proposed were 'offensive to the self respect of Free Citizens'. In several of these letters we find these early articulations of the rights of refugees, their rights, that is, as free, and theoretically equal, citizens. In the interviews, done several years later, by contrast, this right is not asserted so fiercely: it is, I think, taken much more for granted, and understood much more realistically, for citizens have now had a chance to experience the state in all its complexity and even though they may continue to address demands to it, there is an awareness of what they can realistically expect from the state.

III

Once Partition became imminent, people began to move, in large numbers, to places where they felt they would be safer. Much of the movement across the border was collective. As far as possible, communities tried to move *en masse*, and once settled in their new home, tried to recreate the secure bounds of the community as they had been, albeit in altered circumstances. This was essential if people were to recover a sense of security. Several requests were made to the state to rehabilitate people so that they could again be with their own kind. One such letter was written to the Prime Minister of Bombay by the Puj Wawa Panchayat, Karachi. It said:

Worthy Sir

. . . Ours is a small, poor, industrial-cum-mercantile Panchayat of Karachi, founded even before the advent of the British in Sind; and our Panchayat was registered under 'Deti Leti' Act. In consists of about 500 families with congregation of about 1,500 members, males, females and children. We were carrying on our trade and profession viz. chiefly manufacture of confectionery including mithai, all sorts of biscuits, choc[o]lates, toffee etc, and all jaggery preparations and condiments, it being our traditional trade and occupation. We never participated [in] the present political crisis least we had intention of leaving our Sweet Homes and now we have all migrated to this province to the Area of Greater Bombay and are scattered over in various camps viz. Chembur, Pavai, Mulund, Akbar and Kalyan.

Though all of us have lost everything in Pakistan, we have not lost faith in Providence & endeavour. . . . Though poor, we would hesitate to be burden on your most benevolent Govt. and would carry on our trade even on small scale is [if] sufficient financial and housing aid is afforded to us by your honour. We all of us are so customed and habituated that we all used to live in close proximity to each other, and a big mohalla in Karachi was termed unofficially as 'Sawa Para' where most of us had our own buildings. We have been by nature most docile and immobile in our trade and traditions.

We therefore request that a portion of one, the above named camps on G.I.P. Rly., preferably at Matunga, when ready, may be given to our Panchayat people, all in a Group in one camp, on rental system as I am prepared to supply you a list of all such families. This will facilitate us to retain our old customs, trade and traditions & brotherhood and shall be able to help each other through thick and thin.[12]

The need to band together was strong. Many families were now different in composition with one or other member being missing or dead; community leaders were often the first to die in the violence, and there was an extreme sense of vulnerability in being alone—without the support of the community—in a new environment. This request for a piece of land where the original community could be recreated, grew out of this sense of insecurity and the need to recreate old structures. People also became increasingly anxious to ensure that their own representatives, or people of their own kind (and this was usually defined in religious terms) were placed in positions of power. The assumption was that Hindus in power would automatically offer protection and security to Hindus and Muslims would do the same for

Muslims. Partly this perception grew from the fact that people in power who belonged to the 'other' community had, by and large, aligned—either voluntarily or out of lack of choice—with their own community. Thus if the officers in the police and administration in a particular place were Muslim, the Hindu and Sikh population of that area felt vulnerable. If they were Hindu, the Muslim population felt vulnerable.

In June 1947, a Congress worker by the name of Rao (the full name is actually not clear on the letter) wrote to the General Secretary, Provincial Congress Committee in Lahore, expressing his concern that: 'the district administration is completely composed of Mohemmadan officers. Except the D.C. (anti Hindu) and Superintendent of Police who are Europeans, almost all are Mohemmadans. . . . It should be particularly noted in this respect that within a few days four Hindu or Sikh officers have been transferred. . . . These transfers have made to feel Hindus of the district, their hopelessness and a great panic is prevailing everywhere in the Hindu mind particularly at the Headquarters of the District.[13] He pointed out that not only were all officers Muslim but the Hindus felt further trapped because all transport companies were, by and large, owned by Muslims 'who do not book the Hindu passengers and they help Muslims in their sabotaging activities.'[14]

And if Hindus and Muslims demanded that their own people be put into positions of power, the real minorities, the Christians, the Harijans, also had similar requests. In November 1948 the All Christian Welfare Society protested—in a letter addressed to Dr Rajendra Prasad, President of the Union of India—at the fact that the Subcommittee on Minorities Rights convened by the Premier and Speaker of the East Punjab Provincial Assembly had no Christian representative:

Sir

By a Resolution passed in the Emergency Meeting held in Simla on 8 November 1948, I as the President [of the Society] was authorised by the Society to write and inform you the reactions of Christians in East Punjab as contained in my statement given to the Press which appeared in the 'Statesman' dated 3 November 1948. From these statements you will gather that my Society representing the Indian Christians & Anglo Indians in the East Punjab views with concern the manner & the mode in which the Christian interest has been scandalously ignored in the so-called sub-committee for Minorities Rights convened by the Premier & the Speaker of the East Punjab Provincial Assembly. As a matter of fact the name of the sub-committee is a misnomer because it consists of the representatives of two majority communities, the Hindus & Sikhs, who in the last analysis of things are intended to be the ruling class & other minorities & their individuals would be the subject nation according to the present inferences which can be drawn from the reported deliberations of the said sub-committee.

It will perhaps interest you that since 15th August 1947, all the key positions either in the general administration or in the judiciary & the university invariably have been given by the East Punjab Government & Legislature to the Sikhs or Hindus & none whatsoever to a Christian. The unfortunate implication in the opinion of my Society of this is that our Government perhaps considers that merit, ability & sense of civic responsibility are the exclusive embodiments of those citizens of the East Punjab who are either Sikhs or Hindus. This we think is stark communalism in practice and much militates against the practical application of the doctrine of the one nation theory or composite nationalism as contemplated either in the Resolution of our Beloved Prime Minister which was passed by your Constituent Assembly in January last year, or in the declared policy of the Congress High Command & its popular President Dr P. Sitaramaiyaji.[15]

The writer went on to say that his Society had made several attempts to seek representation on various bodies but to no avail. Everywhere Hindus had been favoured and 'no reply is received to the representation made by this Society that the one vacancy which is left unfilled [on the Local Simla Committee] should be given to a Christian in view of the fact that a certain Dr Poyindar & before her Colonel Grant was holding this seat in the Municipal Committee Simla.' He added:

In reply to our representation that the sub-committee for Minorities Rights should include a Christian we are told that the Committee is the creation of the Members of the East Punjab Legislative Assembly & therefore no outsiders can be co-opted. The root trouble is that although

members of the United Punjab were co-opted as members of the Legislature, our Government did not extend the same treatment to Christians
because no Christian M.L.A. came over to the East Punjab. This is a serious
miscarriage of justice resulting in lack of representation on democratic
lines of the Christian interests in our Provincial Legislature who therefore
can ignore with impunity the democratic rights of all Christian citizens in
the East Punjab, in this important period of formative transition in the
building of our Nation.[16]

The letter pleaded for a recognition of the rights of Christians as bona-
fide citizens of a secular state. No matter that they were in a minority,
this did not mean that they could be denied even the 'elementary rights
of citizenship either in theory or in practice'. Like the Christians, the
Scheduled Castes also felt threatened. Long before Partition actually
became a *fait accompli*, they had begun to make representations to
those in power, asking how their interests would be protected in the
new, changed situation. Not only were they a significant minority in
Punjab, they had begun increasingly to represent themselves as being
separate from the Hindus. Since they were an organized group politically, their voices were heard—if only marginally—more than the
voices of individuals or of those, such as Christians, who did not command the same sort of political clout. Among their key concerns was
the fact that Partition was against their real interests because they were
not seen as a separate community, but were rather subsumed under the
more 'general' category of Hindus. In a letter written to the Governor
of Punjab in June 1947 the President of the Punjab Provincial Scheduled Castes Federation said that the scheduled castes would 'prefer
death rather than to be governed or ruled by any other pure majority
of one religion in the divided Punjab.' He put forward the demand
that the scheduled castes needed 'real representatives' in the Legislative
Assembly and said that they had 'no faith in congress and as such the
present congressite Harijan M.L.A. can no longer speak on behalf of
the Scheduled Castes.'[17] Thus, only their own representatives, and
only those elected by them, could represent their interests. Harijans
(scheduled castes) who were in power because of the Congress did not
have the same legitimacy.

IV

The tremendous uncertainty created by the imminence of Partition had the result of making numbers seem particularly important. In moments of tension, people band together, they close ranks against the 'other'. Certain physical spaces are defined as 'safe'—because the greater strength of numbers can enable one or other community to control that space—while others become unsafe. Geography, too, now comes to be seen in terms of 'us' and 'them'—this is our part, this is theirs. Strength, clearly, lies in numbers. For Hindus and Muslims in the years leading up to Partition, one reality that was quite clear at the national level was that the Hindus and Sikhs formed the majority while Muslims were, in relation to them, a minority. This carried with it all the baggage that accompanies articulations of majority/minority status. The terms majority and minority are invested with a sort of power that relates largely to numbers. Majorities refer to a larger numerical strength and the logical assumption is that therefore they are more powerful than minorities whose numbers are similar. In Punjab, however, the situation was not quite so clear cut. If Census statistics were to be believed, Hindus and Sikhs formed a minority—albeit very slight—in the province. Yet they were by no means weak—if anything, they held the bulk of economic, and until 1945, political power. In more 'normal' times they were able to translate this power into control over the majority community. Muslim peasants who worked the lands of Sikh and Hindu landowners for example, were said to be among the most indebted of peasants in India. The writer Krishna Sobti puts this most eloquently when she says:

> Barring a few who were very big landlords, Muslims [in west Punjab] were primarily poor labourers and peasants; they earned just four annas a day. They did all the work, and yet were always in heavy debt. As reported by one of the Lawrence brothers who was given charge of the revenue in Punjab, Muslim peasants were so deep in debt that even if they worked for fifty years, the debt they owed the moneylenders would not be repaid.[18]

Partition changed all this. In the midst of the upheaval and uncertainty lay the promise of a new country, a land which Muslims could call their own, and in which, in theory at least, they would be rid of this kind of serfdom. The tables were effectively turned on the erstwhile powerful Hindus and Sikhs. There were many who now became very fearful. Their lack of numbers became crucial to this sense of fear. Within west Punjab and the NWFP differences in numbers now became particularly important. Although, in overall numbers, the Hindus and Sikhs were only fractionally fewer than the Muslims, in specific cases, the difference was greater. Thus, for example, they formed a minority in the NWFP and were all the more vulnerable as a minority because of the physical space that separated them from the Indian border. Unlike Sikhs and Hindus in west Punjab, they could not move overland because of the distance, nor could they easily make use of any form of transport other than air transport, which only became available towards the end of August and even then, was primarily used to ferry government servants across. While the NWFP as a whole, and this included Hindus and Muslims, had by and large been opposed to Partition, once it became known that it was a *fait accompli*, communal tensions began to escalate here as well. This exacerbated the vulnerability the Hindus and Sikhs felt as a minority. They formed organizations to represent their interests. Through these, and individually, they began to address appeals to those in power. One such appeal came from Sardar Ganesha Singh, Joint Secretary of the Central Hindu/Sikhs Minorities Board, and was addressed to Sardar Patel. It said:

I, on behalf of Hindus and Sikhs of N.W.F.P. lay the following for your immediate consideration and action please.

1. As you are aware, the minorities of this province have made such heroic sacrifices which have got no parallels in the history of India. We have suffered both at the hands of the British imperialists as well [as] Muslim League so that India may be free. But now, at the time of India's rejoicing, we are left in the sinking boat. We have stood at our posts so India may benefit.

In case we had accepted Pakistan three months earlier, we would not have suffered much humiliation and losses, both financial as well as of life. Hundreds of girls have been kidnapped, but still then we have not budged an inch from our stand and we have fought a fight that no body can deny appreciation. We had to fight marauders, Police and Political departments. What is the fruit of all this suffering? What is the end of all this sacrifices and that has been done for us? And to all this, there is only one reply, i.e. nothing. We have been ignored and [are] being terrorised. You can very well know that it were Hindus & Sikhs who were responsible for the fall of Muslim League Ministry. They promised to give us all the facilities but we declined it so that the prestige of Congress may not be lost. But now you have handed over us to the butchers, who are thirsting for our blood, and they are marking time so as to wrought [*sic*] us completely when they hope to get power within a month or so. You people are standing aside and asking us to stay there, but so far we do not see if you have taken any step to think of us. The nature of Muslims of this place is not like that of other Pathans and this can be well known to you by Pandit Nehru's visit to this province. The president and members of the League have told us that they were not offering us any facility and had rather threatened us that those who would not be staying in Pakistan after the 15th will be declared as absconders and steps would be taken to forfeit their all. Our conditions will be like jews in Hitlerite regime.[19]

Ganesha Singh then goes on to say that he has also taken the step of meeting Mohammed Ali Jinnah from whom he learnt that Hindus and Sikhs of the NWFP could not be represented in the Constituent Assembly because their population was less than 101 lakhs. Nor, apparently, could any other province of Pakistan intercede on behalf of the Hindus and Sikhs of NWFP. This circumstance, according to Ganesha Singh, would effectively result in turning the Hindus and Sikhs of the area into hostages in Pakistan. He urges the government to act quickly; time was short and the Hindus and Sikhs also feared that the Pakistan government—because it was bankrupt—would immediately issue orders that no Hindus and Sikhs could take their wealth to Hindustan. In this way, he said, 'we will be ruined both in case and properties.'[20] He put forward three proposals for immediate action, which included the provision of alternative homes in safe areas, and transferring the subsidy given to the NWFP to Hindus and Sikhs in return for their properties.[21]

In terms of actual numbers, there were places where the balance of power shifted, and Hindus and/or Sikhs found themselves in a minority. But what happened then to people whose permanent status, if you like, was—and continues to be—that of a minority. By this I mean the real minorities such as Christians, tribals, scheduled castes and others. Their interests, as I have pointed out earlier, had necessarily to take second place in the face of the travails of more powerful minorities. I do not wish here to dismiss the genuineness of the Hindu or Sikh sense of being a minority in one or other area, only to point to the irony of a historical circumstance which makes majorities insecure enough to feel like minorities, and renders invisible the real minorities in the bargain.

Indeed, the sense of insecurity was further heightened by the so-called 'loss' of people to the 'other' religion. The game of numbers had become so important that any conversions, however small, were a cause for concern. The following letter looks not at conversions to Islam—which is what the Hindus feared so much—but instead at conversions to Sikhism, a religion that was close to Hinduism. The real fear that underlines this apparent concern for conversions, is that of the lower castes (and classes) going over to Sikhism, the conversion, and therefore loss, of the Harijans.

Dear Sir

It is my ill-luck to bring to your generous notice the fact that Sikhs are carrying out mass conversion of ignorant Hindus into Sikhism at a fabulously high rate and their missionary enterprise is gathering momentum by leaps and bounds. Over a lakh has already been converted in UP and Bihar. We are simply conniving at it under a self-deceiving presumption that Hindus and Sikhs are identical. The Sikhs have a separate political entity is now an open secret. Akali leaders cry with the beat of drum that they are not Hindus and it is a term of abuse if applied to them. Their self-admission requires no further amplification. But proofs, based on theory and the day to day life of the two communities, can be multiplied. Some Sikhs go to the length of taking beef just to disown Hinduism. Beyond the ten gurus and their Holy book, viz the Granth Sahib, they alienate with a vengeance all Hindu sages of the past and their spiritualistically philosophic works. They have developed an innate hatred for the Hindus. Their present alliance with the Congress has been made at a heavy cost and is only transitory, selfish and a calm before the storm. The Hindus in the UP and Bihar are patronising Sikhism as if they would be the saviour of the Hindu community. Time would prove that as soon as they amass a calculable strength in these and other provinces, they would demand much greater weightage than what the Hindus would have given to the same people had they continued as Harijans. As Harijans there is every chance of their forming an integral part of the Hindu body politic some day; but as Sikhs, those very people who have been pounded down under Hindu tyranny would, in their new garb, ruthlessly butcher the Hindus. The country would rue the day when such conversions have been treated with leniency. I therefore appeal that steps should be taken to checkmate this non-Hindu grafting. It is a pity that all Hindus are taking it lying down and phlegmatically too. Hindu Sabha is dead; it had lost its hold on the masses. The 'Sangh' and the Congress are the only two Hindu organisations who can grapple with the gravity of the situation. But to our ill-luck the Congress shrugs its shoulders at any such issue. . . .

The cause of these mass conversions are alleged to be the privilege of the Sikhs to keep a sword and the maltreatment of caste Hindus to the Harijans. If this is so, both these handicaps can be overcome by legislating that all men in these provinces can keep swords and all Hindus irrespective of caste and creed can have excess [access] to public space—temples, hotels, etc. I may mention for your information that it was on this very ground that on the request of some of the Muslims the Punjab Government during the tenure of Sikander Ministry legislated that all Punjabis could keep swords.[22]

The sense of betrayal at the Congress' acceptance of Partition ran deep in the NWFP. Many people felt that their interests had been sacrificed: now, they were to be part of the state of Pakistan, simply because geographically, they were located in a place that could not be easily 'connected' with India. Congress leaders, particularly Nehru, had basically decided that the NWFP did not matter. And indeed Nehru faced considerable opposition when he did attempt to visit the NWFP. The following letter, written by a number of people from Abbottabad, District Hazara in July 1947, provides eloquent testimony of this. Written by 'those minority members who are still here in the frying pan,' the letter is addressed to various political leaders and says:

Respected Hon'ble Shriyut Hindusthanpati Maharaj

Subject: Horrible and heart rending scene of Minorities condition of N.W.F.P. (Part of Pakistan) confirmed by your Hon'ble self as a reward to our sacrifice rendered so far for the complete Independence of all Indian[s].

We the depated [*sic*] and placed in a frying pan sacrificed at the altar of your Independence which you sought on our blood . . . we can't appeal after the memorial day of 15th August, when we will be solely at the brutal sword of barbarous Government of Pakistan. . . . There are only now two alternatives after the 15th August, 1947, either we must give our religion for ever or we have to be tortured and put to death. During this transitory period Mullahs and other religious propagandists are preaching openly that they have to clear off (kaffirs, the idol worshippers, i.e. we unfortunate Hindus and Sikhs) by sword of Islam as in the past they have started converting, massacring [*sic*] and what not from this district . . .

Under the circumstances we requested you with folded hands to kindly take mercy on us and save us from this Pakistani Government and make such arrangements so that we may be taken from this place and our property may be transferred. Just a few days ago Hon'ble Pt. Jawaharlal Nehru have given a statement in the press that the India has not suffered too much by division—it is like a tree from which two or three small branches have been cut but it won't affect the tree, similarly Hindustan has not suffered by a separate Government of Pakistan, and it is quite true, but we appeal to him also to take us from this place to somewhere in Hindustan so that we may also enjoy . . . after so many sacrifices what is freedom and our children may be free otherwise they will be chained slaves as in the previous times Negros were sold in the open market of America and Abraham Lincoln gave them freedom. Similarly we are looking forward to free us from the trap of Pakistan and be free after the 15th August. But every thing must be done before the said date, otherwise they have prepared the constitution for us and we can't move from this place and there will be the law of Mullas, the verdict of Fatwa. . . . We hope you will excuse us from what has been said above, but it is from our core of heart and it is not written for any other motive, but to save our skins from this hell.[23]

Hindus and Sikhs in what was now to be a Muslim state, the writers of letters such as the above, saw themselves as a minority. Their wishes were not taken into account in the referendum held in the province, they said, false votes were cast in their names and in the names of their women. Those who had boycotted the referendum found that they had only helped to give away their votes: 'There are persons,' said one letter, 'who were dragged reluctantly to the polling booths, there are persons who were coerced and bribed at the expense of their helplessness and poverty, there are persons who were incited in the name of diplomatic *jihad* against Kuffaristan. Votes of nationalist women who had boy-cotted the referendum were usurped and used by the modernised fashionable "Tom-boys" hired from other provinces of India. The number of such voters is not less than 1500 out of the total of 3000 in the city of Peshawar alone, which is explicit from the fact that almost all the women votes have been polled in Peshawar.' Quite rightly they pointed out that the people of the province had played a major role in the struggle for Independence, and now they were being sacrificed by the Congress.[24]

V

After they came over to India, thousands of people settled in camps until such time as they felt they could move out and set up home on their own, or until such time as the camps were disbanded. For many, the biggest problem now was how to get a job that would enable them to earn enough to live. Although a number of employment exchanges were set up, they were not able to provide or locate enough employment for all those in search of it. The offices of the All India Congress Committee received a number of letters from people seeking help in finding jobs. On 16 January 1948 Satya Dev Kathuria wrote to the Minister of Relief and Rehabilitation, asking for help in securing a government job in the changed circumstances of the country.

Sir

. . . During my school life I was associated with national movements and social work and my inclination was always towards the uplift and the freedom of the motherland. In Jubbulpore too, I took the company of some local social workers who used to see me every now and then. I was taking part in all their activities whenever I got time after the day's work. I was doing this instead of [in spite of] my being a Government servant, who were not allowed by the then Government to have any connections with such persons and their movements. It was not a crime in my views. This somehow came to the notice of our Section Commander, Lt. J.D. Bracken, R.I.A.S.C. who threatened me with dire consequences in the first instance and then made false allegations against me, got me arrested and put me in the quarter-guard. He, however, offered to release me if I would agree to join in the regular forces. I could not do so. After a month or so I was released from the quarter guard as he could not prove anything against me but dismissed me from the service and a report against me was sent to the Police at my native place at Bannu which blocked my entry into any Government service. This was a great injustice done to me for which I have suffered heavily. I took active part in the 1942 movement and was jailed for one month alongwith other students.

Now that the National Government has been established in the country, and those who were rebels in the eyes of the old Governments are now on the helm of the affairs I feel that I am no longer debarred from entering into any Government Service. . . . Under the circumstances, I seek your goodself's help and request you to please consider my case sympathetically and favour me with a suitable permanent Govt. job as other Government servants of long service from Pakistan are being provided with. I also request you to please allot me a suitable accommodation.[25]

Employment was hard to come by, often even for those who were involved in political work and could be said to have had some kind of access. The following letter was written by Bir Vishan Dass, Secretary Congress to the General Secretary of the AICC:

Jai Hind

I am addressing you as one of the unfortunate refugees from the Pakistan with sanguine hope that you will kindly do all you can to alleviate some of my difficulties. At present I am staying in a camp at Kurukshetra with my family members for the last six months. Our leaders speak very loudly re the various schemes to rehabilitate us but we see nothing practical to solve our miserable plight.

If we write to our leaders and sympathisers explaining our problems we get no response from them or even the courtesy of acknowledgement. In the West Punjab I was a leading congress man and social worker. The object of my writing to you now is to find out as to whether you can do anything for the displaced congress workers of Pakistan. I have also addressed some letters to leading congressmen of Jullundur but so far have heard nothing from them. . . .

Having failed in all my attempts for securing some employment, I at last in despair accepted the job of a peon in the above Vocational Training Centre on Rs 30 plus Rs 25. You can well imagine how long can I carry on with this meagre amount when I have to support a long [large] family. I am now requesting you once again firstly to seek your advice and secondly to seek your help in getting a good and secure employment.[26]

Employment, property, home, community—people who wrote in to those in authority expressed concern about all of these issues. As with the writer of the above letter, they sought advice, perhaps even some form of reassurance: it could not have been easy to go from being a social worker, a status that Gandhi had helped to invest with some dignity, to being a peon, a job for the lowly. It is difficult to know how many of these letters were actually dealt with: the state was occupied with so many 'larger' concerns—would its functionaries have had time to attend to these small, individual voices—voices that raised demands for small things, a few hundred rupees, a small job, a roof over their heads? The files which contain these letters do not include responses on the part of the state. Many of the letters themselves, as the one from Bishan Das above, speak of the indifference of the government, the lack of response on the part of the Congress.

To me these letters represent more than just the immediate tragedy and pathos of Partition: they speak of material losses, of different expectations, but they speak also of a particular kind of relationship with, and expectation of the state—a sense of 'family'—where the state is seen as the benevolent parent of whom such demands can be made. The expectations were myriad, as the following letter from Chaman Lal Roshanlal from Batala, to the Deputy Commissioner, Gurdaspur shows:

1. That I am a refugee from Lahore Proper.
2. That my brother, Banarsi Dass was arrested in a murder case in communal riots at Lahore in March 1947 and remained as undertrial prisoner in Lahore till March 1948 when he was released on bail and came to Batala.
3. That inspite of great efforts I could not get any shop at Batala allotted to me as a refugee and therefore I and my brother remained without work since their coming from Pakistan in August 1947.
4. That I got a shop (Hindu Property) on rent recently at Batala near the Lorry Stand from M/S Harbans Lal and Bros. in the building known as Sham Lal Building and alongwith my brothers has started a business in brass utensils to earn an honest living for myself and my family.
5. That the aforesaid shop has been allotted to a Beer merchant namely Panna Lal of Batala who is a non-refugee . . .
8. That the public is protesting against liquor shop on the main road.

I therefore most humbly prayeth to please intervene in order to save me and my family from starvation.[27]

As is evident, there are barely any letters by women, which is hardly surprising. Unused as they were to negotiating the public world, women would, in all likelihood, have found it difficult to write. Many were also not literate, and in Punjab, many women were literate in Gurmukhi, a language that did not have much official currency. I believe that for those people who wrote letters, just the fact that they could write, and that on the odd occasion they could even expect to receive a reply, served as an outlet for their most immediate concerns. For women, and other marginalized people, even this access was hardly available. This is why their silences lie much deeper, and need to be probed much more carefully. Even in the course of doing my interviews, while I consciously looked for women, it was extremely difficult to actually find women who were willing to speak.

Conclusion: Some Reflections

The decision to partition India was a political decision. But its impact and ramifications were felt not only in the political arena, but also, and most deeply, in the lives of people. Today, a half century after Partition, as we try to recover a sense of what the experience of division actually meant to people, it is sources such as the one I have explored here to which we need to turn if we are to excavate the many histories that lie beneath mainstream, official history. A sense of how people felt—how, if at all, these feelings found expression, what emotions were paramount—these, to me, are a crucial part of what makes up the history of an event.

In the letters that we have looked at above, we see a reflection of people's immediate concerns. But we see more than that as well. We see, if we look beyond those concerns, a slow, hesitant, articulation of a sense of self, an awareness of, or an involvement as, citizens of a new nation, the bewilderment at what many perceive as a betrayal on the part of the newly-formed state, a sense of the vulnerability of the citizen-subject when the protective arm of the state is removed. This is especially important because of the kind of energy, both physical and emotional, that people had invested in the realization of this state. It was their state, created—in a manner of speaking—by their own hands, created also to replace the oppressive and unjust colonial state. For such a state to fail, or to be seen to fail, almost as soon as it had come into being, led to a profound sense of betrayal, and it is this that we see in several of these letters.

In the interviews that took place four, sometimes five, decades later, this acute sense of betrayal is not so predominant. It has been replaced, instead, sometimes with resignation and sometimes with anger at the functioning of the state, tempered by an understanding of the complex nature of the state. No longer do people express such a sense of betrayal or even closeness. Instead, there is a kind of alienation from the state, a comprehension of its authoritarian character, and a much clearer understanding of the kinds of claims people can make and expect to have attended to by the state. For most people, the meanings of Partition were not fixed once and for all. As time passes, meanings shift, change, develop. The letters we have looked at here, the interviews that I explore in detail elsewhere, suggest such shifts. To those who lived through it, Partition may have meant something very different then from what it means to them now. Thus, letters written in those difficult years, as well as interviews, diaries, memoirs, produced during and shortly after Partition, help us better flesh out the lives, experiences, and concerns of people then. Letters—both in informal and formal archives—are undoubtedly important to this process, but we need also to note their limitations. As I have said earlier, a large number of people were unable to write letters to those in authority—women, the illiterate, even those unused to this form of giving expression to grievances and feelings. Just as their voices have remained traditionally unheard in political histories, and their stories unwritten in other historical documents and records, so too can these marginalized groups disappear even from these 'alternative' sources. Our task of recovery thus continues to be tentative and incomplete, but equally, urgent and necessary.

NOTES AND REFERENCES

1. See, for example, *Economic and Political Weekly: Review of Women's Studies*, Mumbai, April 1993; Urvashi Butalia, *The Other Side of Silence: Voices from the Partition of India*, New Delhi: Penguin India, 1998. Mushirul Hasan (ed.), *India Partitioned: The Other Face of Freedom*, New Delhi: Roli Books, 1997; Ritu Menon and Kamla Bhasin, *Borders and Boundaries: Women in India's Partition*, New Delhi: Kali for Women, 1998.
2. Butalia, *The Other Side of Silence*, New Delhi, 1998.
3. Arif Shamim, 'Writing Home to a Stranger', *The News*, Lahore, 4 May 1997.
4. See Stephen Keller, *Uprooting and Social Change*, New Delhi: Manohar Publishers, 1975; U. Bhaskar Rao, *The Story of Rehabilitation*, New Delhi, 1967, the Department of Rehabilitation.
5. U. Bhaskar Rao, *The Story of Rehabilitation*.
6. Manmohan Singh, personal interview.
7. Sherna Berger Gluck and Daphne Patai, *Women's Words: The Feminist Practice of Oral History*, New York: Routledge, 1991.
8. Punjab: AICC Papers, File No G 26, 1948.
9. AICC Papers, File No. G 39.
10. Punjab: AICC Papers, File No. G 26, 1948.
11. Ibid.
12. Ibid.
13. Punjab: AICC Papers, File No. G 19, 1947.
14. Ibid.
15. Punjab: AICC Papers, File No. G 17, 1948.
16. Ibid.
17. Punjab: AICC Papers, File No. P-14 (Pt. I and II), 1947–48.

18. Krishna Sobti, personal interview.
19. NWFP: AICC Papers, File No. G 14, 1946–47.
20. Ibid.
21. Ibid.
22. Punjab: AICC Papers, File No. G 11, 1946–48.
23. Punjab: AICC Papers, File No. CL 9 (Part I), 1946.
24. NWFP: AICC Papers.
25. Punjab: AICC Papers, File No. G 39, 1948.
26. Ibid.
27. Ibid.

Bodies Inflicting Pain:
Masculinity, Morality and Cultural Identity in Manto's 'Cold Meat'

PRIYAMVADA GOPAL

Slicing through the abdomen, the knife went all the way up to just below the nose. The pant cords were cut. From the mouth of the knife-user came immediate words of regret, 'tsk, tsk, tsk, tsk! A *mistake* has taken place!'

(Manto, 'Mistake' in *Black Marginalia*)

Accounts of violence . . . are vulnerable to taking on a prurient form. How does an anthropologist write an ethnography—or to borrow a more apt term from Jean Paul Dumont—an anthropology of violence without its becoming a pornography of violence?

(Valentine Daniel, *Charred Lullabies*)

If this isn't an insult, what is it? A girl appears naked before a man and says 'what's the harm . . . It's only Khushia . . .' Khushia? . . . he couldn't be a man, but a tom cat, like the one that is always yawning on Kanta's bed . . . yes, what else?

I would like to thank Suvir Kaul for his helpful editorial comments, Raza Mir for help with one especially tricky translation and Devendra Issar for some important clarifications on transliteration. Biodun Jeyifo, Hortense Spillers and Laura Brown have helped me greatly with earlier versions of this work. I also thank Daniel Kim and Cheryl Higashida for being so generous with work space and computer time. Discussions with Ed White have been very useful in thinking through some of these issues.

I N SAADAT HASAN MANTO'S eponymous early story, the pimp Khushia sits brooding on a deserted platform that serves by day as a car repair station.[1] He is thinking about his call that morning on Kanta, one of the girls in his 'circuit'. After he had announced himself, she had opened the door to let him in; she was wearing nothing but a small towel. Khushia finds himself petrified and his gaze shifts away quickly from her nude form. When he tells her that she shouldn't have opened the door in that state, her reply is a mortifying one: 'I thought what's the harm [. . .]? It's only Khushia; I'll let him in.'[2] Beating a hasty retreat, he spends the evening on the deserted car repair platform pondering the implications of what has just taken place. He surmises that had Kanta really considered him a man rather than 'only' her pimp, she would never have allowed herself to appear 'unceremoniously naked' as she opens the door to let him in: 'She was a prostitute, of course, but even they didn't behave like this.'[3] Chewing paan with tobacco, he swirls the accumulated spittle around his mouth and as though enacting his new-found sense of sexual inadequacy, finds himself unable to spit out the liquid. The rest of the story finds Khushia attempting to resolve the situation.

Narratives of sexual encounter and ensuing crises of (male) self and sexuality are central to the prodigious body of work produced by Indo-Pakistani writer Saadat Hasan Manto, during his short life (1912–55). Aside from fighting court cases over the alleged obscenity of five of his short stories, Manto enjoyed (and assiduously cultivated) the reputation of a maverick and rebel who generated controversy. In essay after essay, from 'Pase-Manzar' [Behind the Scenes] to 'Taraqqi-Pasand Socha Nahin Karte' [Progressives Don't Think], he paints himself as a lone rebel unfettered by ideological constraints either from the Right or the Left.[4] Hailed most recently by Salman Rushdie 'as the only Indian writer in translation whom I would place on a par with the Indo-Anglian,' Manto is described by Rushdie as a 'writer of low-life fictions whom conservative critics sometimes scorn for his choice of characters and milieus.'[5] Leaving aside the doubtful and arrogant compliment to Manto, Rushdie's comments are problematic in at least two symptomatic ways: they reduce an extremely uneven and diverse body of work to 'low-life fictions', and are unhelpful about what precisely came to be controversial about Manto's writings. In fact, the controversies generated by his stories had little do with his choice of characters and milieus *per se*. After all, established literary greats such as Premchand had already set their fiction in contexts of 'low-life', engaging in issues such as prostitution and sexual exploitation. I would argue instead, that what Manto's most controversial texts—'Cold Meat' ['Thanda Gosht'], 'Smoke' ['Dhuan'], 'Black Salwar' ['Kali Shalwar'] and 'Open It' ['Khol Do']—generated were, rather, arguments about gender and sexuality in their fraught intersection with questions of cultural identity.[6] If it is now axiomatic that nationalism was a gendered and sexualized process, less critical attention has been paid to the ways in which nation-formation was also the flashpoint for struggles over the meaning of community, morality and even the nature of reality itself.[7] These struggles were also gendered and if they were visibly about women and female subjectivity, they were also implicitly about men as national subjects and as both agents and bearers of cultural values. It is this latter aspect that Manto was to make salient in several of his Partition stories.

In line with Rushdie's celebration of Manto's uniqueness, other critics have also lauded what they see as Manto's avoidance of committed social analysis, a fierce individualism that apparently distinguishes him from the other progressive writers who 'were busy trying to connect men and women's social and economic status to their characters' lives and to provide systemic solutions to their problems.'[8] This ubiquitous celebration of an apparently individualist and even apolitical Manto ends up, however, doing a disservice to its own idol by flattening the historical range of Manto's output into a singular and synchronic anti-Progressivism. Manto was undoubtedly a self-appointed maverick, but his relationship to other Progressive writers (themselves hardly a homogeneous bunch) was never one of simple alienation as even polemical essays like 'Progressives Don't Think' suggest. Moreover, Manto's writing ranges from complex psychobiographical stories like 'Cold Meat' to stories like 'Babu Gopinath' that are just as simplistic and 'vulgar' as some of those written by the 'social engineers [. . .] turned litterateurs' that critics finds so appalling.[9] Even in the more sophisticated stories of prostitute life such as 'Black Salwar' and 'The Insult' ['Hatak'], Manto resorts to stock characters and narratives drawn from the pool of both 'human drama' stories and 'social engineering' literature.[10] More useful than celebratory or denunciatory approaches to either Manto's 'individualism' or his 'social commitment' would be a nuanced critical understanding of how his work changes in response to historical exigencies. Manto's engagement with masculinity and morality in the context of Partition is a case in point. Faced with catastrophe and breakdown, Manto's response, as of many of his contemporaries, was to grieve. At the same time, however, he found himself preoccupied with the question of reconstruction: could different ways of being and relating emerge out of the destruction and disorientation he saw around him? What is fundamental in Manto's exploration of the issue is his eventual realization that regeneration and transformation would take more than 'social commitment' and emancipatory agendas; equally necessary would be far-reaching psychic transformation at the level of the individual and his community.

I have argued elsewhere that much of Manto's pre-Partition work can be broadly divided into two kinds of gendered narratives.[11] There are, on the one hand, stories of male sensual experience such as 'Smoke' and 'Odour' (not discussed here), which celebrate a pre-cognitive, purely experiential mode of male being-in-the-world. On the other, there are the more conventional emancipatory accounts of social exploitation and oppression which typically have a female figure at their centre.[12] 'Woman', in these latter stories, becomes a type of shorthand for the 'real', functioning both as metaphor for her own degraded condition and for the lamentable state of society. All through his prodigious corpus, Manto's best stories show signs of his endeavour to overcome these dichotomies by self-reflexively articulating psychobiography and historical analysis, sense-experience and intellection. But it is really in his post-Partition work, which came to focus on the male experience of violence (as perpetrator, victim, or both), that Manto begins to achieve some success in this regard. In stories like 'Cold

Meat' and 'Open it', which deal with gendered communal violence, Manto is impelled and inspired to bring together those previously intractable elements in his work: self, psyche, pre-cognitive sensuality and masculinity on the one hand, and on the other, structure, society, self-reflexive analysis and (suffering) femininity. While some of his feminist contemporaries like Rashid Jahan and Ismat Chughtai engaged the reconstitution of female bodies and psyches in modern urban spaces in their work, it was Manto who took up, most visibly and force-fully, the tasks hinted at by writers like Sajjad Zaheer and Mahmuduzafar in the *Angarey* collection.[13] This was the idea that social transformation would require not only the 'emancipation' of female subjects but also the reconstitution of male subjects and psyches.

In the following reading of 'Cold Meat' and of issues thrown up by litigation against the story on obscenity charges, I trace the connections between the author's attempts to work through gendered dichotomies in his own output and that of his contemporaries, and his reflections on masculinity as the site and object of necessary transformation in the wake of Partition. If such a transformation would, on the one hand, entail reworking masculine psyches, it would simultaneously realign the relationship between individual and society toward a more organic, democratic and humanist moral order. Manto's delineation and implicit advocacy of these connections—radical for their times and, arguably, for our own—might well be what accounts for the intensity of the controversies around the story and the protracted litigation that the author underwent on its behalf. In their zeal to appropriate Manto as a brilliantly iconoclastic individualist who abstains from social commitment, critics like Shashi Joshi miss out on this crucial dimension of the 'perversity' that got Manto into trouble. It is precisely Manto's attempts to work out the necessary relation between an individual's critical processing of his own experience and the sociopolitical order at large that a newly-entrenched political and legal system came to see as an untenable challenge; indeed, therein lay the 'obscenity' of Manto's work. Like many other writers of the time, Manto gives us stories of women who have been the victims of brutal gendered and sexual violence. But what, he finally seems to ask, of the men who are as much part of these processes? And the state that rests its claim on representing them and a common morality? What was at stake in Manto's attempts to forge a kind of organic and critical transformative vision which brought into articulation, psyche and history, emotion and morality, individual and society? The story of 'Cold Meat' and its trial tells us something about this.

From Man to Human

Read typically as 'exclamations of horror' or 'documents of barbarism' (to use Peter Bradbury's and Walter Benjamin's terms respectively), stories like 'Cold Meat' and 'Open it' are brief and intense in their representation of the violence of Partition.[14] While many of Manto's Partition stories, including his aphoristic sketches in *Black Marginalia* ['Siyah Hashiye'], are undoubtedly powerful evocations of the sheer horror and human brutality that marked nation-formation in 1947, these narratives also tell us something about the changes that historical processes effected in Manto's thinking about human and social existence in general and violence in particular.[15] If, at one level, violence put the writer in a position of paralysis where the act always exceeded its possible representation, at another level, it forced him to think in more complex ways about its origins and its consequences. Those consequences were undoubtedly horrific but for Manto, they also raised questions about the potential for transformation in both man and society. (I use the gendered noun advisedly.) Who was affected by violence? Was there only one kind of victim? Could trauma have a rebound action on the perpetrator of violence and push him to face his own contradictions as brute ('haivaan') and as human being ('insaan')? In a way, the cataclysmic events of Partition generated in Manto (after a period of real disorientation), a profound re-examination of the ways in which gender and gendered social relations had figured in his earlier work. The inadequacy of the lyrical stories of male sexual experience as well as those more analytical ones of female sexual subjection seemed even starker in this context of complete ethical breakdown. In the stories that emerged out of the violence of Partition, the traumatic moment of the loss of masculine identity which we first saw in 'Khushia' now also signals a moment of cognition and self-realization out of which transformation *might* occur. The stories are far from utopian and in many ways, do fit the rubric of a literature of 'mourning' where 'what we witnessed was not just the British policy of divide and rule [. . .] but our own willingness to break up our civilizational unity, to kill our neighbours, to forgo that civic ethos, that moral bond with each other, without which human community is impossible.'[16] At the same time, these are narratives that require us to read them for what they also tell us about the possibilities for recovery and reconstruction of those very human and communitarian bonds.

'Cold Meat', which after its publication in 1949, became the target of a year-long court battle, is a story about an all-too-brief rendezvous between two Sikh lovers, Ishwar Singh and Kulwant Kaur.[17] In the world outside, looting and arson are rife, and Ishwar has participated in them fully, periodically bringing the spoils home to Kulwant. The air between the two lovers in the hotel room is tense. For some time now, Kulwant has sensed that not all is well between the two of them. Suspicious that he has been seeing another woman, she badgers him aggressively about his whereabouts of the past few days. He manages to evade the question and pacify her by initiating a bout of lovemaking. However, when the foreplay reaches fever-pitch and Kulwant is like a 'pot ready to boil over,' Ishwar is unable to 'play the trump card' and bring their sexual play to a climax.[18] Now hysterical with rage (for this is the second time that Ishwar has been unable to consummate their love-making), Kulwant confronts him about the 'other woman.' Ishwar Singh finally confesses to her existence. At this, she grabs his dagger and stabs him in the neck, still demanding details. With blood spurting from his veins, Ishwar Singh tell her:

> In the house that I . . . looted . . . there were seven . . . seven men there. Six . . . I . . . murdered . . . with this very dagger, with which you . . . never mind . . . listen . . . There was a girl, very beautiful, who I picked up and took with me . . .[19]

He had taken the girl to a road where there were bushes behind which he intended to 'taste this delicacy.' As he finally 'plays his trump,' a terrible realization dawned on him.

'. . . but . . . but . . . .'

His voice became faint.

Kulwant asked again, 'Then what happened?'

Ishwar Singh opened his closed eyes and looked at Kulwant Kaur's body, every part of which was heaving, 'She . . . she was a dead body, a corpse . . . Absolutely cold meat . . . my love, give me your hand.'

Kulwant Kaur placed her hand on Ishwar Singh's hand which was now colder than ice.[20]

The story was rejected as too dangerous for the times even by sympathetic publishers of progressive Pakistani journals. It was finally published in the journal *Javed*. Within a month, it became the target of protracted litigation. Read together with accounts of the legal trials it underwent and the various judgements handed down on the obscenity charge, 'Cold Meat' provides valuable insights not only into Manto's own evolving literary politics, but also the gendered politics of cultural identity in the context of Partition.

The sexual explicitness of 'Cold Meat' is striking even for a late-twentieth-century reader. The narrative dwells in great detail on the physical proclivities of the two main characters as well as the minutiae of their intimacies. Both Ishwar and Kulwant are deeply sexualized characters, defined as 'man' and 'woman' precisely in terms of their hyper-heterosexuality. Curiously, at the same time as each is described as an excellent specimen of their respective sexes, sex roles themselves seem to become fluid as the narrative unfolds, oscillating between the two lovers until there is a more or less complete exchange at the end of the story. Kulwant Kaur is first introduced as an extremely womanly figure with a hint of the latent masculine. She is 'large of limb [. . .] with big hips, full with quivering flesh. Breasts lifted high, flashing eyes, a faint shadow on her upper lips. From the set of her jaw it is clear that she is a woman who fears nothing.'[21] Ishwar Singh's masculinity on the other hand, is emphasized at the precise moment that it is being undermined: 'his turban coming undone, holding a dagger in hands that are trembling slightly.'[22] Ishwar's masculinity, as Manto delineates it, is indistinguishable from his heterosexuality, his physical affect in relation to his lover as 'the most fit man for a woman like Kulwant.'[23] But as Ishwar nervously unties and reties his long hair, he feels the competing forces of desire and suffering (figured as 'tyrant' and 'victim' later on in the narrative) vying for supremacy within himself. Similarly, the narrative's own rhythms oscillate between strained tension and libidinous energy. First, Ishwar's silences are punctuated by Kulwant's aggressive questions about his whereabouts; then her comment—'[y]ou are not who you were eight days ago,' is met by a burst of physical assertion on his part:

> Ishwar took Kulwant's upper lips with his teeth and started to nibble them. Kulwant melted completely. Ishwar pulled off his own kurta and said 'Let the card game begin.' [. . .] With both hands, he took the folds of her tunic and just as one might skin a goat, pulled it off and put it to one side. Leering at her naked body, he gave her a hard slap on her side and said: 'Kulwant, in the name of the Great Gurus! You are one solid woman!'[24]

Recovered masculinity is conveyed, not surprisingly, through sexual aggression and violence and Ishwar's playful reappropriation of the role of the 'tyrant'.

Why then, does the discovery of cold flesh and an act of near-necrophilia have such a debilitating effect on a man who, we are told, has shown neither mercy nor humanity as he participates in the killing frenzy of the riots? Even the lovemaking of Ishwar is filled with violent machismo, contrasting sharply with the impotence of the would-be rapist:

> Having said that, he decided to punish her some more. He bit her upper lips, her earlobes, grabbed her heaving breasts, slapped her buttocks, filled his mouth with her cheeks to kiss them, and sucking her breasts, he slathered them with saliva. Like a pot on high heat, Kulwant was starting to boil over. But for all this frenetic activity he was unable to stir any desire in himself. He tried all the tricks and moves he could remember, he tried them out like a losing wrestler might, but to no avail.[25]

In the face of Kulwant's impatience and sexual assertiveness, it is now Ishwar who turns into 'cold meat' like his erstwhile victim. To his lover's angry question about the identity of 'the slut [. . .] who has sucked you dry', Ishwar's answer—'no one'—has a ring of ironic truth to it. Just as his violent communal acts have reduced his victims to 'no one,' his punishment from himself is that he too will lose his identity as man. Manto describes this loss as one where 'a human being is handed down a great punishment by his own remaining humanity' ('Written Testimony').[26]

Writing in the context of communal violence in Sri Lanka, anthropologist Valentine Daniel has pointed out that violence in the pursuit of cultural recognition leads to a paradox whereby 'what the "victorious" group [. . .] has gained is the recognition of a corpse, which is no recognition at all.'[27] The moment of near-necrophiliac rape becomes the moment when Ishwar Singh is forced to confront the possibility of his own annihilation, for the coldness of the corpse resists and circumvents the 'heat' that defines him as a man and a sexual being. Manto asserts that sexuality and the concomitant opposition of hot and cold are central to the story not as a means of eroticizing the text but in order that the contrast between life and death may emerge forcefully: 'if Ishwar Singh himself had been a cold man then the effect of this incident related to a forced sexual act would not have been so strong.'[28] Stalled by the death of his victim, Ishwar must now reckon with the implications of what he has been doing all along in taking life with such reckless abandon. This is a reckoning not only brought about by the humanity that supercedes the brutality within Ishwar, but one which results in a renewed allegiance to this humanity. Humanism, for Manto, as we shall see over and over again, is born out of and against the very contradictions that texture human existence.

Civilized Masculinity and its Discontents

Despite its relatively explicit engagement with the erotic, the tribulations undergone by 'Cold Meat' and its author in the courts of law cannot be accounted for by the story's references to sex acts alone. During his defence, Manto himself pointed out quite correctly that there are far more sexually titillating passages in other widely-available texts ranging from religious tomes to classical love poetry.[29] Reading accounts of the no less than three trials that the story withstood, it becomes apparent that the 'obscenity' charge itself was a point of condensation and displacement for all kinds of other concerns ranging from cultural identity, masculinity and morality, to the nature of reality itself. The state's interest, it becomes clear, was not with the text's engagement with sex and sexuality *per se*, but with the specific implications of that engagement. In this regard 'Cold Meat' seems to have generated anxiety on two broad counts. The first of these is the story's contention that humane values, indeed moral bearings themselves, can be developed by working through contradictions, especially when these are made salient through trauma. A man like Ishwar Singh is traumatized precisely at the moment that he confronts his own contradictions: he is simultaneously perpetrator and victim, deeply inhumane and yet fundamentally connected to other human beings in a context where alienation and difference are the order of the day. As he engages with his own trauma and the contradictions that engendered it, he finds himself not only *feeling* his situation intensively but also reflecting— self-consciously and self-reflexively—on who he is and what he has done. Out of these negotiations between emotion and cognition emerge, for Manto, the possibilities for transformation. This contention, which emphasizes both the emotional and the cognitive abilities of the subject, was directly at odds with the prevalent argument, made by the prosecution and the two judges sympathetic to it, that moral norms could be determined by a cultural elite who alone know the difference between wrong and right. The second related cause for controversy was that even as it drew on existing narratives of women as victims and men as either predators or protectors, the story placed the burden of scrutiny on masculinity as such. To the potential discomfort of its readers, 'Cold Meat' examined men in relation not only to female bodies, but to their own bodies and manner of being.

In his studies of masculinity and violence, Peter Bradbury points to a problem also pertinent to Left engagements with feminism and the 'women question'. He suggests that the rhetoric of *female* emancipation has allowed men 'to distance [them]selves through professionalism or exclamations of horror, and to evade the crucial issue which women cannot confront for us,' namely, what it means to be a male in the context of patriarchal violence.[30] Though many of Manto's own stories lend themselves to being read precisely as such exclamations of horror at what is being done *to* women, in stories like 'Cold Meat' and 'Open it' he was attempting, albeit in a limited way, to confront an issue less salient in the familiar emancipatory discourse of his day: the question of 'what it is to *be* violent; and what that violence means for our existence *as men.*'[31] As incipient attempts to break out of more conventional rescue-and-reform narratives that emphasize female violation and male horror, narratives like 'Cold Meat' also offer insights into what Philip Mellor and Chris Schilling have termed 're-forming the body', in this instance, the male body. 'Cold Meat' is notable for the ways in which it makes manliness and masculinity—terms that tend to be unmarked in progressive and, certainly, nationalist discourses of gender—visible.[32]

Ishwar Singh's incomprehension and powerlessness in the face of sexual paralysis forces him (and us) to think about himself *as a man* in relation to gendered violence. This is indicated most powerfully by the shift in reference of the story's title from the female victim to the male perpetrator. Indeed, Manto writes at one point, it is 'Ishwar Singh [who] becomes the victim of a shock related to forced sexual relations.'[33] Without absolving Ishwar Singh of his role in this violent encounter, the story suggests that under certain conditions of resistance, the trauma of being the violator/the aggressor/the brutalizer may engender psychological consequences of its own and epistemological insights that in turn can clear the ground for re-formations of the self. In this instance, the victimizer is forcibly made aware of the fragility of his power and subject position: Ishwar Singh's own masculinity is denaturalized and destabilized by the death of the gendered other who cannot perform the cognitive act of acknowledging the aggressor's power and difference from herself. By dying, by literally becoming 'not woman' and 'not human,' the potential rape victim disallows the enactment of gendered power relations. The burden of cognition falls then on Ishwar himself and the result is trauma. As with Khushia, whose gaze returns to himself and his own destabilized masculinity, Ishwar Singh's scrutiny at the end of this violent encounter returns to himself, a self whose endeavours to draw cultural and sexual boundaries through violence have just been foiled.

Manto, one should be clear, has no interest in dismantling the entire apparatus of cultural masculinity. But it is important to recognize the ways in which the events of Partition would seem to have driven him toward the conclusion that masculinity must be radically reconstituted if there is to be any meaningful social transformation, and certainly, if the horrors of 1947–48 are not to repeat themselves. What makes this vision of psychic and social transformation radical in comparison to a more pervasive awareness in Left discourse that men need to eschew violence and adopt responsible attitudes, are the organic connections that Manto emphasizes here between mind, body and morality. Ishwar is a particularly compelling character for the ways in which his emotions and his behaviour, his reasoning and his actions, are at war with each other until he finally comes to make some kind of peace between them and with himself. As readers, our own first encounter with Ishwar is mediated through his emotions and the effect they are having on his body. As he stands holding his dagger in one corner of the room, we seen him 'unraveling the threads of his troubled thoughts,' head cast down, a trembling voice filled with pain, colour gone from his face. His sexual failures, as we have already seen, are intimately related to his ethical transgressions and his sudden rediscovery of his own human capacities for empathy and compassion. It is towards the end, as Ishwar Singh dies tasting his own blood, that the potential in him for a regenerative transformation into a decent human being becomes evident. This moment of potential regeneration is one, as Manto claims, 'where he comes to a realization, or let's say, *becomes capable of realizing* that the dagger which just slit my throat is one that I used to kill six people.'[34] This awareness of those other six human beings in a metonymic tasting of human blood is a moment that Valentine Daniel, drawing on Piotr Hoffman's work on violence, might describe as the 'transcendence of narcissistic particularity'.[35] Inasmuch as this transcendence entails 'the emergence of a universal/communal being, [it] is the mark of becoming truly human.'

Morality, Nation, Culture

Masculinity, needless to say, is a culture-specific mode of being. The argument that a story like 'Cold Meat' is, therefore, intimately bound up with issues of gendered cultural identity and national character can be substantiated both through Manto's own reflections on the story and various accounts of the obscenity trials themselves. *In the Dock of the Law* [Adaalat ke Katghare Mein], an edited compilation of testimony, reports, and judgements on the five court cases that were fought over his work, contains an essay by Manto on 'Cold Meat' which opens with a long meditation on his move to Pakistan in 1948. The rambling observations on shifting locations, writer's block, literature, and nation seem to have no immediate or apparent connection to the subsequent account of how he came to write 'Cold Meat,' the difficulties he had in getting it published, and the awful predictability with which the story was impounded:

> For three months, my mind was in an odd state. I couldn't tell if I was in Karachi in my friend Hassan Abbas' house or sitting in a restaurant in Lahore where there were frequent soirees to benefit the Prime Minister's fund. [. . .] For three months, my mind couldn't decide anything. It felt as though on the screen, several movies were running simultaneously. Clashing with each other. Sometimes Bombay and its bazaars and streets. Sometimes Karachi with its small, swift trams and donkey carts and sometimes the noisy restaurants of Lahore—I couldn't figure where I was. I would sit all day long on a chair, lost in thought.[36]

This dislocation and disorientation produce for him a series of questions on what to write, how to write, indeed, the very nature of writing and literature in this changing context:

> Will Pakistan's literature be different? If so, then in what way? Who will be the owner of all that was once written in undivided Hindustan? Will this be divided too? Are not the basic realities and problems that Pakistanis and Hindustanis face, one and the same?.[37]

As Manto ponders the fate of the Urdu language itself (he was prescient in believing that its contours would change in each of those new nations) and worries about the possibility of living in a theocratic state, it becomes clear that his writing from this point on will inevitably be inflected by these philosophical and political questions. In several other passages that precede the relatively brief discussion of the actual genesis of 'Cold Meat,' Manto describes the pervasive dissatisfaction he can sense around him as two streams flow together, that of life and death. Life becomes a constant mingling of opposites such that it is hard to distinguish between them: hunger and gluttony, sadness and joy, expressions of happiness and cries of pain. Even slogans cheering the new nation and its new prime minister have a ring of sadness to them.[38]

It is out of this sense of life as structured by contradictions and Manto's personal disorientation as his 'pen ambles around in the general twilight, looking for a path,'[39] that 'Cold Meat' is finally born. This tightly-woven story about a rioter who confronts his humanity through crisis is, if not exactly allegorical, certainly deeply connected to Manto's concerns about the shape of national culture and the form that the new nation-state will take beyond its strange and violent beginnings. The story, as suggested earlier, is one that takes up the possibility of reconstruction through changes in individual and collective structures of feeling. Unlike the 'rescue-and-reform' narratives of nation or the 'emancipation-of-women narratives' more familiar to Left writing, change here entails a painful psychic reconstruction of male subjectivity. Even so, 'Cold Meat' is less a thorough-going critique of masculinity than an attempt to critically realign masculinity with both humanity and humanism. Ishwar's impotence is as much a signal that masculinity must be articulated with the best kinds of human(e) impulses as it is a self-inflicted punishment for his inhumanity. The reconstitution of masculinity and the development of humanity-as-humanism (insaaniyat) become preconditions for each other. It is, in fact, through the somewhat gratuitous and misogynist contrast that the text makes between Kulwant's and Ishwar's different attitudes toward the potential rape victim that the point about Ishwar's newfound humanism is underscored. Reading his own story, Manto points out that it is precisely when Ishwar Singh loses his 'masculine sexual ability,' that 'he feels a new turn inside him—in contrast to which Kulwant Kaur is still obsessed with one thought', and that is the identity of the other woman. If for her that Other woman is a 'whore's daughter,' the alien object of hatred, Ishwar Singh has come to experience empathy and to think about his and his victim's common humanity. This realization is a cognitive act to which both mind and body, reason and emotion are integral. It is the experience of violence, as both perpetrator and victim, that finally brings Ishwar Singh to moral understanding.

Inasmuch as it brings culture and moral understanding back into the ambit of the people at large, the kind of psychic reconstruction that Ishwar Singh senses as a possibility within himself has disruptive implications for the nexus of state, nation, and culture, attempts to consolidate which were taking place in both nation-states at this historical juncture. It is important to point out here that Manto was neither an anti-statist in any simple way nor a votary of 'the people' as an abstract and homogeneous entity. In fact, early on in his musings, he feels impelled to claim that he will remain 'loyal to the state under any circumstances' but also to ask at the same time whether he may have an independent and democratic relationship with it: 'will we be given the leave to criticize its rule?'[40] And far from delineating 'the people' as an abstraction, Manto's sense of heterogeneity and difference impels him to advocate the importance of re-formations of bodies and psyches, and working through contradictions—as against simply legislating moral codes from above. It is precisely his sense that the state can and must be part of a democratic moral vision and cultural practice that enables Manto to make the connections between individual psychic transformation and social reconstruction. As such, it is not surprising that the legal debates around the story come to focus on various inflections of the term 'character': the character of the author (pornographer or conscientious litterateur?); the character of the story's protagonist (violent sex maniac or noble savage?); the character of the reader (impressionable or critical? Is he likely to be turned-on or disgusted by what happens in the story?); and the character of the state (the keeper of national culture or part of the self-critical process of cultural reconstruction? Democratic organ of newly-won freedom or authoritarian replacement for colonial rule?).[41] What is remarkable about the entire debate, in comparison to other discussions of national culture in the same period, is the complete absence of any reference to female sexuality and womanhood. For all concerned at this point, the burden of scrutiny is on the character of the state and its male citizens.

Morality, Masculinity and Reality

Given the centrality of questions of character, both individual and collective, the courtroom drama over the alleged obscenity of 'Cold Meat' returns quite logically, in arguments made by both prosecution and defence, to the issue of what is *real*. Since questions of character, morality and ethics are connected to both actual practice and ideal conditions, the debates focused on at least aspects of literary engagements with reality: what constitutes the real; how literature should engage with it; the effect of the story on the reader's reality; and, by implication, literature's relationship to cultural and political reconstruction. The prosecution's charge against 'Cold Meat' rested on two contentions: first, that the actions shown and words used in the story and by the character were indecent, and secondly, that this indecency would have the effect of inciting lewd behaviour among its readers (presumed to be male) by inflaming their senses. According to the judgement by presiding magistrate A.M. Saeed, which upheld the prosecution's claims, 'in this story, scenes which inflame the desires are presented and sensual gestures are referred to all the time.'[42] The magistrate's ruling on the story cited, by way of definition, another judgement made by Lord Cockburn in the eighteenth century, describing 'obscenity' as a 'subject which incites bad character and behaviour in those who are receptive to such deleterious influences and in whose hands such works might fall.'[43] The defence argued that the language and actions portrayed by the story were true to the milieu in which it was set and that the effect on the reader would be one of palpable revulsion.

Magistrate A.M. Saeed's judgement condemning the story relies on a dual move. Even as it cites a universalized definition of 'obscenity,' it is quick to assert that obscenity is also a culture-specific concept: 'each society has its own notions about character and those things that are part of one society's folk character may be considered deleterious to character in another society.'[44] As though aware of the contradiction in bringing together universal definitions of obscenity and culture-specific arguments against the depiction of sex, the magistrate was quick to point out that Cockburn's definition was only a measuring rod, and not a comprehensive guideline. The situation, he writes, also calls for an evaluation of cultural norms and the damage done to these culture-specific norms and sensitivities by stories like 'Cold Meat.' This means that even if the story represents actually existing conditions and therefore might be good *literature*, it still does damage to the cultural norms of the society it emerges from.

> It is true that improprieties, sensual tendencies and sexual activities, and crudeness are to be found in everyday life. But if literature takes on these standards as acceptable, as the witnesses for the defence have testified, then presenting different aspects of real may be good literature, but it will be opposed to the moral condition of *our domain*.[45]

Magistrate Saeed's argument concedes that reality itself is differentiated, but that when literary engagements with 'their' reality clash with the prevalent norms of 'our' circles, then the law must necessarily uphold the latter. If literature and moral codes are both attempts at shaping reality, then the prerogative of the state is to assert the dominance of the latter as more 'real' than other realities.

The distinction made here between 'different aspects of real life' and 'the moral condition of our domain' indicates the real bone of contention between the state's prosecution and Manto's defence. If for the latter, moral practice is forged out of the heterogeneous and contentious arena of daily life, for the former, morality is an ideology that self-consciously abstracts itself from such practice. 'Cold Meat' attempts to explain how moral understanding might develop, as a cognitive and emotional process, out of a working through of the contradictions that structure everyday existence. This emphasis on cognition and process threatens the moral*ism* of the nationalist state whose own authority ('the moral condition of our domain' in Saeed's words) might come under scrutiny should its subjects develop analytical apparatus that enable them to work through their experiences and emotions. This danger is intensified in the case of a state which draws its authority from an elite cultural nationalism which also relies on acquiescence to abstract and commodified notions of normativity. Should the subjects of such a state develop the kinds of critical faculties that enable them to analyse and even rework their own emotions, ideological investments, and experiences, then such a state faces the daunting prospect of engaging with reasoned and impassioned democratic action.

Low-Life and the Limits of the Text .

In his written testimony and report on the trial, Manto's take on the question of differentiated realities is ambiguous and not without its own set of problems. Asserting only that the moral perspective of those who arrested him and confiscated the story is 'different' from his, Manto winds up arguing that 'raw brutality' as an aspect of the real is best exemplified by lower-class characters and life. His own investments, he claims, are in 'Modern Literature', where aesthetics cannot be limited to beautiful things. While defending himself here from charges of obscenity by insisting that he has merely been faithful to life and the demands of authenticity, Manto also asserts that lower-class life is the site where life's truths may be best engaged with. This is why the portrait of Ishwar Singh is necessarily that of an unrefined rural villager or 'rube':

> The question is why not present things just as they are? Why make jute into silk? Why make a heap of garbage into a heap of perfume? Will turning our faces from reality help us become better people? Absolutely not—so why take umbrage at the character of Ishwar Singh and his way of talking?[46]

The claims that Manto makes here suggest an advocacy of a literalism quite at odds with the delicate moral and psychological realism that characterize his more complex stories and characters, including 'Cold Meat' itself:

We cannot expect that Ishwar Singh express his thoughts and emotions in a refined way. He is a crude man, a rube, but from the way he speaks, he testifies to all that he is coming to understand and this way of talking is, in its own place, appropriate and necessary.[47]

On the other hand, Manto will argue, Ishwar Singh's crudeness and unrefined language are that much more effective in highlighting the humanity that he is capable of after all:

[D]o we not see a glimpse of the humanity in Ishwar Singh's dark heart which causes him to negate his own desires—and it is a healthy thing that the writer of the story has not lost faith in human beings and humanity. If the writer had not made sensuousness integral to Ishwar Singh's way of feeling and thinking, then truly 'Cold Meat' would be a very base thing.[48]

As he goes on to argue that what happens to Ishwar Singh can happen to anyone, Manto's claims exhibit a tension between exceptionalizing this character and his experience, and generalizing them in order to explore further possibilities for individual and social transformation. In this regard, sexual desire becomes simultaneously an index of Ishwar Singh's classed existence as well as a marker of that which is common to all human beings. In an essay entitled, 'The Story Writer and Sexual Matters' [Afsana Nigar aur Jinsi Masail], Manto elaborates this dual use of sex in his stories.[49] Sex epitomizes the contradictions of modernity itself where 'woman is both near and far [. . .] sometimes appearing naked, sometimes clothed. In some places you see women in the guise of men and in others, men in the guise of women.'[50] But if sex, historicized like this, is metonymic for the ambiguities and conflicts that mark modern gender relations and even gender itself, sexual desire is also that which (somewhat melodramatically and with implacable heterocentrism) withstands history and politics: 'Two lands can be separated from each other by a law but no administration, no decree, no law can keep man and woman apart from each other.'[51] Sex, in Manto's work, is both symbol and site: the place and manner in which historical specificity and basic human capabilities can be articulated together.[52]

Though sexual desire performs a crucial aesthetic and political function in 'Cold Meat,' that of eliciting from the reader an identificatory emotional response which will have epistemological consequences, Manto's own interpretation of his story is, in places, startlingly reductive. For instance, in his written defence, he downplays the complexity of the sexual in his story in favour of according it a simple instrumental role. Insisting that the story has no erotic charge and that only a pervert would gain any sexual thrill from a reading of the story, Manto writes: 'Of abnormal people, I can say nothing, for there are people who would find it possible to have sex with a corpse.'[53] Normal people, he insists, would have only the clinical reaction that one of his own defence witnesses (a doctor, no less) claimed to have had: the story would render them 'cold meat,' i.e. impotent. Though such a claim clearly has a tactical use in fending off the charge that Manto was a pornographic writer, it also contradicts his prior claim that in order for the story to have the effect that it does, the cold, the dead and the inhuman(e) must necessarily be contrasted with the warm, the alive, the sensual. The reader, he suggests earlier, must *feel* this contrast in order to understand the ways in which the humane and the inhumane can co-exist in the same person's (their own) heart. In distancing himself thus from the erotic, Manto undermines one of the strongest aspects of his work, a keen sense of the role of libidinal energies in reworking psychic and political existence.

It is tempting, given a defence of the story which argues that different realities engender different narratives, to read Manto as a contingency artist, a purveyor of radical relativism. Such a reading would, however, underestimate the extent of Manto's investments in coming up with a moral vision and articulating a humanism for what he saw as his barbaric, though redeemable, times. The ways in which a story like 'Cold Meat' manages to function simultaneously as an account of a particular incident and as a more generalizable parable of human behaviour are significant here. In attempting to articulate the exceptional and the average, the particular and the general, Manto elaborates a vision which accepts human and social complexity but one which is also invested in working through that complexity to arrive at common ethical concerns. This dynamic scenario contrasts with the normative goals of the state whose interests, as articulated by one judge during Manto's trials, are to impose a moral code developed by an elite circle. In this instance, the implications are that this code would be inflected by religious valences that would sharpen communal borders. Magistrate A.M. Saeed notes in his judgement that 'obscenity and the inflammation of the passion is considered to be the work of the devil';[54] the meeting of the Press Advisory Council to discuss 'Cold Meat' brought up the charge that the story would 'disturb the public peace' (quoted in 'Troubles', p. 99).[55] Even as Manto was to continue to examine the possibilities for a reconstruction that might emerge from the violence and moral breakdown of Partition, he was to come down hard both on nationalist claims to unified cultural identity and on the narrow moralism that circumscribed such visions. Accordingly, his next story, 'Open It', written after the 'Cold Meat' debacle, found Manto back in the docks of the law.

In many of his post-Partition essays, Manto moves from a more or less descriptive interest in 'the human condition' to discussing the psychic and political potential of *humanism*; a story like 'Cold Meat' is one instance of this movement. The somewhat pedestrian approach to the former in earlier stories like 'Black Salwar' or 'Odour' is reworked into a sense that neither the human nor the social can be captured by formula. At the same time, there is an increasing, urgent need to think about how individual and systemic transformation might take place. If Partition violence, with its perverse combination of mindless hysteria and twisted rationality (recall the epigram at the beginning of this article drawn from Manto's 'Black Marginalia,' where a killer acknowledges a '*mistake*' after seeing the genitals of his victim), is evidence of that which must be overcome in ourselves, then transformation will also require a radical and critical realignment of emotion and reason.

Manto, it must be remembered, was also responding to what he perceived as the increasing ossification of Progressive writing into formulaic and 'sterile' work based on manifestos and statements inspired by 'external political diktat'.[56] But despite his disillusionment with official 'Red' writing and his hurt at the condemnatory hostility of some of its votaries towards his *Black Marginalia*, Manto does not respond with a retreat into the anti-representational or the apolitical, even as he mulls over the challenges of representing violence and theorizing transformation:

> For a long time I refused to accept the consequences of the revolution, which was set off by the Partition of the country. I still feel the same way; but I suppose in the end I came to accept this nightmarish reality without self-pity or despair. In the process, I tried to retrieve from this man-made sea of blood, pearls of a rare hue, by writing about the single minded dedication with which men had killed men, about the remorse felt by some of them, about the tears shed by murderers who could not understand why they still had some human feelings left.[57]

While there is a strand of narcissism that erupts periodically both in Manto's stories and his self-portraiture, leading him every once in a while to denounce any connection between politics and literature, Manto never finally retreated from thinking about what must be said and what needed to be done. The *Black Marginalia* themselves, as well as Partition stories like 'Cold Meat,' are essays in a critical humanism which takes both affect and reason, individual and collective, seriously. Each irony-laden sketch in *Black Marginalia*, for instance, is a play on traditional values like 'politeness', 'propriety', 'decency', 'consideration', 'equity', 'fair trade', and 'neatness'. Take, for instance, 'The Grouse,' a single line sketch from the *Marginalia*:

> Look my friend, you charged me black market prices and still gave me such low-grade petrol that not even one shop got burned down.[58]

In observing the perversions of these values, Manto simultaneously attacks the twisted emptiness of conventional moral imperatives and yet seems to hint at some possibility of ethical reconstruction out of them.

The best of Manto's post-Partition work, despite its birth out of 'nightmare', still attempts to resurrect and deepen what he had once described as the explanatory importance of writing: '[. . .] I will not only offer a picture of this incident but will also attempt to show why it comes to pass.'[59] In stories like 'Cold Meat' and 'Open It,' Manto engages not only with how things have came to pass but what other directions they might take. Like Paul Celan, accused by Adorno of 'writing a poem after Auschwitz,' Manto was condemned by some of his former comrades for making a career out of death. Manto might, like Celan, have not only replied that '[o]nly faithless am I true,' but also that it was in trying to understand, and in not always succeeding, that he remained true.[60] The vast and uneven corpus of this writer, whose explicit wish that he not be deified after his death continues to be disregarded by those who write about him, requires of us a critical apparatus that evades both the celebratory and the condemnatory. We may read him, not for the conclusions that we can arrive at, but for the insights that we might glean with regard to 'the ongoing process of becoming human or at least renewing one's humanity'.[61]

NOTES AND REFERENCES

1. Saadat Hasan Manto, 'Khushia', *Black Milk*, trans. Hamid Jalal, Lahore: Sang-e-Meel Publications, 1996, pp. 57–64.

2. Ibid., p. 58.

3. Ibid., p. 59.

4. Both articles can be found in *Mantonaama* [The Life and Work of Manto], ed., Devendra Issar, Delhi: Indraprastha, 1991, pp. 19–23, 353–5. Unless otherwise specified, all translations into the English are mine.

5. Salman Rushdie, 'Damme, This is the Oriental Scene for You!', *The New Yorker*, 23–39 June 1997, pp. 50–61, p. 52.

6. All these stories as well as accounts of the legal controversies that Manto became embroiled in can be found in Devendra Issar, ed., *Adaalat Ke Katghare Mein [In the Dock of the Law]*, Delhi: Indraprastha, 1991.

7. For a sampling of recent work on the topic of nationalism and sexuality in postcolonial contexts, see Partha Chatterjee, *The Nation and Its Fragments: Colonial and Postcolonial Histories*, Princeton: Princeton University Press, 1993; Andrew Parker *et al.*, eds, *Nationalisms and Sexualities*, London: Routledge, 1992; Elaine Kim and Chungmoo Choi, eds, *Dangerous Women: Gender and Korean Nationalism*, London: Routledge, 1998; Doris Sommer, *Foundational Fictions: National Romances of Latin America*, Berkeley: University of California Press, 1991.

8. Shashi Joshi, 'The World of Saadat Hasan Manto', *Life and Works of Saadat Hasan Manto*, ed. Alok Bhalla, Shimla: Indian Institute of Advanced Study, 1997, p. 155.

9. 'Babu Gopinath', *Mantonaama*, pp. 122–5. See Joshi, 'The World of . . .', p. 155.

10. 'Hatak' [The Insult], *Mantonaama*, pp. 91–108.

11. Priyamvada Gopal, *Midnight's Labors: Gender, Nation and Narratives of Social Transformation in Transitional India, 1932–1954*, Dissertation, Cornell University, 2000.

12. I am referring here in particular to the works of Munshi Premchand as well as other writers affiliated with the Indian Progressive Writers Association (the PWA, established in 1936), including Mulk Raj Anand and Rajinder Singh Bedi. Female exploitation and degradation was a familiar trope in the work of writers associated with the PWA although, as with Manto, each writer's corpus is complex and deserves careful, differentiated reading.

13. The *Angarey [Embers]* collection was a pioneering, controversial and successful attempt to inaugurate a climate of literary radicalism. Edited by Sajjad Zaheer who would go on to be a co-founder of the Progressive Writers Association, the collection included stories like 'Dulari' (Zaheer) and 'Gallantry' (Mahmuduzaffar) which began to probe male experience and masculinity in the context of social inequities.

14. Peter Bradbury, 'Sexuality and Male Violence', *Men, Sex and Relationships: Writings from Achilles Heel*, ed. Victor J. Seidler, London: Routledge, 1992, pp. 156–71; Walter Benjamin, 'Theses on History', *Illuminations*, trans. Harry Zone, ed. Hannah Arendt, New York: Schocken Books, 1968, p. 256.

15. 'Siyah Hashiye', *Mantonaama*, pp. 277–81.

16. Aijaz Ahmad, *In Theory: Classes, Nations, Literatures*, London: Verso, 1992, p. 119.

17. 'Thanda Gosht' [Cold Meat], *Mantonaama*, pp. 88–92.

18. Ibid., pp. 90–1.

19. Ibid., p. 93.

20. Ibid., p. 97.

21. Ibid., p. 88.

22. Ibid.

23. Ibid., p. 88.

24. Ibid., pp. 90–1.

25. Ibid.

26. 'Tahriri Bayan aur Report' [Written Testimony and Report], *Mantonaama*, pp. 111–18, p. 116.

27. E. Valentine Daniel, *Charred Lullabies: Chapters in an Anthropography of Violence*, Princeton: Princeton University Press, 1996, p. 69.

28. 'Written Testimony', p. 114.
29. Ibid.
30. Bradbury, 'Sexuality and Male Violence', p. 156.
31. Ibid., my emphasis.
32. Philip A. Mellor and Chris Shilling, *Re-forming the Body: Religion, Community and Modernity*, London: Thousand Oaks, California: Sage Publications, 1997. The last few years have shown increasing scholarly interest in this area, most prominently in studies of fascism. For work in the Indian context, see especially Ashis Nandy, *The Intimate Enemy*, Delhi: Oxford University Press, 1983, 1989; Anand Patwardhan's documentary, *Father, Son and Holy War*, Icarus Films, 1995.
33. Written Testimony, p. 113.
34. 'Exegesis', p. 130, my emphasis.
35. Daniel, *Charred Lullabies*, p. 68.
36. 'Zahmat-e-Meher-e-Darkhshan: Thanda Gosht par Mukadme ki Kahani Manto ki Jabani'. [Tribulations of the Shining Sun: The 'Cold Meat' Trials in Manto's Own Words'.] *Mantonaama*, pp. 94–111, p. 95.
37. Ibid.
38. Ibid.
39. Ibid., p. 96.
40. Ibid.
41. See the account of the controversy over 'Cold Meat' in two essays and a report by Manto and the transcriptions of the two judgements in *In the Dock of the Law*, pp. 94–145. In one of his essays here, Manto asks: 'Having just won our freedom, will our condition be any different from the way it was under foreign rule? ('Tribulations', p. 95).
42. A.M. Saeed, 'Judgement', *In the Dock of the Law*, pp. 123—27, p. 123.
43. Ibid.
44. Ibid.
45. Ibid., p. 124, my emphasis.
46. 'Written Testimony', p. 115.
47. 'Sameeksha' [Exegesis], pp. 128–32.
48. 'Written Testimony', p. 115.
49. 'Afsana Nigar aur Jinsi Masail'. [The Short Story Writer and Sexual Matters], *In the Dock of the Law*, pp. 349–52.
50. Ibid., p. 352.
51. Ibid.
52. 'Cold Meat' is 'a story whose topic is apparently the recent riots but in fact whose roots are really in man's sexual desires and which is intimately linked to human desires and sexual relations' ('Written Testimony', p. 113).
53. 'Exegesis', p. 129.

54. 'Judgement', p. 125.
55. Ibid.
56. Khalid Hasan, 'About the Book', *Partition: Stories and Sketches*, ed., Khalid Hasan, Delhi: Viking, 1991, p. xiii.
57. Ibid., p. xii.
58. 'Ulahna' ['The Grouse'], from *Black Marginalia*, in *Mantonaama*, p. 280.
59. Ibid., p. 352.
60. Paul Celan, quoted in Daniel, *Charred Lullabies*, p. 211.
61. Ibid., p. 69.

Children and the Partition

NITA KUMAR

F OR INDIANS BORN after 1980,* the Partition of the country into
many nations is not an earth-shaking event. It is a distant happening with which they have, at best, tenuous relationships. To in-
vestigate these relationships is to raise questions about the way history
and histories are created and how the arts of memory are exercised. At
the very least there is an official history with which all historians have
a certain relationship. Set beside these official histories are other ways
of grouping the events of the past and we experience or observe their
presence as alternative or competing histories.

The children of modern India may be (i) aware of their official

*At the date of writing, they would all have been below seventeen years of age.

I would like to thank the following children and schools for their generous cooperation:

Shahzad Akhtar, Naushad Ahmad, Shamina Khatoon, Sonya Khatoon, Tarranum
Jahan, Samiya Sabohi, Fatma Zohra, Neha Parveen, Shabnoor Nazeen, Alavina
Naseer, Shahina Parveen, Nilofer Meena, Tarranum Fatima, Irfana Majumdar,
Sriparna Majumdar, Saraswati Nandini, Rudra Majumdar, Dibyarka Basu, Shudhir
Das, and Saba Parveen.

In Banaras: Jamia Salfiya, Jamia Islamiya, Jamia Hamidia Rizvia, Qudrutullah
Gulzar-e-Talim, Central Hindu Girls School, Tulsi Vidya Niketan, Kiddy Convent.

In Calcutta: Archana Primary School, Loreto House.

history which they integrate into other aspects of their being; or (ii) aware of their national history but separate from and uninvolved in it. 'Alternatively', they may be (iii) unaware of their official national history but aware of other histories; or (iv) unaware of their official history and of any history.

This essay is chiefly about children in the first three categories, and indeed these may be the only three that are socially possible. In the first and longer section, we look at children of category (iii), children who clearly have other histories. How are the arts of memory exercised in their case? This section, prefaced by a set of two interviews, concerns the children of Muslim weavers in Banaras. I have chosen weavers because this community has been historically regarded as 'communal', 'bigoted', and 'backward', and today are regarded as much of the same, but more eloquently, as resistant to the secularizing and modernizing efforts of the nation.

In the second section we look at children of categories (i) and (ii). The community and class background of these children, as befits a 'mainstream' group, has not been discussed at any length. They are from the class that forms 'the backbone of the nation', that wants liberal education and secure 'service' jobs for its sons, marriages into service families for its daughters and now maybe careers as well, if in proper establishments. It reads and comments on national politics and takes issues of inflation, corruption, production, distribution, and so on, very much to heart. The children confidently regard the lessons of history, society, culture, etc., which they learn in school, to be gospel truth, and in any case there is no contradiction at home.

Of the many patterns that may be discerned within this discussion only some are relevant for the present argument. We see how weavers' children fall between the inadequate arts of memory of a pre-modern and a modern epoch. Secularization and disciplining into a nationalist identity occurs through suppression of a minority or local or deviant culture. Given this, the weavers are losing out on their legitimate place in the nation, but it is the middle-class children who are losing out on memories and cultural funds.

Interview 1: The Son of a Weaver in Banaras,
About Thirteen Years Old

'Who are you?'

'My name is Shahzad Akhtar. I am in class IV, in Jamia Hamidia Rizvia'.

'What do you like doing?'

'I like to play marbles in my free time. I play bat and ball in the field (*maidan*) occasionally. I don't like to stay at home.'

'What do you know about 1947?'

'1947? I can't remember. I don't know.'

'You must have studied it in your History?'

'History?' We don't do much. . . . Nothing much is taught in our school. We will have our exams soon. Yes, I know, the Slave Dynasty . . . the Slave Dynasty . . .'

'Yes?'

'I don't remember. The Slave Dynasty . . . [swears]. Many of our periods go free (*khali jaten hain*). Let me tell you what happens. The teachers get together in groups, talk, eat and drink. They eat in the classroom and don't let the children eat anything. No, we don't have tiffin time. If we try anything, they beat us.'

'You do have a History book don't you? Maybe *Hamari Duniya Hamara Samaj*? (*Our World and Our Society*—the UP textbook in Social Studies).'

'Yes, but we—er—we haven't begun it yet.'

(Shahzad is then asked many random questions in History but cannot answer a *single* one of them. He keeps explaining that he has forgotten or that they haven't 'done' it yet. Then he volunteers certain answers he remembers, in a subject called 'Malumat-e-Amma' (General Knowledge). He repeats the answers in a monotone, accompanied by a swaying of his body, as habitually done by those reciting what is learnt purely by rote.)

'What is *haj*?. . . . What is *namaz*?. . . . What is *roza*?. . . . Who invented the needle?. . . . Who invented soap?. . . .'

(The speed of his answers precludes getting them down exactly, and he is unable to repeat them slower. His mother enters at this point and interrupts occasionally.)

(Mother): 'How will you do your exams?'

(doubtfully) 'Yes, they are in May, no, in June . . .'

(Mother): 'We want him to change schools. He is not learning anything.'

'Is he fond of learning?'

(Mother): 'No, his father is very fond of having him learn (*bahut shauk hai*).'

'Are there any activities or functions in the school? Do they celebrate 15 August? 26 January?'

'Nothing. Nothing at all.'

(Mother): 'There were when I was small. I studied in the same madrasa you know. On 15 August we were all taken to Jai Narain (the oldest 'modern' school in Banaras) to participate in a parade. The management of this madrasa eats up all the money. They do not bother about studies at all.'

'Can you not complain about this as a guardian? And about their not getting time for a snack?'

(Mother): 'No, because we are "low".' (Mother leaves the room).

Shahzad has a little sister of six or seven, whose doll has recently had a wedding with a doll in her paternal aunt's house. Shahzad recounts it with enthusiasm. The two children, with two other siblings, show off all the store of things now owned by the doll: fridge and kitchen items, clothes, jewellery, furniture. . . . Shahzad is very interested in every part of the proceedings and exhibits a necklace, one of many such pieces of the doll's apparel that he has made.

'Do you have any teachers at all who teach?'

'Mansoor master is a good teacher. He even jokes a little.'

Interview 2:
Teacher in Jamia Hamidia Rizvia

'Who are you?'

'Mohammad Mansoor Alam Khan, from Bihar, here for ten years.

I teach Maths in VI and VII, Urdu in IX and X, History in VI and VII, Geography in V, VI, VII.'

'What is special or different about the teaching in the school?'

'For a long time, this school went up to class V–VI only. Those who are in the sarı business do not want their children to get ahead. Then it was till VIII for a long time. For the last four years we have IX and X. There are obstacles from guardians.'

'What kind of obstacles?'

'Greed for money (*paise ka lobh*). Also, the economic condition is not too good.'

'Regarding that—if the children need to sit at the loom—why not adjust the school timings?'

'We have. The timings are 7.30 a.m. to 12. About 40 per cent work at the loom plus studying.'

'How are the studies here?'

'Good.'

'Which subjects are good?'

'Hindi and Urdu are good. Sociology [*sic*] is okay. Science is not. It is tough for them. They cannot work hard enough.'

'What is the advantage of learning these things if they will only weave in the future?'

'Oh, there has been *some* improvement in the condition of the people.'

'Is there any direct teaching on the subject of citizenship, social interaction, behaviour, etc.?'

'There is Diniyat (Religion), a subject from class II onwards. There is Civics, part of the UP Board syllabus from VI onwards.'

'Is there any indirect teaching? Do you have any functions or programmes?'

'On Republic and Independence Days we have flag hoisting, sweets. On 23 December, ten days before Ramazan, we had our annual function. We gave awards and a farewell to class X. There were seven students this year. Their guardians came. No, we have no plays, music, recitation, satire, and so on.

'What are the main problems you encounter as a teacher?'

'There are many. Guardians don't take enough responsibility. There is poor attendance at parents meetings, or the guardians simply never come. We tried monthly meetings, class-wise. There is great illiteracy among them. In my own class, V, out of some twenty-eight twenty do come. They listen, but they cannot do what they are told. They drop out after class V because they've finished the Quran Sharif. This place has no society, no culture. Since this madrasa is free, only the poor send their children to it. They are also indifferent to other schools because there is no Urdu there.'

'What do the children learn at home?'

'How to weave. The traditional work (*gharelu karobar*). Things related to weaving.'

'Anything else? What about from TV?'

'That influence is restricted to clothes.'

'No, what about cricket?'

'Yes, now cricket is such a thing that you can get carried away during a game. But it only lasts as long as the game. They cheer for the Pakistani team. Then they forget. It is a temporary phenomenon. One of my friends currently supports the South African team.'

'So it is not an indication of communalism?'

'No, it is only cricket.'

The ideally balanced recollections demanded of memory perhaps exceed the capacities of the untrained human mind. The victims of history, the bodies of the human beings on whose backs achievements are carried out in the name of progress are not automatically given a space in human memory. They need constant battle against forgetfulness. If we believe that the feel of people's experiences must be transmitted, that the ethical value of that experience must be respected, then there are many tasks that remain for many kinds of history.[1] But before we discuss that further, let us explore the arts of memory as they are exercized by the weavers.

Weavers's children, like Shahzad, have the following experience. A son, for a weaver, is an extension of himself. As an infant he is only semi-human, the other half of him divine, toy-like, prince-like (*bachche to badshah hote hain*).[2] Fathers give sufficient indication of this by enthusiastically playing with their infant children in their free time, cuddling them, commenting on their abilities, indulging their whims. From as early as four or five years onwards, a weaver's son becomes street-wise. He is sent to the shops for tea and *pan*, for small purchases, to send and bring messages. He is not disciplined regarding his use of space or time, and is expected to be mobile. In this respect he is a miniature version of his father and and other males in the family and begins to resemble them more and more.

Of the many leisure activities of the weavers, such as fairs, festivals, processions, annual celebrations at shrines, gatherings for music and poetry, and wrestling and body building, the most important for them is *ghumna phirna* (wandering around), including both wandering around the city and going 'outside' for *saill-sapata* (pleasure trips). In the case of all the activities, especially the last, there is a structure of signification with certain key relationships: between the body and freedom, the outdoors and freedom, season and mood. 'Freedom' is a concept idealized by weavers and all other artisans. It reflects partly the actual freedom inherent in the piece work that characterizes artisan production, and is partly an ideological reflex to the insecurity and inflexibility of such labour. That the idealization of 'freedom' reaches the heights it does is a testimony to the self-conscious ethic of the city, based on its corporate character, its patronage of the arts and letters, its pride in more mundane pleasures with open air, mud, and water; and a refinement of 'tradition' as expressing the excellent in many areas of cultural life.[3]

While Muslim weavers hold this view of the city, of freedom, and of themselves as inheritors of this tradition in conjunction with other artisans, their view of 'history' and 'geography' is parallel but separate. Certainly, if we reflect upon it, they could not be expected to share in the familiar, dominant Hindu view of the city as the centre of civilization and the bestower of release after death, or in its fecundity with regard to temples and icons and holy bathing places.

For the Muslim weavers, history dawns with the coming of Islam to the region, approximately around AD 1000, when Salar Masaud

Ghazi was martyred nearby and the remnant of his force settled down in the region. They became the kernel of the present population of Muslims. As evidence of this history are scores of graves, shrines, and mosques to the *shahids* (martyrs) who sacrificed their lives to the spread of Islam. This history is kept alive in everyday existence by the weekly worship and annual celebrations that mark the most popular of these shrines, as well as in their quieter role as places of rest and meditation at any given time.[4]

While women, children, and whole families go together to shrines on special days, the places are typically cultural centres for males as are mosques and *chabutaras* (open cemented platforms) in every neighbourhood. A little boy may accompany his male relatives and experience to progressively increasing degrees the openness and benignity of the city. Like them, he can wander around anywhere in his free time, may be traced to one or two favourite haunts, like an outdoor space, at friends' homes, playing or watching cricket, or simply 'in the lane' (*gali men hai*). He does not get embroiled in domestic activities, unless, like shopping, they involve the outdoors. The reports of teenage boys, when interviewed, are identical to those of adults in describing the joys of the outdoors, of free time, and open space.

Shahzad Akhtar stands at a bridge between infancy-childhood and teenage. He was 'caught' by me on the street, engaged in nothing in particular, accompanied by a few friends who hastened to blend into the background. Rather than surround me with curiosity, they preferred to remain 'free'. To shake me off, Shahzad first reported that he was on his way to weave. But when my insistence made him surrender and we were sitting and chatting in his home, two of his friends looked in to find out where he had disappeared. At the same time, he showed evidence of enjoying quieter pastimes at home, including sewing and threading necklaces for his little sister's doll, although he did not mention any such interest when reporting on his pleasures.

His weaving began at least two years ago. The vocation of the weavers lies with the pit loom and training for all of them starts with their sitting at the loom from about the age of eight onwards. This may be with the father or with a master weaver in exchange for a small apprenticeship. He starts with the simplest processes and is made to 'embroider' the narrow borders at each end of the sari under the adult's guidance. He is simply inadequate physically to use the loom fully until he matures.[5]

Shahzad Akhtar lives in Madanpura, the centre of the silk weaving industry. If asked who he is, he is more likely to say 'I am a resident of Madanpura,' than 'I am a Muslim,' or 'I am from Banaras,' or 'I am an Indian.' This identification with a mohalla or neighbourhood is a correlate of poverty, illiteracy, and backwardness. It plays itself out in self-identification at a daily level, such as in the common question to strangers, 'Where are you from?'[6] and in all cultural activity. Wrestling matches, poetry competitions, Baqr Id sacrifices, Moharram tazias, and Barwafat decorations all take the form of competitions between mohallas.

To be from a weaver's family is to 'be' an Ansari, a nomenclature adopted by weavers in preference to the derogatory '*Julaha*' in the 1930s. The process of upward mobility through a change in name and the composition of a valedictory history is one that characterizes every caste and caste-like group in twentieth-century India, and is old enough for the weavers to retain no oral memory of it. Ansaris consider themselves a lineage and an endogamous group. They cite as their specific personality traits pacificity, kind-heartedness, and a love for freedom. The last is expressed and reconfirmed in lifestyle and leisure activities. Pacificity and the more untranslatable *narmdil* or *dilraham* ('kindheartedness') are perhaps demonstrated in their relations with middlemen and agents. Weavers are consensually accepted as being easy to deal with in matters of buying and selling. Their love of freedom does pose a danger in that they miss deadlines and shut up shop at any small pretext, but during the process of transaction, they display no acerbity or aggressiveness.[7]

It is difficult to state precisely where a weaver's son like Shahzad would pick up these preferred qualities of Ansaris except to say that he does spend hours with male relatives, first in the dusky workshop marked only by the clatter of eight looms, then during occasional trips with his father to Chauk, the central wholesale and retail market of Banaras, carrying finished saris. Otherwise he hangs around in his mohalla and rarely goes outside, if ever at all.

Shahzad studies in Jamia Hamidia Rizvia which means that if a Sunni, he is a Barelwi, as opposed to being a Deobandi or Ahl-e-hadis, and a Shia if not. His school was founded in 1897 by an association called Anjuman Taraqqi Ahl-e-Sunnat.[8] In opposition to the reformist groups, they represent a continuity with the past, while 'in their very self-consciousness, representing a departure from it.'[9] To some extent Ahmad Riza Khan participated in the defence of Sunni Islam against the Arya Samaj brand of militant Hinduism, but he opposed even more militantly the Shias and the reformist Deobandis and Ahl-e-hadis.

The founding of Hamidia Rizvia and other major madrasas in Banaras are part and result of the educational history of colonialism. After Wood's Despatch in 1854, local Muslims failed to 'take advantage' of the new government scheme of grants-in-aid for both vocational and ethical reasons. The new schools were favoured by some because they trained boys for an official or professional career, but, as the government was told by assorted members of the public, 'the Ansaris already have a profession.'[10] Nor could the weavers resign themselves to sending their children to schools where no character formation would take place. Together with other castes and communities, Ansaris came to found their own institutions, in which, they believed, a synthesis between the spiritual (*dini*) and the worldly (*duniyayi*) could be effected.[11] In the process of doing this, they worked along denominational lines: the Deobandis and Ahl-e-hadis set up separate madrasas, as did the Barelwis. Their teachers were hired accordingly and their textbooks chosen or even written according to sectarian loyalties.

Shahzad Akhtar's fate is affected in ironic ways by this. For us, he is entirely part of the popular culture of Banaras that is shared wholeheartedly by all weavers and all artisans (along with some other occupational groups), and his primary identity is that of 'Banarasi'. As a school-goer he is also subject to a teaching that defines him as a 'Muslim' and as a 'Barelwi'. He is constantly made aware of his own sectarian identity and that of his school; his friends (at least in school) are all Barelwis, and he adopts an unquestioned sense of righteousness regarding other sects—attributes shared by all my informants.

Jamia Hamidia Rizvia, like other madrasas, had to develop its own curriculum once the accepted classical Islamic syllabus, the *dars-e-nizamiya*, was substituted by a government board syllabus.[12] Histories and Geographies had to be written, since such subjects did not traditionally form part of the Islamic syllabus.[13] The text used at present by Hamidia Rizvia is 'Geography District Varanasi' for 'the fourth grade of Islamic maktabs' written by Maulana Abdus Salam, author of two larger works on the subject, *Tarikh Asar-e-Banaras* (The History of Banaras) and *Tazkara Mushayakh Banaras* (Narrative of the Great Men (Sheikhs) of Banaras).[14] Let us look at only one issue as it is treated by the maktab's social studies book.

The Gyanvapi mosque, the Jama Masjid of the city, is in the heart of Banaras, next to the Vishwanath temple. It is of signal interest to historians in the threat it poses today as a target for the wrath of fundamentalist Hindus who consider it symbolic of Islamic iconoclasm. The book discusses the mosque's name and location, then goes on to say: 'This Jama Masjid was built approximately 315 years ago in 1070 hijri (*c.* AD 1664) by the renowned badshah of Hindustan, Alamgir. Hindus claim that it was built by destroying a temple on this site. This is wrong. The foundations of this mosque were laid by the great grandfather of Badshah Alamgir, Akbar, and Alamgir's father, Shah Jahan, had started a madrasa in the mosque in 1048 hijri which was named Imam-e-Sharifat.'[15]

Of course the status of the iconoclastic activities of Alamgir, better known as Aurangzeb, as well as the origins of the Gyanvapi mosque are far from resolved. Indian textbooks have unreflectively presented, and continue to present, Aurangzeb as among the most fanatic of Muslim rulers (and for them there are many to choose from) and the destruction of any temple by him as a most credible, unquestionable fact. Meanwhile, contemporary research has shown that complex political motives usually lie behind seemingly simple religious ones. The Hamidia Rizvia textbook is therefore 'right' in its denial of guilt to Aurangzeb but 'wrong' in the reasons it gives for this.

What is of immediate relevance here is that textbooks of this kind create a history and consciousness on questionable premises. In this case a community is being set up which includes Alamgir, an Emperor whose sway extended over the whole of Hindustan, and weavers in Banaras, mostly poor and illiterate. The dividing line is laid between this community, which worships at and therefore builds mosques, and those who worship at temples and therefore mourn their destruction. Such divisions and constructions do not have to be anything more than suggestive and associative to make an impression on minds of every age. Evidence from the fantastic and dramatic epochs of the past are powerfully used in these constructions, being in stark contrast to the humdrum existence of poverty-ridden everyday life.

Madrasas, depending on their sectarian affiliations, stress their separate identity constructions, however. Jamia Salfia (Ahl-e-hadis) or Jamia Islamiya (Deobandi) would never accept the definitions, the reasoning, or even the form and layout of a textbook published by Jamia Rizvia. The community remains therefore a burgeoning 'Muslim' one, but one qualified by a sectarian identity.

Does all this at all match what we hear from Shahzad Akhtar about his own experiences? We can discount his mother's testimony that things were much 'better' in her student days as the romantic nostalgia of a parent frustrated by a child's failure. But while in conversation Shahzad and I were surrounded by four other children from the same madrasa who agreed with everything he was saying, qualifying it for their own teachers and classes. Shahzad is an attractive, cheerful, intelligent, sociable boy, who is articulate on all subjects, but specially effective on certain chosen ones (his teachers' injustices, his sister's doll).

Shahzad does not know what happened in 1947. Shahzad cannot remember any episode or personality from Indian history. Furthermore, he cannot make up, improvise or just invent anything as a child with an active imagination and elementary training in answering questions of a 'textbook' character might be expected to do.

His responses constitute a damning indictment of his school. First, that no History has apparently been taught him even within the rote-learning system. Second, that no overall pattern has been revealed to his regarding how to field questions or spin tales, that is, to construct narratives. Third, and where the madrasa shares the fault with most other schools in our country, no connections have been suggested between his own life and larger historical developments.

If we turn to the second interview, with the teacher that Shahzad admires, we find part of the key to the puzzle. If Master Mansoor may be taken as spokesman for the madrasa, as he and I both consider him to be, his answer to the poor learning of students like Shahzad is that Ansaris in general are apathetic to learning. They should support the schools and the students. In 'other' schools (i.e., where guardians are more active), schools do twenty-five per cent of the teaching, guardians the rest, and here the school has to do ninety-five per cent of the teaching.[16] The Ansari guardians are not only lacking in 'society' and 'culture' (i.e., they do not share in middle-class ideals of progress), towards education they are particularly *udasin* (indifferent, because interested only in the child's learning the Quran).

The guardians, on the other hand, imagine that the child's learning will naturally take place in the school (what percentage was not specified to me, but I repeatedly got the impression that it was almost a hundred). Since madrasas are known to be aided institutions, which receive in addition charitable endowments, it is a common speculation that their funds are being misused by their managers. Why else would the kind of descriptions that Shahzad gives of classroom conditions be given? Why else would the child learn so little?

Our approach to the 'problem' is to try and see it as a condition of a certain faultline between modern and pre-modern discourses. The madrasa would like to expect the guardians to behave like modern, participating citizens and prepare their children socially and psychologically for an educated future. Such a future would be bounded by practical considerations such as health, nutrition, and family planning; and by ideological ones such as awareness of constitutional rights (distinguishing between the hierarchical values of 'freedom') and participation as a full citizen of a democracy (distinguishing between 'myth' and 'history'). The guardians, on the other hand, are still part of a 'pre-modern' world, one that has been trying for at least the whole of the twentieth century to come to terms with the demands of modernization. If indeed it was an older world where an Ansari world-view was fully legitimate and the outside world condemnable, socialization could be left to the family. If, similarly, it was a newer world where a modern nationalist world-view was hegemonic, social-ization could be left to the schools.

As things stand, Shahzad learns little in the school. The school blames the parents for their ignorance of the modern educational agenda. The parents blame the school for not fulfilling the agenda, conscious that they are being treated as inferior in this old-new dicho-tomy.

Of course, while Shahzad does not know what happened in 1947, what is important is that he does know and is learning many other things. Together with other Ansari boys, he is learning the craft of weaving, both its technique and its ethic, or how a weaver is expected to conduct himself. He is learning the pleasures of the outdoors and established pastimes in the popular culture of Banaras. He is gradually being socialized into gender role-playing (even the sewing and necklace-making that impressed me so much, on later consideration, has much to do with his learning to weave and embroider). Every part of his work and leisure underlines his maleness first. And since he does go to school and passes exams, he is learning to think of himself as 'educated'. An educated person is necessarily superior to an uneducated person, but inferior to others educated in more normative ways. Madrasa education is on the brink between non-education and education in the eyes of the system and its supporters, and almost everyone else as well.

There is a structural congruity here. Shahzad will never become a well-educated person—or he will never become a good weaver. Good weavers, the majority of weavers, are those who are tied to their occu-pation as a given, an inevitability that is justified by its being the 'best occupation' in the world. They are free and unreformed, sceptical of the values of control, discipline, citizenship, and progress. The practices of Jamia Hamidia Rizvia effortlessly guarantee Shahzad's fit for this role. And all madrasas are like that, according to educators: in the balance they try to maintain between *dini* and *duniyayi* instruction, they go on the side of religion.[17]

One conclusion that emerges effortlessly is that community-based schools such as the madrasas of Banaras must be sacrificed for national(ist) schools. The needs of a community, whether religious, occupational, or linguistic, have to be erased before the needs of the nation. This is a violent, arbitrary, colonial solution. Madrasas and other schools may be pedagogically weak, but they are not 'symbolically violent;'[18] they do not impose the 'culture arbitrary' of the dominant group of society onto other groups. At the same time, they are repressive in that they restrict the choices of children. If we acknowledge the value of freedom, not in the weavers' sense of strolling around and spitting everywhere, but in the sense of the equality with other citizens to choose occupation and lifestyle, then it is the madrasa that precludes such freedom totally.

Part of being a good weaver is to be rooted in local culture, protective of a particular history, ignorant of and indifferent to the nation and its history, unaware of 1947. A good weaver is aware instead of being a Muslim, a Barelwi, a Banarasi, and an Ansari, an unreflective supporter of the Pakistani cricket team, and resistant to the condemnations of ignorance and backwardness because self-sufficient in himself. There is a close tie between history-teaching and citizenship. The madrasa children reproduce their lower class-identities directly through their madrasas, and not through resistance to them, as would the working-class children in a modern British school.[19]

II

This section is prefaced by a set of two descriptions of participant-observation situations and two interviews.

Participant Observation 1

I teach History in Class V in Qudrutullah Gulzar-e-Talim, a Muslim school for girls in Banaras.

Class V has fifty students, of which some five are absent. It is a spacious, well-lit, airy classroom, with bare walls, serviceable desks and benches, a large blackboard (for which a child produces the chalk from inside her desk). They are all wary of me in the beginning, and warm up slowly.

I ask them about 1947. There is a prompt response from the same child concerning aspects of the event, Independence and Partition, as well as to my third question, regarding five important freedom fighters. The hesitation in answering is so extreme, with the same child attempting the next few questions as well, that I wonder aloud if she stands first or second in the class. She does not. Now the two who do shake themselves up slightly.

I ask them to attempt a map of India on the blackboard. They will not. I show them the trick of making it with a triangle. With vast prodding and help from me, some two or three come up and make a hash of it. None of them have a mental picture of India, its neighbours, or its states. They cannot place any of them on the map, or any cities, or anything else. When questioned orally, they know the main mountains, rivers, and cities. They have obviously never used the blackboard, drawn anything, or attempted anything visually or tactically.

Does anyone know a story or song regarding 1947? No. With some help from me, a couple of girls mention a song or two, such as *Sare jahan se achha*. Has anyone heard a story? No. I mention stories, songs and scenes familiar to me from television. It seems to me that their general knowledge, even of TV and film content, is very poor. Even more, their *level of interest* in what is shown or could be shown on TV is very poor.

I try to probe their identities. What is their father's occupation? After a long bout of tongue-tiedness, one ventures the euphemism, 'loom *ka kam*' (the work of the loom). Almost all are from weavers' families. Do their mothers work? Upon their saying 'no,' it goes to their credit that they all look embarassed when I wonder aloud if housework is not work. They vow to never consider their mothers non-workers again.

Their identities are securely gender-based. They laugh heartily when I suggest that their fathers may supply them clean uniforms for school. They associate intimately with their mothers. All are eager to claim sharing in her work: washing and ironing clothes, washing dishes, cooking, cleaning up. They love it when I ask questions about their dolls and how many were married. Hands shoot up with alacrity. Smiles flash on most faces.

Their subjects are all the same as in a madrasa, including Urdu, Diniyat, and Arabic in addition to the Board subjects. Equal numbers raise their hands for Urdu, Maths, and English as their favourite subjects. Many of them have tutors.

When I discover they have no music, dance, or drama, and that the school merely gave a holiday on Republic Day instead of celebrating it, I heave an involuntary sigh of disappointment. 'One *should* have some music, dance, or drama' escapes me. Such is the rapport built up in the class by now that they wistfully agree with me.

Participant Observation 2

I interact with class XI in the same school, Qudrutullah.

There are eighteen girls, some fifteen or seventeen years old, sensible, confident, and pleasant-looking. They are sitting temporarily in a classroom not theirs, so when I look around for their *naqabs* (veils), I don't see them; they have hung them in their own room. A couple of voices murmur, 'We don't all wear naqabs.' (The Principal had earlier told me that naqabs were compulsory). Throughout the class, the teacher of Economics, Indrani Tripathi, sits with me. They have no choice of subjects: all do Hindi, Economics, and Home Science. They are just the second or third batch to be in class XI, and the second one from whom some hope of future collegians can be held.

They answer promptly all my questions regarding 1947 and freedom fighters. They remember at least the film *Gandhi* and have heard nationalistic songs on TV. They even have some idea of what to do for the country, especially one who is a doctor's daughter.

They are unselfconscious about Pakistan. Many have relatives there who visit often. One, who narrates the tale of an aunt who does not like it in Pakistan because she does not feel at home (*apnapan*) there, is greeted with empathy by others.

All help at home. One even makes candles and pickles, presumably helping in her mother's work.

They meet each other, go out shopping, watch TV, read Urdu magazines and *Stardust.* Two respond with a 'yes' to having Hindu friends: for one it is the daughter of her father's friend, for the other, a neighbour in the mixed Hindu-Muslim mohalla of Shivala.

The girls seem relaxed about themselves and their future. Some five plan to do a B.A. from Basanta College. One can *picture* them as promising undergraduates, in burqa or not.

In my view the greater 'secularization' and 'national identification' of these girls is due partly to their belonging to a different class of Ansaris, those who would prefer non-madrasa to madrasa schools. Within these schools, it is due further to their having some Hindu teachers, like Indrani. These are modern, secular, nationalist women who are subtly Hindu; they are friendly observers of the girls, but their critics and reformers as well. My most powerful impression of the teacher was that she was a trifle bemused by Muslim customs, none of which happens with Hindu children getting a Muslim teacher. The students learn in a myriad subtle ways how to conform to 'majority religion' and 'national' culture, and because they and their families have the will to do so, they conform and 'progress'.

The second part of this second section moves to a different stage of action, Calcutta. The children studied here are all sons and daughters of refugees from East Pakistan in 1947–48, who live in the colonies of Tollygunj like Netaji Nagar and Kudghat. The families are Hindu, but secular and liberal. They are upwardly mobile and universalist, and believe in progress. All the children go to schools that are overtly religious: Loreto House (Christian), Future Foundations (Hindu, based on Sri Aurobindo's philosophy), and Ramakrishna Mission Vidyalaya (Hindu). These schools are taken by me as typical of those that project a national, secular version of India's history. The families concur in this version, regardless (or some may say because) of the past that individuals have experienced.

*Interview 3: Daughter of a Refugee from
East Bengal, Ten Years Old, Student of Loreto House,
a Christian Missionary School*

'Who are you?'

'I am a girl. I like badminton and cycling and my favourite food is cheese. My hobby is reading. My favourite subject is Science. . . . I'm short, I have black hair and brown eyes (there was no response to stimulus from my side for more community-oriented definitions of the self)'.

'What do you know about 1947?'

'It was an important year but I can't remember what happened. Yes, India got Independence from British rule.'

'Do you know about Partition?'

'There were lots of riots going around. India got divided into two. All the Hindus came to India and all the Muslims went to Pakistan.'

'What are Hindus?'

'It's a religion?' (I encourage her) 'Hindus are a kind of people.'

'What kind?'

'Their language is Hindi and most of them live in India.'

'Who are they different from?'

'Sikhs.'

'Anyone else?'

'Muslims?'

'What are Muslims?'

'Muslim are just another kind of people. They go to mosques and do a few other things differently.'

'Do you know any Muslims?'

'No.'

'How would you know a Muslim if you saw one?'

'They dress differently. The girls wear veils. The boys wear salwar-kameez—no, kurta-pyjama—and caps.'

'Do they speak Hindi?'

'Yes' (realizes that earlier she had said only Hindus did).

'What about Masroor? (a friend of hers who is Muslim) How is he different from you? What is the difference?'

'He is not. There is no difference.'

'What is your father?'

'He is the director . . . (gives occupation) His religion? He is a Hindu.'

'How do you know?'

'I *know* he is.'

'Does he do *puja*? Go to temples?'

'He doesn't go to mosques. No, he doesn't go to temples. He *visits* temples.'

'*Puja?*'

(Doubtfully, then humorously) 'I've seen him light a wick.'

'Tell me about your father's father.'

'He was a zamindar and used to own a lot of property and then he sold it all. I don't know when. Was he a Hindu? I don't know. I think he was. No, I have not seen any pictures of him or his house' (I know that such pictures hang in their family house).

'How do you know all this?'

'My father told me.'

'Do you know where he lived? Anything else?'

'In Bengal, but I don't know where. I don't know anything else.'

'Would you like to know?'

'Yes.'

'Do you know any stories about Muslims?'

'Id is their festival. They go to mosques and they pray. Once in my old school on Id we had a poetry competition. In one book I saw they were hugging in a special way, on both sides of the neck.'

'Do you know that Hindu and Muslims fight?'

'Yaah, I don't know about what. I know that one of our neighbouring countries wanted to take Kashmir . . . it was China or Pakistan. . . . Why Kashmir? It makes a lot of things. It's clean and pretty.'

'Would you like to fight? For Kashmir?'

'Yaah, (grins) No! I don't like fighting. I would not do it because I would like to do something else.'

'For yourself? Or for India?'

'I don't know. Yes, for both.'

Interview No. 4: Son of a Refugee from East Bengal, Thirteen Years Old, Student of Class VIII in Ramakrishna Mission Association

'Who are you?'

'My name is Dibyarka Basu. There is not much to say about me. I am a boy. I read in RKMA Vidyalaya. My hobbies are reading story books and watching cricket.'

'What do you know about 1947?'

'It was a year that brought much hope to the Indian common people. But the Independence of India also brought the Partition of Bengal. A catastrophic (pauses, gropes for word) riot began. It gave the Indian people an opportunity to develop their country, but it gave the political leaders a way of exploiting the country.'

'Who is to blame?'

'Mahatma Gandhi is partially involved but I think the real. . . . was Zinnah [*sic*].'

'How do you know all this?'

'General information . . . what I hear from people, what I read in books.'

'Do you study about it in History?'

'No, our textbooks have nothing on this. Our syllabus is not so much attached with politics.'

'Do your teachers talk about it?'

'Our History teacher is not so good, although he has knowledge, but my English teacher in my previous school was very good.'

'Did you see anything on TV in this connection?'

'Yes, two or three films . . . I can't remember which. *Gandhi*? Yes. Yes, I know some songs. Which ones? "Bande Mataram. "Bharat *amar janani*." On 15 August we have a march or parade, and flag hoisting.'

'Do your parents tell you about this?'

'My father does. No, he is not like the textbook.'

'Do you know anything about your grandfathers?'

'Yes, he [*sic*] was Professor of English. I heard that he was wise. He lived nearby. The second grandfather I have forgotten. At one time, at *one time* he lived in Bangladesh. I don't know where. His occupation? I don't know.'

'Would you like to know?'

'Yes. I am interested.'

'Are you a Hindu?'

'Yes.'

'How is that different from others?'

'There is no difference. Customs are different. That is not very important. All the gods of all the religions are the same. My father and mother are Hindu *by name*. They celebrate Durga *puja*. They worship Goddess Kali. But all the gods are the same.'

'Do you know any Muslims?'

'Yes. (Names cricketers, at least four of them.) No, I have no friends. I have one uncle. Not a direct relation. A friend of my father's. No, there is no difference between his house and mine . . . yes, the construction is different. There are no attached bathrooms. The kitchen is very big. There is a big roof. The house is large. They are rich.'

'Why do Hindus and Muslims fight?'

'It is a perfect example of stupidity. There is no reason to fight. It is due to orthodoxies. They are stubborn. No, I don't know this from my teachers, but in general . . . but I don't know the way of removing this.'

'Would you like to do something about it when you grow up?'

'It depends on the political situation of the time. There may be no need.'

'What religious books do you know or have read?'

'The Veda. We have shlokas in our school. "*Amader Gan*" has Veda-*path*. We have a subject, "Indian culture". We memorize shlokas and learn the meanings. No, I have not read the Quran.'

'Would you like to read it?'
'No. I mean I have not decided.'

In the first participant-observation above, the Muslim school described sets itself apart from madrasas, and places itself in the tradition of Sir Syed Ahmad Khan. Together with about a score of other such institutions in Banaras, it states its intention to produce a well-rounded, modern, progressive person, but one who is also a good Muslim. Those running the best-endowed and respected madrasas would say that that was their intention as well. But the differences in the two kinds of schools are quite apparent to all. We could name them for our present purposes as two: one, that the principal and teachers of Qudrutullah depend far more on the guardians of their students to accomplish their purposes than the madrasas can. The Qudrutullah guardians are required to cooperate in the school's mission of having students perform daily scholastic duties and pass periodic exams, and the guardians in fact do so—or remove their wards to a madrasa. The guardians' failure to thus perform is exactly what madrasa teachers deplore but have to tolerate.

The second difference is a corollary of this greater cooperation: the undermining of the arts of memory in daily life. The school, in performing its job better, co-opts the home, weakens home culture, and weakens the world of intangible traditions, rituals, practices, and role-playing that helped—and continues to help in the case of madrasa children—in the perpetuation of histories. Students in modern schools will not have the time or inclination to learn, and her guardians will not have the will, the coherence, and sometimes even the courage, to teach in any way an identity and relationship to the past that is different from the one officially preferred. The project of modernization, secularization, and nationalization becomes a family project, with the child at the vanguard.

Interviews 3 and 4 demonstrate—indeed, highlight—the second process at work. The school's history teaching is imbibed by the child but with no connection to the child's own identity. Nor does the child have an alternative culture or history. The schools these two students belong to are, respectively, an old, well-established Christian missionary school, a model for a kind of modern English medium institution; and a Hindu reformist school, which denominational differences aside, has an Annie Besant philosophy of producing modern, scientific Hindu citizens. In both cases the overwhelming experience of the child is one of homogenization, where no part of the home culture is acknowledged or tolerated, unless it be targeted for reform.[20]

Since a child's experiential sensitivity is probably greater even than our imagination—only our memories of childhood sometimes give us a glimpse of this sensitivity—the child succumbs to these homogenizing influences. Children of modern public and missionary schools (of whatever denomination) assimilate the daily routine and rituals of their schools much more completely than envisioned by educationists.[21] All of home culture becomes a trace, a mark fading with time. Guardians of children in these public or missionary schools cooperate with the project of homogenization far more fully than in the modern Muslim school. In such public schools, they are likely not to follow, but to lead the school in its mission, being either products of such institutions themselves, or consumed by the ambition of seeing their children 'succeed' in a frankly competitive world. In the case of the above interviewees, the parents were refugees from East Bengal in 1947—but whatever they retain of an alternative history is consigned slowly to oblivion. All linguistic, regional, sectarian, and caste identities of the child and her family are purposefully erased.

Guardians in fact concede this readily, although with different points of emphasis. The parents of interviewees no. 3 and 4 agreed that we in India do not respect history, we keep no documents in the house, we believe little in story-telling about or ritualizing the past. One father regarded this as an economic problem, people in general being preoccupied with mundane worries, with no time for more 'abstract' thoughts. The other parent regarded it as a cultural problem that stood out starkly when contrasted with the case of England or America. Neither would have agreed that they, the middle class, compared unfavourably in this respect with people like the poorer weavers of Banaras, who quite successfully transmit their history to their children, defying all demands of homogenization.

In defiance of their own logic, however, but not the larger logic of their class-position, they would have maintained that they compared *favourably* with lower classes such as the weavers in that they had made the more rewarding choice of moulding themselves into a secular, nationalist identity—even at the expense of having their children grow up with no notion of the caste, cultural, or even existentially formed historical identities of their families. The class loyalties behind particular positions on 'history' are profoundly important—even as the regional and sectarian are not—but are not the focus of the present essay. Here I wish to only arouse us dealers with 'history' to a greater reflexivity about our enterprise, and do not properly analyse the causes that give rise to nationalist versus alternative histories.

In order to tease out the analyses from these interviews further, we have to remind ourselves of some implications of a nationalist system of education which necessarily includes a nationalist history. That the exercise that schools are engaged in is a violence in which control of the minds of children is achieved and notions of what is true, proper, credible are imprinted on them, is too well understood to need elaboration.[22] As long as we speak of the nationalist system, we are stuck with the problem of colonization. As long as we subscribe to its values, we are acting colonially.

It is perhaps natural for us to regard the socialization effected by Qudrutullah, Loreto, and Ramakrishna Mission Vidyalaya, as more successful than that of Jamia Hamidia Rizviya. The Muslim, Christian, and Hindu reformist schools—all claiming to be secular in practice within their sectarian ideological pronouncements—teach students with more professional acumen. They are closer to the model of a modern institution, with less soul-searching and conflict regarding the validity of the model.[23] Their students are better able to answer factual questions regarding their history, and they are better trained in the art of answering questions altogether. As one student responded,

I think Partition was the fault of some leaders who wanted to satisfy their own interests, like Jinnah; they knew they were in a minority in India, they would never become big leaders—now I'm talking like my textbook—they aroused communal feeling among Muslims. The Congress had to agree. (Were some of the Congress leaders not at fault?) (Pause) Some of the Congress leaders might have also wanted Partition but the aim of the Congress was to keep India united so they couldn't openly support that demand.[24]

Both the level of knowledge of the student and her self-consciousness that she sounds like her textbooks are noteworthy. Also noteworthy, in interview 3 especially, is the reflexive sense of humour as the child admits that she would 'rather do something else' than fight for her country even to save the 'clean and pretty' Kashmir,[25] or as another child of the same age responded, 'I do not want to fight because I might die, and I prefer to be alive than to be dead.'[26] Similarly the self-conscious dignity of interviewee number 4 is remarkable when he refuses to commit himself to what he would do to resolve the communal question when he grew up: 'It would depend on the political situation of the time.'[27]

How far the 'History' learnt as a subject gets assimilated by the child as part of his or her identity is not possible for us to say conclusively, given our relatively simple ethnography here.[28] The evident indifference in response to questions related to History in general and 'Indian History' in particular, points to a weak relationship between the subject as studied and the child's sense of the self. The child's world does not incorporate a sense of the nation and its birth. But then there are the occasional insights which obviously draw upon and play between school lessons and personal experiences; these indicate at least the possibility of a relationship between taught subject and self. For instance, a fourteen-year-old in Future Foundation (the school based on Aurobindo's teaching) said:

Yes, I am a Hindu. I am first an Indian, then a Hindu. It doesn't feel good to think of oneself as a Hindu. For example, a dada (senior male student) in our school is a Muslim. One day my friend Reoti called him a 'mollah' . . . it felt very bad. My friend also called Azharuddin a 'mollah' because he didn't play well. Not that I am a supporter of Azharuddin, but I don't have that bad impression about Muslims. I wanted to object but my friend Rishika didn't want me to. *Thak* (let it be), she said, these are matters of caste and community. Our miss says, '*tomra to bheto Bangali*' ('you are all cowardly Bengalis')—you are communal and prejudiced but don't dare to show it. She said that in matches, Muslims support Pakistan, but we would not dare to. I like it that India is secular. I could be a Muslim or anything, it would be the same, but I wouldn't wear the burqa, I hate that.[29]

Or as another child of an immigrant father from Pakistan and a non-immigrant mother explained:

Am I sorry about Partition? My grandfather was a zamindar, he had a lot of property. They had to leave all their property. Later on, the government gave some of the money to the refugees, not all the money, that would have been too much. My grandfather had a really nice library which they had to leave behind. (Pause) My father seems sorry about Partition. Since they had a big library, I'm sorry. But, (pause) if it hadn't happened, if they'd stayed there, our lives would have been different. He wouldn't have met my mother, I wouldn't have been born. It must have been very sad for them though. My father said my grandfather didn't want to leave.[30]

This interesting philosophical point came quite unself-consciously to the child: what happens in history, when seen from our personal vantage point, is very likely the best, since if things had happened differently, we personally wouldn't be here at all to to discuss these questions.

Conclusion

The problem for historians arises in the impossibility of distancing themselves from a judgemental involvement in the historical process. What we say will suggest, partly by implication, whether we are personally wedded to a one-nation, a two-nation, or a multi-nation theory, whether we believe in the continuity of history and a nationalistic historiography or not, what content we prefer this nationalistic historiography to have, and whether we celebrate the efforts of communities to reproduce their local identities at the expense of a national one, or consider it a regrettable attribute of their marginalization.[31]

The conclusion of this essay is two-fold, both related to history-writing and history-teaching. While inter-related, the first has to do with the technology of education, and the second with its politics.

The child in South Asia—both the advantaged middle class child who learns school history lessons well, and the disadvantaged working class child whose school has not yet developed a technique to teach national history—grows up without a sense of certainty about his national history, where he belongs in it, and what his 'duties' within it are.[32] The home, in such a country, a postcolonial, underdeveloped country, is greatly impoverished. The modern state and its appurtenances may not have scored a total victory, but fight a tough battle. Their voice is loud and clear, if not always comprehensible. So, many of the earlier socialization functions of the home are meddled with and written over by the state.

But the school, ostensibly part of a universalist modern system of education, fails because of its pedagogic poverty. While the trappings of the school are modernistic, its 'hidden curricula' falters. Also, there is little reflection or debate about the actual processes by which children may be wooed to participate in the construction of an identity. The approaches that are adopted are not informed by any remarkable pedagogical expertise or respect for children's developmental levels.[33] The schools' aim is to build up historically conscious nationalistic individuals, but the school fails. Its products either do not learn a national history, or they do not assimilate the history they learn as truth; in neither case do they internalize it as part of their identities. At both extremes, that of the minimally modern institution of Jamia Rizviya, and of the acknowledged leader-in-the-field modern institution of Loreto, educators agree with this assessment. Those of the former school put the blame on guardians: these educators appear yet to learn the other lesson of modernism that such obstacles must be crushed into submission. Those of the latter school accept that they probably emphasize the universal and the comparative (which should more precisely be read as the Western) at the expense of the national and the local, but maintain that it is a good choice.[34] This 'failure' of the school—and I use the word in a restricted, contextualized sense— is for pedagogues to overcome through the particular practices in their classrooms. They need to take to heart the lesson that they all know intimately from their teaching experience, that (i) a pedagogue has made a choice of strategy as soon as he begins his class; (ii) this strategy is not limited to the content of the textbook but infuses every process in the classroom space; and (iii) that even the contents of the chapters are assimilated only to the degree that they capture what we call the child's 'imagination'.

Secondly, as professional historians who do not quake before a questioning of the outdated scientism of our discipline, we must ask of our history writing if we are willing to risk experimentation, to collapse, for instance, history's boundaries with aesthetics, tradition, story-telling, and other arts of memory. Can we confront the peculiar task before us, to be nationalists without denying other histories? Can we improvise upon the forgotten techniques by which histories were always transmitted, in the interests of making our nationalist history interact with personal and community histories? History has not come to an end anywhere. Yet the difference that marks societies where a nationalist vision of the self and one's country predominates (say, in Britain or the USA), and those where many alternate histories co-exist (say, India), is not reflected in any parallel difference in the history-writing of the respective societies, namely the ex-metropolises and the ex-colonies. Historians of India could reflect on this for their own craft, and, together with pedagogues, for the sake of the nation's culture. How must we formulate the relationship between our official History and the senses of history created in a routine, everyday way? How could one write or teach about the nation in ways that do the least possible violence, indeed, that respect and celebrate other higher and lower level un-mixing and un-matching histories?

This relationship is ironically left un-problematized at both extremes of viewing the question of children and history. A modernizer like Myron Weiner[35] assumes that only a state or a bureaucratic will is needed to make all people choose to educate their children in a similar way. A critic of modernism like Dipesh Chakrabarty[36] suggests that to propose lessons in sanitation or the germ theory, or by implication, other lessons in modern self-worth, is to outrage some 'natural' 'indigenous' dimension of thought that should be left free. The first steps towards a problematization should subject these assumptions to scrutiny.

As practising historians, and not to mince matters, brick and mortar *constructors of the nation*, it would defeat our purposes to claim that answers exist, but only remain to be found. Answers have to be made up. But many starting points exist. For instance, the knowledge that we might be seeking approval from some unnamed god of 'science' when we set about delineating the margins even as we define the centre. Or the knowledge that we may be so rooted in the class prejudices that decide our gains and losses that we cannot even recognize alternative wills to action. Or even the knowledge that to hear other voices is not to root for their naturalness. If politics lies within the historian's domain, it also lies elsewhere in the memories and identity constructions of the dominated others.

These and other starting points have already been mapped and the task is not so much to belabour the difficulties before us as to appreciate the need for incorporating such problematization into our practice.[37] How, after all, do we educate a child about her nation and yet protect that brilliant innocence which makes her admit that she would not like to fight to preserve its boundaries because she 'would rather do something else?'

NOTES AND REFERENCES

1. See Angelika Rauch, 'The Broken Vessel of Tradition', *Representations* 53, Winter 1996, pp. 74–96, a paper with which I only partly agree.
2. Zafar Sadiq, weaver, Madanpura; Khaliqulzamman Khan, Police Sub Inspector, observer of weavers, Adampura.
3. N. Kumar, *The Artisans of Banaras: Popular Culture and Identity*, Princeton: Princeton University Press, 1988; rpt., Hyderabad: Orient Longman, 1994.

4. N. Kumar, 'The "Truth" About Muslims in Banaras', *Social Analysis*, Special Issue no. 23, 1990, pp. 82–96.

5. This has been the 'traditional' way of teaching weaving for at least the whole of the twentieth century; see B.P. Singh, *Banaras ke Vyavsayi*, Kashi: Gyan Mandal, 1920, pp. 4–6.

6. See N. Kumar, 'D'ou venez-vous?' Le *mohalla* de Benaras' ('Where are you from?' The *mohalla* of Benares'), in *Benares: un Voyage d'architecture*, Paris: Editions Creaphis, 1989.

7. See Kumar, *The Artisans*.

8. This and all other information on Hamidia Rizvia and other madrasas is obtained from the members of their managing committees: here chiefly from Janab Moinuddin, Secretary.

9. Barbara Metcalf, *Islamic Revival in British India: The Madrasa at Deoband*, Princeton: Princeton University Press, 1984.

10. File 728 GD Block 1887, UP Archives.

11. File 7 Education A 1917, UP Archives, File 14, Education A, 1911, UP Archives.

12. I thank the late Maulana Abdus Salam Nomani for explaining to me the *dars-e-nizamiyya's* role in Banaras education; see also Francis Robinson, 'The Ulama of Farangi Mahall and Their Adab', in B. Metcalf, ed., *Moral Conduct and Authority*, Berkeley: University of California Press, 1984.

13. See B. Metcalf, *Islamic Revival*, Maulana A.S. Nomani.

14. Abdus Salam Nomani, *Tarikh' Asar-e-Banaras*, Banaras: Maktaba Nadvatulma'arif , 1963.

15. Abdus Salam Nomani, *Geographia Zila Varanasi: A Textbook for Darza IV of Islamic Maktabs*.

16. Mohammad Iqbal and Mohammad Siddiqi, teachers, Jamia Islamia.

17. Among many others, the following prominent educationists may be mentioned as sharing this view: Salamullah of Farogh-e-Urdu; Abdul Aziz of Mazhar-ul-uloom; Hafiz ur Rahman of National Inter College; Badruddin Ansari of National Inter College.

18. Pierre Bourdieu, *Outline of a Theory of Practice*, trans. Richard Nice, Cambridge: Cambridge University Press, 1977.

19. Paul Willis, *Learning to Labour: How Working Class Children Get Working Class Jobs*, Westmead: Saxon House, 1977.

20. Described eloquently by Jerome Christensen as 'The Revolutionary Vernacularizing Thrust of Capitalism' which peremptorily determines native intelligence by censoring unruly, demotic speech as gibberish; in 'The Romantic Movement at the End of History', *Critical Inquiry*, 20, no. 3 Spring 1994, 452–76.

21. I discuss this in detail in N. Kumar, *Lessons from Schools: The History of Education in Banaras*, Delhi: Sage, 2000.

22. It is difficult, therefore, to see how Ashis Nandy makes a thesis of this point in 'Reconstructing Childhood; A Critique of the Ideology of Adulthood', in his *Traditions, Tyranny, and Utopias: Essays in the Politics of Awareness*, Delhi: Oxford University Press, 1987. The literature on education is replete with discussions of precisely this function of education. For references and overall discussion, see Kathleen Lynch, *The Hidden Curriculum: Reproduction in Education—An Appraisal*, London: The Falmer Press, 1989; Peter Woods, *The Divided School*, London: Routledge & Kegan Paul, 1979.

23. Educational institutions in India have hardly been discussed in light of their distance or proximity to the modern model they are based on. For a preliminary but interesting discussion see Edward Shils, 'The Academic Profession in India', in Edmund Leach and S.N. Mukherjee, eds, *Elites in South Asia*, Cambridge: Cambridge University Press, 1979.

24. Irfana Majumdar, student of Class X, Loreto House, Calcutta.

25. Saraswati Nandini, student of Class V, Loreto House, Calcutta.

26. Rudra Majumdar, student of Class V, Future Foundation School, Calcutta.

27. Dibyarka Basu, student of Class VII, Ramakrishna Mission Vidyalaya, Calcutta.

28. Discussions of childhood show a deplorable thinness; see for instance, Anja Forssen, ed., *Childhood in Four Societies Part I: Tanzania and Finland*, Helsinki: The Finnish Anthropological Society, 1985, and Frederick Ellen and Gerald Handel, *The Child and Society: The Process of Socialization*, New York: Random House, 1978.

29. Sriparna Majumdar, student of Class IX, Future Foundation School, Calcutta.

30. Irfana Majumdar.

31. See Avril Powell, 'Perceptions of the South Asian Past: Ideology, Nationalism and School History Textbooks', in Nigel Crook, ed., *The Transmission of Knowledge in South Asia*, Delhi: Oxford University Press, 1996, pp. 190–228.

32. For the more interesting discussions along these lines, see E. Valentine Daniel, 'Three Dispositions Towards the Past: One Sinhala, Two Tamil', in H.L. Seneviratne, ed., *Identity, Consciousness and the Past, Social Analysis*, Special Issue Series no. 25, September 1985, 22–41; Terence Ranger, 'The Invention of Tradition Revisited', in Preben Kaarholm and Jan Hultin, eds, *Inventions and Boundaries: Historical and Anthropological Approaches to the Study of Ethnicity and Nationalism*, Roskilde: Roskilde University International Development Studies, 1994. For an indigenous, non-academic view,

C.G. Kolhatkar, 'Bahurupi', in D.D. Karve, trans. and Ellen McDonald, ed., *The New Brahmans: Five Maharashtrian Families*, Berkeley: University of California Press, 1963, p. 143.

33. For two opposed explanations, see Robin W. Levin, 'The School and the Articulation of Values', *American Journal of Education*, 96, no. 2, February 1988, 143—61; and Krishna Kumar, 'Origins of India's "Textbook Culture" ', *Comparative Education Review* 32, no. 4, November 1988, pp. 452–64.

34. Mrs Janette D'Souza, History teacher at Loreto House, Calcutta.

35. Myron Weiner, *The Child and the State in India*, Princeton: Princeton University Press, 1991.

36. Dipesh Chakrabarty, 'On Modernity, Garbage, and the Citizen's Gaze', *Economic and Political Weekly*, 7–14 March 1992.

37. See Kumar, *Lessons from Schools*.